Thorstein Veblen in the Twenty-First Century

For my son and daughter,
Mathieu and Sierra,
who learned early on that life is about being humble,
not about playing the game of
invidious distinction.

Thorstein Veblen in the Twenty-First Century

A Commemoration of *The Theory of the Leisure Class* (1899–1999)

Edited by

Doug Brown

Professor of Economics
Northern Arizona University, USA

Edward Elgar
Cheltenham, UK • Northampton, MA, USA

Published by
Edward Elgar Publishing Limited
Glensanda House
Montpellier Parade
Cheltenham
Glos GL50 1UA
UK

Edward Elgar Publishing, Inc.
6 Market Street
Northampton
Massachusetts 01060
USA

A catalogue record for this book
is available from the British Library

Library of Congress Cataloguing in Publication Data

Thorstein Veblen in the twenty-first century: a commemoration of The
  theory of the leisure class, 1899–1999 / edited by Doug Brown.
    Includes bibliographical references and index.
    1. Leisure class. 2. Institutional economics. 3. Veblen,
  Thorstein, 1857–1929. I. Brown, Douglas M., 1947–
  HB831.T48 1998
  330'.092—dc21
  [B]   98–29683
                                                             CIP

ISBN 1 85898 613 3

Printed and bound in Great Britain by Bookcraft (Bath) Ltd.

Contents

PART IV: VEBLEN AND THE GLOBAL ECONOMY

List of Contributors

Doug Brown is Professor of Economics in the College of Business at Northern Arizona University, where he has been teaching since 1985. He has previously written *Towards a Radical Democracy* (1988) and co-edited with Janice Peterson, *The Economic Status of Women Under Capitalism* (London: Edward Elgar, 1994). He has published articles on institutional economics and Marxism in *The Journal of Economic Issues, The Review of Social Economy* and other academic journals. His current research interests concern sustainability and the political economy of global capitalism.

William M. Dugger is Professor of Economics at the University of Tulsa. He is the author of *An Alternative to Economic Retrenchment, Corporate Hegemony,* and *Underground Economics.* He is the editor of *Radical Institutionalism and Inequality.* He is the co-editor, with William Waller, of *The Stratified State.* He has served as President of the Association for Social Economics, Association for Institutional Thought, and Association for Evolutionary Economics.

Gladys Parker Foster is retired and lives in the Denver area, where she has taught at several institutions of higher education and serves on a number of boards. Metropolitan State College of Denver awarded her an honorary Doctor of Public Service degree. She has contributed chapters to books on Institutional Economics and has published in *The Journal of Economic Issues, The American Journal of Economics and Sociology,* and *Economies et Societes.* Her major interests are in monetary theory, feminist economics, and value theory in Institutional Economics.

William Hildred is Professor of Economics at Northern Arizona University, where he has taught since 1988. Previously, he was on the faculty of the University of Central Oklahoma and the staff of the Denver Research Institute (DRI) at the University of Denver, and operated his own consulting firm. In addition to his DRI and consulting work in regional economic development, economic and educational planning, various aspects of technology development and diffusion, and corporate R&D, his academic publishing includes articles in business and tax journals and the *Journal of Economic Issues* concerning tax expenditures and methodological issues.

Ann Mari May is Associate Professor of Economics at the University of Nebraska-Lincoln where she teaches courses in US Economic History and Women and the Economy. She has published numerous articles on political economy and feminist economics and has been actively involved in faculty governance and efforts to increase the representation of women faculty at UNL.

Phillip Anthony O'Hara is a Senior Lecturer in Economics at Curtin University, Perth, Australia. He has published in a number of journals, including *The Journal of Economic Issues, The Review of Social Economy,* and *The European Journal of the History of Economic Thought.* During 1998 he received from the Association for Evolutionary Economics (AFEE) the Ayres Visiting International Scholar Award. Recently he has edited *The Encyclopedia of Political Economy* (London and New York: Routledge, 1998) and forthcoming is *Marx, Veblen and Modern Institutional Economics: Principles and Dynamics of Capitalism* (Aldershot: Edward Elgar).

Paulette Olson is Associate Professor of Economics and Women's Studies at Wright State University where she teaches labor markets, labor history, the political economy of women and American economic history. Her research interests include women's economic status, the working poor, corporate welfare, environmental issues and the postcolonial critique of development. She is currently writing a book documenting the oral histories of women economists who received their PhDs between 1950 and 1975.

Janice Peterson is Associate Professor at the State University of New York, College at Fredonia. Her current research interests include institutional and feminist economics, poverty and social welfare policy, and economics education. Her work has been published in *The Journal of Economic Issues, The Review of Social Economy, The Social Science Journal,* and in collections such as *Introducing Race and Gender Into Economics* (Robin Bartlett, ed.), *Inequality* (William Dugger, ed.) and *The Stratified State* (William Dugger and William Waller, eds). She is the co-editor of *The Economic Status of Women Under Capitalism* (with Doug Brown) and *The Elgar Companion to Feminist Economics* (with Meg

Lewis), and contributor to *Institutional Economics: Principles and Dynamics of Capitalism* (Aldershot: Edward Elgar).

Yngve Ramstad is Professor of Economics at the University of Rhode Island, where he teaches the history of economic thought. He has published numerous articles on the thought of John R. Commons and on institutional economics in general.

Linda Robertson received her doctorate in 1976 in English renaissance literature. As a consequence of her insterest in the rhetoric of the academic disciplines, she began collaborating with William Waller in 1991 on the critical analysis of economic discourses. She has published a number of collaborative articles with William Waller and teaches a course with him on women's economic narratives. She is currently at work on a book length study on the social construction of the warrior, entitled, *The Myth of Civilized Violence*.

Jacqueline B. Stanfield is Chair and Associate Professor of Sociology at the University of Northern Colorado. She is the author of *Married with Careers: Coping with Role Strain*, and has published on family policy in *The Review of Social Economy*, role strain in *the American Journal of Economics and Sociology*, and dual career couples in the *Social Science Journal*.

James Ronald Stanfield is Professor of Economics at Colorado State University. He is the author of *John Kenneth Galbraith; Economics, Power, and Culture: Essays in the Development of Radical Institutionalism; The Economic Thought of Karl Polanyi: Lives and Livelihood; Economic Thought and Social Change*; and *The Economic Surplus and Neo-Marxism*.

Rick Tilman is Professor of Public Administration at the University of Nevada, Las Vegas. He has published four books and many articles on Thorstein Veblen and was until recently the Director of the International Thorstein Veblen Association.

Ruth Porter Tilman is finishing her Masters in Public Administration at the University of Nevada, Las Vegas. Together they have lived in Nevada for more than sixty years.

William Waller is Professor of Economics at Hobart and William Smith Colleges where he has taught since 1982. He is past-president of the Association for Institutional Thought, a past trustee of the Association for Social Economics, a past member of the editorial board of *The Journal of Economic Issues*, and a member of the board of directors of the Association for Evolutionary Economics. He has co-edited two books *Alternatives to Economic Orthodoxy* (M.E. Sharpe, 1987) and *The Stratified State* (M.E. Sharpe, 1992). His articles have been published in *The Journal of Economic Issues, The Review of Social Economy, History of Political Economy, Review of Institutional Thought* as well as a number of edited collections.

Kimberly Wheatley-Mann completed graduate work in economics at Colorado State University and is now an entrepreneur in Novato, California. Her MA research paper examined Marxian and Veblenian conceptions of gender inequality.

Acknowledgements

The idea for this book occurred to me about three or four years ago. Since that time numerous people have played important roles in the process of bringing it all together. First, there is the Economics Department at Curtin University in Perth, Australia. When I took a sabbatical for the 1995–96 academic year, the Economics folks at Curtin hosted me and provided me with an office and computer. This was clearly nothing they had to do, but it gave me the opportunity to write my chapter for this book and begin putting the project together. To all of the staff and faculty that made me feel at home and helped me that year, I thank all of you for your care and generosity.

Next I want to thank the contributors to this volume. Their friendship is much more important to me than the fact that they are my colleagues. They are good colleagues, but they are even better friends. I thank all of you for your excellent contributions to this volume.

I want to thank also the Northern Arizona University, College of Business Administration, for their help and support. This is my home and these folks who make decisions about financial support and who have provided me with the resources for this project are my academic family. In particular, I owe a debt of gratitude to our dean, Patricia Myers, for her support for this project.

Finally, I want to thank in a special way, Terri Peters, who is the College's Master of Hard-Core Formatting! She prepared the camera-ready-copy for Edward Elgar Publishing. No one else in the Business College could do what she did. Terri deserves the highest praise for a terrific job. Her skills are the best!

So to all of the above: thank you very much!

Introduction

Doug Brown

The twelve chapters that comprise this commemorative volume are intentionally focused on the ideas in Thorstein Veblen's first book, *The Theory of the Leisure Class*, and specifically whether or not what Veblen said 100 years ago has relevance for us today. In assembling and editing a piece such as this, I asked the contributors to take the time to reread *Leisure Class* and think about it with respect to its meaning for the twenty-first century. There were other options as an editor that could have been pursued. One of these is the assembling of a commemorative volume that includes chapters that focus on Veblen's ideas in general and thus draws from all of his career writings. Another option was to focus a volume on what Veblen meant for the twentieth century, in other words how prophetic was *Leisure Class* for this past century. A volume such as this would analyze what *Leisure Class was*, rather than *what it continues to be*. So one important point that the reader will want to keep in mind is the central organizing theme of this book: what does *The Theory of the Leisure Class* mean for us as we enter the next century? To what extent can we find ideas in it that will help us to solve our social and economic problems in the twenty-first century? Is it worth rereading *Leisure Class* if we are trying to get a handle on what's in front of us? What is in front of us that I will return to in the Conclusion is the globalization of capitalism and all that it entails.

Before offering any more suggestions for what to think about in reading our volume, it seems useful to examine some of the events that led up to Veblen's writing of *Leisure Class* and that culminated in its publication in 1899. An intriguing but no doubt unanswerable question is this: what goes on in someone's mind that makes him/her want to write a book like *Leisure Class*? It is not a book that is very typical of the period. Joseph Dorfman, whose intellectual biography of Veblen still stands as the definitive work on Veblen's life, stated in the 1934 Preface to *Thorstein Veblen and his America*, 'The realm of scholarship knows of few cases like that of Thorstein Veblen. Thirty-five years have passed since the publication of

The Theory of the Leisure Class, but its author remains a figure of mystery and his views an object of controversy' (Dorfman 1934). Now a hundred years have passed since its publication and there is still a bit of mystique associated with Veblen.

More specifically, it is hard to read *Leisure Class* today and not sense that Veblen was a rather alienated individual. He was an outsider both in academia and in the mainstream of American life at the turn of the century. Of course as we recognize throughout history much of what has turned out to be an outstanding or truly creative contribution to knowledge and culture comes from very alienated people. Certainly not all of it has come from these kinds of folks, but I suspect that in terms of alienation Veblen stands somewhere between Karl Marx and Vincent van Gogh. With respect to the discipline of economics Veblen was to America what Marx was to Europe. Both were outsiders; both were in this world but not of it. Both were alienated individuals whose academic backgrounds were in philosophy rather than economics. Since Marxism in the economics discipline never took hold in the United States, it was Veblen's evolutionary approach that founded the heterodox and essentially left-wing branch of economics known as Institutionalism. The Europeans had Marx, who died in 1883, and the US had Veblen. In some ways, Veblen is Marx without economic determinism, and this in fact may be the result of Marx's assimilation of Hegelianism and Veblen's exposure to American pragmatism. They were also a generation apart, and there was more evidence to support deterministic thinking in the first half of the nineteenth century than in the latter half.

But the alienation that creative people suffer is not all the same. One might consider the differences between the alienation of Marx and that of Veblen's contemporary, Vincent van Gogh. This may strike you as an odd comparison at first, but it has merit when trying to get inside the head of one who would write a piece like *Leisure Class*. Clearly, Marx's alienation was very political in nature. He was thrown out of all but the most liberal nation in Europe. Then without a secure livelihood he was cloistered in the British Museum for most of his active years, venturing outside for frequent vitriolic public debates with other labor leaders and activists. Marx's alienation is not one that kept him isolated from others. But it energized him and gave his writing a forceful character. He was a man on attack.

Van Gogh suffered from a more psychological alienation. Born just four years before Veblen in 1853, he too was an outsider, who tried as much as possible to be engaged with the world around him, yet eventually gave it up and took his own life in 1890. Veblen was 33 at the time. His alienation seems to lie somewhere between the extreme political alienation of Marx and the extreme psychological alienation of van Gogh. You cannot help but read *Leisure Class* and sense the alienation that Veblen must have felt from mainstream American life, the lives of the 'rich and famous' and his academic environment and colleagues. And to be alienated from what the 'rich and famous' were about was to be alienated from the rest of mainstream America, because the rest of the mainstream was spending a lot of time trying to emulate the leisure class above them. That left academia as a haven for Veblen, but this too was alienating and no sanctuary for him. For example, in 1892 the newly-formed University of Chicago (1891), that gave Veblen his first real job and from where he wrote *Leisure Class*, was also the recipient of a multi-million-dollar endowment by John D. Rockefeller and officially recognized him as its founder. On the one hand Veblen had the esteemable gratification of being asked by his Cornell colleague, J. Laurence Laughlin, to come to Chicago for $520 a year as a reader, while on the other hand, he was beholden to the invidious behavior of J.D. Rockefeller for making it all possible! Now whether or not these are the kinds of things that went through Veblen's mind is the issue and part of the mystique that surrounds his life. I would like to suggest that there is a type of alienation that informed *Leisure Class* that is somewhere between Marx and van Gogh and is what is behind Charlotte P. Gilman's comment that *Leisure Class* was the 'most brilliant penetrating satire' she had ever seen (Dorfman 1934, p. 196).

Veblen did not have to write his first book about what rich folks are doing and why they are doing it. But you can sense that there is more than aloof satire going on with him as he wrote this. The conventional wisdom is that Veblen was iconoclastic but also a detached, disinterested observer of the social scene of his time. This does not strike me as the case as I read *Leisure Class* today. There is clearly resentment, anger and disgust in his style. He too was a man on attack. There is another commonality between Marx, van Gogh and Veblen and that is the passion that invigorated the work of all three. My suspicion is that Veblen suffered more from the psychological alienation of van Gogh than from the political alienation of Marx.

Whether or not Veblen was the passionate but alienated soul as suggested here will no doubt remain unknown. But there are some events and experiences of his life before 1899 that are worth mentioning as they do tell us a little more about why he wrote *Leisure Class* and what must have gone on in his mind as he wrote it. As most readers recall, he was born on a farm in Manitowac County, Wisconsin in 1857. His Norwegian ancestry was farming stock and they were into self-sufficiency and simplicity. But by 1899, the direction of US capitalism was *not* toward either of these old-world and agrarian values. Also his family, before moving to Manitowac

County, was in Sheboygan County to the south where there were few Norwegians. Here they were scornfully referred to as 'Scandihoofians' (Dorfman 1934, p. 5).

As Norwegian farmers in Wisconsin there were social forces early on that suggest a sense of alienation. But Thorstein escaped the farm and graduated from Carleton College in Northfield, Minnesota in 1880. But when he went to Johns Hopkins University after the midwest years, 'Veblen found himself in the culture of the South, with its highly developed leisure class' (Dorfman 1934, p. 38). There he lived with a family 'which still clung to its aristocratic traditions' (Dorfman 1934, p. 38). When he failed to receive a scholarship at Johns Hopkins he went to Yale where he was called a 'foreigner.' Although he obtained a PhD he then left academia and with his new wife, Ellen Rolfe, returned to rural life on her family's farm in Stacyville, Iowa. He applied for a position at the University of Iowa in 1889 and was turned down. By 1891 he had seven years of academic isolation and was forced to go to Cornell as a post-doctoral *student* as a way to re-enter academic life.

At Cornell when he met J. Laurence Laughlin, who befriended him, Laughlin said that he was 'anemic-looking' and 'wearing a coonskin cap and corduroy trousers' (Dorfman 1934, p. 80). This suggests that Veblen was not only an alienated outsider, but that he intentionally refused to abide by the dictates of 'ceremonial adequacy' in mainstream life. Also at Cornell, according to Dorfman, Veblen read Alfred Marshall's text. Marshall quoted Nassau Senior's statement that 'the desire for distinction is "the most powerful of human passions since it affects all men at all times"' (Dorfman 1934, p. 80). Of course, the question is the extent to which all of this left an impression on Veblen that was later to find its way into *Leisure Class*. In all of this, there is evidence of the makings of alienation.

But then Veblen's fortunes took a turn for the better. When Laughlin was appointed as the head economics professor at the University of Chicago, he invited Veblen to go along. The first president of Chicago was William Rainey who was only thirty-six years old. Rainey was a great sports enthusiast and publicly stated that there were essentially only two branches to the university: athletics and academics. He then appointed a nationally-known collegiate athlete to be Athletic Director. This fact, along with the Rockefeller publicity, must have been difficult for Veblen to handle. It may in part explain, as is suggested at least in Dorfman, why Veblen wrote Chapter Ten, 'Modern Survivals of Prowess,' on sports and the last chapter, 'The Higher Learning as an Expression of the Pecuniary Culture.' There is clearly an element of disgust and sarcasm in his Chapter Ten statement that 'the addiction to sports, therefore, in a peculiar degree marks an arrested development of the man's moral nature' (Veblen 1945[1899], p. 256).

In 1894 Veblen wrote an article for *The Popular Science Monthly* entitled, 'The Theory of Women's Dress,' and in this piece he stated that the first principle of dress is 'conspicuous waste.' In the same year Volume Three of Marx's *Kapital* appeared and Veblen criticized it for failing to explain the loopholes in the theory of surplus value. So by 1895 when he first began talking about writing *Leisure Class*, he was fixated on both the issues surrounding Marxism and socialism *and* those related to what rich people do that causes everyone else to want to emulate them. It must have been clear to him at this point that the real problem of capitalism was not exploitation but the observable waste of resources and energy that result from an economic system driven by the manic desire for status. Marx saw working people as exploited while Veblen began to see them as captivated status-conscious consumers. There is no doubt that if anyone stood in the middle of Europe in 1850 what would jump out at them is the sight of workers in factories being exploited. By 1900, if one stood in the middle of the USA (Chicago) what would be obvious are workers-turned-consumers trying conspicuously to be something they are not. Veblen was ready to write *The Theory of the Leisure Class*.

But there were other problems that can foster alienation. His wife, Ellen, mentioned that she might be pregnant. Dorfman says that 'Veblen fell into a panic' and wanted her to go into seclusion if she was pregnant (Dorfman 1934, p. 120). As it turned out she was not, and although Veblen was promoted to Instructor in 1895, Ellen left him the next year for a farm life in Idaho. He continued to work on *Leisure Class* as well as other articles for *The American Journal of Sociology*, which along with *The Journal of Political Economy* (for which Veblen had been editor) was published from the University of Chicago.

In 1899 Veblen was forty-two and had been an Instructor for three years. He asked for a raise. President Harper told him to look elsewhere, because Veblen was not a good promoter of the University. So Veblen wrote a letter of resignation. Laughlin intervened on Veblen's behalf and got him the raise. Veblen then wrote his former student friend, Henry Stuart, that the ideas for *Leisure Class*, actually originated in his boyhood from his father's remarks (Dorfman 1934, p. 174).

When the book was reviewed it was initially slammed. C. Collin Wells of Dartmouth in *The Yale Review* said it was 'unexampled as a "collection of things that are not so"' (Dorfman 1934, p. 191). Yet despite this reaction, by 1900 it was considered successful by most of Veblen's colleagues and other left-leaning sympathizers. He was promoted to Assistant Professor. His career continued, of course, with the publication of *The Theory of Business Enterprise* in 1904 through the publication of *Absentee Ownership and Business Enterprise in Recent Times* in 1923. Veblen died in 1929. How much of what he wrote was the product of an estranged individual living on the cusp of an emerging capitalist world of alienated mass consumerism? There is perhaps some evidence offered here that his early life suggests that Veblen shared both the passion and 'bourgeois' alienation of both his predecessor, Karl Marx, and his contemporary, Vincent van Gogh. For readers of our volume I would also recommend a reread of *The Theory of the Leisure Class*, bearing in mind that passion and alienation not only seem to be integral to the insatiable quest for esteem, status and invidious comparisons that keep capitalism going, but they are also ingrained in the psychological makeup for those of us who, like some before us, want to challenge the mainstream of life.

Finally, with respect to our volume, its format, style and structure, there are twelve chapters and the book is divided into four parts. Part One, 'The Path of Contemporary Culture,' concerns one of Veblen's main arguments in *Leisure Class*: invidious distinction and the extent to which people's consumer behavior continues to reflect needs for status and esteem. From the three chapters in this section I think you will find that our current globalized capitalism continues to be one in which invidious behavior is raging as ever before. The objects of invidious distinction and pecuniary emulation have changed in the last 100 years, but we still have an economic system that is driven by more than the necessity to meet material needs.

Part Two of the book, 'What is the Leisure Class Up To?' also addresses status-seeking behavior, but these three chapters focus on today's 'leisure class' and the kinds of behaviors that we find characteristic of our wealthiest groups. In assessing the relevance of *The Theory of the Leisure Class* for the next century, we need to consider who the 'rich and famous' are today, how their cultural and economic composition has changed in the last century, and what they do differently today than in Veblen's time. William Dugger in Chapter Four gives us a broad outline of who and what today's 'upper class' is and what it is doing. Then William Hildred suggests that although invidious behaviors are as strong as ever, there are ways in which corporate managers would like to conceal their extravagance and not be conspicuous about it. Finally, the Tilmans discuss today's 'gaming' industry and they speak from experience as they have spent most of their adult lives in Las Vegas, Nevada.

The third part of the volume is about the women's movement and how *Leisure Class* continues to speak to the issues of sexism and patriarchy. As we are aware, the problem of gender justice between men and women continues to plague our contemporary economies the world over. Unfortunately, it cannot be said that Veblen's rather extensive analysis and observations about these issues in *Leisure Class* are antiquated. The four chapters in this part give you a good comparison between what Veblen talked about 100 years ago and what women are talking about today. There have been gains by and for women in the last century. Veblen's discussion of women as the objects of men's pecuniary prowess may not be the dominant issue for women today. For example, Veblen says, 'it grates painfully on our nerves to contemplate the necessity of any well-bred woman's earning a livelihood by useful work. It is not "woman's sphere"' (Veblen 1945[1899], p. 179). Yet it is clear today that women have entered the labor force in great numbers and that they have pursued careers in professional occupations along with men. But they are continuing to do most of the domestic labor as well. Then of women's apparel he says in 1899 that 'the high heel, the skirt, the impracticable bonnet, the corset, and the general disregard of the wearer's comfort which is an obvious feature of all civilized women's apparel, are so many items of evidence to the effect that in the modern civilized scheme of life the woman is still, in theory, the economic dependent of the man, — that, perhaps in a highly idealized sense, she is still the man's chattel' (Veblen 1945[1899], p. 182). As the chapters in Part Three suggest women are less economically dependent upon men but their independence has not yet been the effective means to material security, equal pay, or equal sharing of parenting and household responsibilities.

The last part of our volume concerns *Leisure Class*'s relationship to the new global economy. When Veblen wrote at the turn of the nineteenth century, capitalism in the USA was in the midst of its industrialization process and maturing as a domestic economy. Although capitalism as it began in Europe and the UK in the sixteenth century has always had an international dimension, it has only been in the last quarter century that it has gone global with production itself. Before now what has been global has been trade, mostly based upon exports and imports. With the high-tech revolution in communication, transportation, and production, the factors of production are more mobile. The speed of the economy has accelerated and interaction of all kinds has intensified. Cultural barriers continue to break down and the extent to which global capitalism can bring its central message of 'shop til you drop' has increased. These last two chapters focus on two issues: the growing inequality in the world and the spread of invidious behavior to all parts of it. These are important problems because they both reveal something humanity has never before asked: is humankind sustainable on the basis of the new global capitalism?

REFERENCES

Dorfman, Joseph (1934), *Thorstein Veblen and His America,* New York: The Viking Press.
Veblen, Thorstein (1945[1899]), *The Theory of the Leisure Class,* New York: The Viking Press.

PART I

The Path of Contemporary Culture

1. Veblen's Propensity for Emulation: Is it Passé?

Yngve Ramstad

1 INTRODUCTION

Thorstein Veblen's enduring reputation among those outside institutional economics is as a satirist and incisive critic of the modern pecuniary economy who emphasized the role of status competition. Throughout his long career, Veblen exposed and decried the wasteful expenditure of human effort at the very core of the capitalist system and also the unproductive, even dysfunctional, class of 'absentee owners' controlling its operation. In his first major work, *The Theory of the Leisure Class* (1899), whose centenary is now being celebrated, Veblen brought to light the symbolic rather than 'instrumental' nature of much consumption spending and, on its own utilitarian grounds, largely laid in ruins the philosophical warrant for the market system. In truth, Veblen's demolition of utilitarianism has never been adequately answered (cf. Tilman 1992, Chap. 12).

But Veblen, of course, was far more than a critic of the pecuniary economy. Indeed, he intended through his own work to fundamentally redirect economic theory itself. In a remarkable essay, 'Why is Economics Not An Evolutionary Science?', which appeared in the year preceding the publication of *Leisure Class*, Veblen had urged economists to follow the lead of biological scientists by adopting an evolutionary standpoint toward their subject matter. Veblen insisted that economists could make their science an 'up-to-date' one only by, first, renouncing their 'natural law' preconceptions and conceiving of economic life as a process, an 'unfolding sequence' (Veblen 1919[1898], p. 58); second, abandoning the 'taxonomic' method of analysis in favor of the genetic method (Veblen 1919[1898], p. 72); and, third, casting off the 'hedonistic conception of man' in favor of a conception of the individual as 'a coherent structure of propensities and habits' whose 'realization and expression in unfolding activity' is governed

3

4

The Path of Contemporary Culture

by institutions' (Veblen 1919[1898], p. 74) – that is, governed by means of shared 'habits of thought' derived from ongoing social processes (Veblen 1919[1898], p. 75). Only by adopting this alternative standpoint, Veblen argued, would it become possible for economists to develop 'a theory of a cumulative sequence of economic institutions stated in terms of the process itself' (Veblen 1919[1898], p. 77) and thereby satisfy the central requirement of the evolutionary standpoint.

It is important to keep in mind that as indicated by its subtitle, *An Economic Study of Institutions*, Veblen clearly considered *Leisure Class* to be a theoretical work manifesting the 'up-to-date' scientific standpoint he had called for the previous year. Accordingly, *Leisure Class* must be understood as containing a theoretical account of the consumption process in which the evolution of its controlling institution(s) is accounted for in terms of a process of cumulative change. That demonstration, in turn, was clearly conceived by him to illustrate a general theory of economic evolution – one presented in chapters 8 and 9 of *Leisure Class* – juxtaposing the progressive influence of evolving technology and the conservative influence of institutions.

It should also be recognized that while Veblen understood *Leisure Class* to be a contribution to economic theory (Veblen 1899, p. xiii), it can also be construed as an essay in cultural anthropology (cf. McFarland 1991, p. 89). It was a mark of Veblen's genius that he recognized that consumption enters into the system of symbolic communication employed within human communities. But since there was almost no scholarly work that Veblen could draw upon to provide him with an adequate anthropological understanding of the symbolic function of material objects and services, he made inferences about their meaning and social significance from his reading of historical tracts and of recent work by cultural anthropologists relating to life in 'primitive' societies – in short, by means of a 'speculative anthropology' (Haight 1997, p. 30).[1] Veblen 'confirmed' those inferences by means of examples arising out of his own incisive, yet clearly pejorative, dissection of the consumption practices he observed in the United States of his day.

Significantly, a growing body of work by anthropologists and social theorists is calling into question the adequacy of Veblen's standpoint as a framework for understanding the logic of contemporary consumption. Certainly, there can be no doubt that consumption plays a role in individual and social life that is on a whole different scale and of a different character today than in Veblen's day. It is now widely accepted that the nascent industrial society Veblen observed around him was succeeded and superseded by consumerism ('I shop, therefore I am'; or, 'The good life is the goods life') (cf. Leiss, Kline and Jhally 1990, pp. 59ff), which, it is increasingly being argued, has in turn been superseded by a 'postmodern' society. These developments have produced dramatic changes in the consumption process. When *Leisure Class* was being written, individuals satisfied their needs by using a relatively fixed set of goods and services. In today's consumerist economy, in contrast, individuals are confronted by a seemingly infinite array of choices, and they are seemingly forced to incorporate an endless stream of new items into their activities that possess no clear power to satisfy their established needs and whose use mandates a transformation of their 'spiritual framework.' Scholars who have sought to gain an understanding of these new modes of existence have applauded Veblen for emphasizing the symbolic function of consumption activities. But, the collective impression arising out of the emergent 'new perspective' on consumption is that Veblen's conception of consumption's symbolic meaning is now *passé*.   Indeed, one sympathetic non-institutionalist familiar with the recent consumption literature has gone so far as to assert that 'Veblen's anthropology is not salvageable' in that it provides a set of meanings unable to illuminate the true nature of consumption in the lives of present-day 'postmodern' individuals (McIntyre 1992, p. 59).

How have institutional economists, the supposed intellectual descendants of Veblen, responded to the challenges posed by the burgeoning post-1970s theoretical literature addressing the topic of consumption's cultural and individual meaning?   Surprisingly, prominent identified institutionalists, with Doug Brown (1991; 1992a; 1992b) and J. Ron Stanfield (Stanfield and Stanfield 1980) perhaps being the most notable exceptions, have shown very little interest in addressing the issues raised by the new theories. Indeed, since the publication in 1958 of John Kenneth Galbraith's *The Affluent Society* and in 1962 of David Hamilton's *The Consumer in Our Society*, institutional economists have had remarkably little to say about the consumption process[2] or even about concrete issues relating to consumer behavior.

Given these realities, the centenary of *Leisure Class* provides an opportunity not only to celebrate Veblen's achievement in breaking out of the apologetic utilitarian straightjacket in which economics was becoming enmeshed, but also to re-examine the serviceability for this age of the theoretical perspective Veblen fashioned.   In particular, I want to explore from an 'internalist' perspective[3] whether the late twentieth-century scholars who have spawned the 'new' way of looking at consumption's role in individual and social life have in fact provided a compelling rationale for concluding that Veblen's theory of pecuniary emulation is outworn.   Or more positively, I want to explore whether Veblen's propensity for emulation can still be construed to provide scholars with a warranted 'conceptual point of entry' (cf. Resnick and Wolff 1987, p. 25) into the analysis of consumption processes.

'The propensity for emulation – for invidious comparison,' Veblen (1899, p. 109) declared, 'is of ancient growth and is a pervading trait of human nature.'   Indeed, 'with the exception of the instinct of self-preservation, the propensity for emulation is probably the strongest and most alert and persistent of the economic motives proper' (Veblen 1899, p. 110). As these passages make evident, the propensity for emulation was in Veblen's assessment an established element of 'human nature' and a central motive force of volitional 'economic' activity.   Veblen was always extremely precise in his choice of terms.   Hence it is worth noting that emulation is defined in *The Random House Dictionary of the English Language* as: 'to try to equal or excel; imitate with effort to equal or surpass. Syn: follow, copy.' Thus defined, emulation may entail: (1) equaling or outdoing someone else in general terms on an abstract continuum ('prowess') or (2) following or copying a specific usage or activity in an attempt to equal or excel someone else ('reputability').[4] As implied by the 'with effort to equal or surpass,' emulation entails an impulse or 'propensity' for invidious comparisons with an eye toward gaining equal or superior status in comparison to others. Within Veblen's theory, in short, emulation is a drive impelling individuals to engage in status competition.

It has previously been noted that *Leisure Class* was intended by Veblen to provide a theoretical standpoint depicting the unfolding evolution of the institution(s) manifest in consumption behavior in 'terms of the process itself.' Significantly, Veblen understood emulation to be the 'dominant incentive' for acquisition and deemed it to be 'primary' in guiding the accumulation of wealth and consumption of goods (Veblen 1899, pp. 25–26). In other words, in Veblen's evolutionary theory of consumption, emulation is the principal motive force underlying the evolution of prevailing usage. It was also noted previously that Veblen conceived human behavior to arise out of drives (such as emulation) that are given behavioral direction by means of institutions. Accordingly, the propensity for emulation is given behavioral direction in Veblen's theory through the institution of 'conspicuous waste.'

Early in human prehistory, Veblen determined, high status had been accorded those who possessed 'prowess' in combat or the hunt rather than to those who engaged in activities making a direct contribution to the provisioning of society (Veblen 1899, p. 43). Since 'property' or 'wealth' in the form of goods or producers (slaves) symbolically signaled one's degree of prowess, it became the conventional basis of self-esteem and self-respect (Veblen 1899, pp. 30–31). Veblen allowed, however, that in addition to the 'desire to excel in pecuniary standing and so gain the esteem and envy of one's fellow-men,' other motives, particularly, 'the desire for added comfort and security of want' are also present 'at every stage of the process of accumulation' (Veblen 1899, p. 32). Still, it was Veblen's contention that early in humankind's history the conspicuous abstention from productive labor, or 'conspicuous leisure,' and also the conspicuous use of wealth in a non-serviceable manner,[5] or 'conspicuous consumption,' became the conventional status markers separating those with super-ordinate status — the 'leisure class' — from other members of society.

Under the stimulus of the propensity for emulation, Veblen maintained, members of the leisure class adopted various symbolic representations of their power to waste time and wealth. Due to respect for their 'prowess,' the leisure class's enduring 'wasteful' practices became honorific. And, again under the stimulus of emulation, as members of lower ranks gradually imitated the symbols associated with leisure class status to the extent possible (Veblen 1899, pp. 84–85; 103–104), the principle of conspicuous waste inexorably penetrated the conventional scheme of life at all levels of society – 'no class of society,' Veblen averred, 'even the most abjectly poor, foregoes all customary conspicuous consumption' (Veblen 1899, p. 85). Accordingly, invidious conspicuous waste became institutionalized as a habit of thought governing the expression of emulation and, eventually, with the full emergence of a highly developed industrial community, pecuniary achievement in order to create 'an invidious pecuniary comparison with other men' came to be 'the conventional end of action' (Veblen 1899, p. 33). Concomitantly, 'waste' — non-functionality[6] — became a desirable, that is, 'honorific,' characteristic of consumption usage subject to observation by other members of the community and thereby an inherent element of 'taste.' Significantly, Veblen saw both serviceability and waste as entering into the utility of produced goods from the owner/user's point of view:

> Goods are produced and consumed as a means to the fuller unfolding of human life; and their utility consists, in the first instance, in their efficiency as a means to this end. The end is, in the first instance, the fullness of life of the individual, taken in absolute (impersonal) terms. But the human proclivity to emulation has seized upon the consumption of goods as a means to an invidious comparison, and has thereby invested consumable goods with a secondary utility as evidence of relative ability to pay. This indirect or secondary use of consumable goods lends an honorific character to consumption, and presently also to the goods which best serve this emulative end of consumption. The consumption of

expensive goods is meritorious, and the goods which contain an appreciable element of cost in excess of what goes to give them serviceability for the ostensible mechanical purpose are honorific. The marks of superfluous costliness in the goods are therefore marks of worth – of high efficiency for the indirect, invidious end to be served by their consumption. In order to appeal to the cultivated sense of utility, an article must contain a modicum of this indirect utility (Veblen 1899, pp. 154–155).

As previously noted, Veblen's foremost objective in writing *Leisure Class* was to forward a scientifically-adequate theory of evolving consumption usage 'in terms of the process itself.' But, being an 'arch-enemy of waste' (Tilman 1985, p. 890), he also sought to formulate that theory in terms allowing for a critique of the wasteful consumption practices he associated with the capitalist system. It will be helpful in light of what follows to briefly sketch out how Veblen attained this second end. According to Veblen, the satisfaction derived from one's consumption activities rises and falls both with one's success in maintaining a standard of living exceeding what one has become accustomed to and one's success in maintaining a standard of living equal to or better than the customary standard associated with one's class status (or, in modern language, one's reference group) (Veblen 1899, p. 31). Both of these motives provide a compelling explanation for the seeming insatiability for 'more' evident throughout the modern period (cf. Veblen 1899, p. 111). Presuming that an individual quickly becomes accustomed to any enduring increase in living standards (Veblen 1899, p. 31), and that mutual status-motivated consumption is intrinsically a self-canceling exercise in futility, Veblen concluded that increased consumption is essentially a treadmill phenomenon – one must successively consume (waste) more just to stay in the same status location. In other words, increased consumption does not translate into a general increase in self-perceived subjective well-being. But, if this is so, as Veblen clearly presumed, the utilitarian defense of laissez-faire and economic growth is vitiated.

In light of the foregoing, it seems clear that Veblen associated the propensity for emulation with the following occurrences. First, the standard of reputability (the degree and general form of conspicuous waste) symbolized in the usage and activities of the leisure class becomes prescriptive for all – that is, the pecuniary standard of life enjoyed at a particular time by the leisure class becomes the 'conventional standard of (full) decency to the amount and grade of goods consumed' aspired to by all classes of people within the same community (Veblen 1899, p. 102); second, self-conscious status competition induces individuals at all levels to display as much 'pecuniary prowess' as possible; third, self-conscious status competition within the leisure class induces individuals to seize upon new methods of demonstrating their prowess (emulatory waste), and some of those methods will be imitated by others and gradually become conventional elements of the leisure class mode of life; fourth, as specific consumption usage become conventional within the leisure class, self-conscious status competition assures their imitation, to the extent possible, down the social ladder; and, fifth, that a general lifting of the material scheme of life will not produce a general increase in the average level of self-perceived well-being.

2 PECUNIARY EMULATION AND THE NEW PERSPECTIVES ON MATERIAL CULTURE

We have seen that Veblen forwarded a dichotomized conception of the role of purchased commodities in human conduct. They are useful, first, as a technological 'means to the fuller unfolding of human life' and, second, as honorific 'evidence of (one's) relative ability to pay.' These denotative categories of meaning constitute the very heart of Veblen's theoretical standpoint, and indeed, his critique of the pecuniary economy cannot be comprehended if they are disregarded.

Anthropologists have never questioned Veblen's contention that, in addition to being technologically useful, goods and services have symbolic usage. But some recent attempts by anthropologists to reexamine the cultural significance of material items have implicitly called into question whether Veblen's system adequately conveys the symbolic function of produced goods and services. Arguing that it is only through the acquisition, use, and exchange of material things that human beings acquire a social life, Mary Douglas and Baron Isherwood (1979) have proposed that goods are 'communicators' carrying meanings that are far more fundamental to social existence than Veblen apprehended. Using the metaphor of a ritual, Douglas and Isherwood demonstrate that material items help 'give shape and substance to social relations, fix or anchor social relationships,' and provide markers containing the meanings that allow individuals to make sense of the flux of events (Lury 1996, p. 12). Moreover, according to Douglas and Isherwood, goods make visible and stabilize all the basic categories that are used to classify people in society — parent and child, husband and wife, teacher and student, and so on (Lury 1996, p. 13).

A related, but somewhat different, conception of the role that material items play in social communication was put forward at approximately the same time by Marshall Sahlins (1976). Whereas Douglas and Isherwood use the anthropological concept of rituals to illuminate the social significance of material items, Sahlins employs the concept of totemism — the practice of symbolically associating plants, animals or objects with individuals or groups. According to Sahlins, individuals have an intrinsic need to display their membership in a particular social group and their adherence to the shared values of the group. In the modern era, he argues, manufactured rather than natural objects have come to comprise the symbolic code – the totems – by which group affiliation is communicated to others (Lury 1996, p. 15). Thus clothing and other material items are used to signify one's 'tribe' and its values. For example, by this interpretation motorcycles function as totems of working class masculinity.

Significantly, there is now widespread agreement among scholars studying material culture that the work of Douglas and Isherwood, Sahlins, and others has allowed 'the field of person-object relations (to escape) the limitations imposed upon it by its founding father, Thorstein Veblen' (McCracken, 1988, p. 89). And it is now generally accepted by those scholars that 'the cultural meaning carried by consumer goods is enormously more various and complex than the Veblenian attention to status was capable of recognizing' (ibid). Or, alternatively, *as symbols*, their role goes far beyond that of communicating relative 'pecuniary prowess.' Veblen never suggested that the symbolic significance of material items is limited to their function as signs of pecuniary prowess. What he actually asserted, as noted earlier, is that the principle of conspicuous waste 'guides the formation of habits of thought as to what is honest and reputable in life and in commodities.' In so doing, he added, 'this principle will traverse other norms of conduct which do not primarily have to do with the code of pecuniary honor, but which have, directly or incidentally, an economic significance of some magnitude (as in exchange rituals). So the canon of honorific waste may, immediately or remotely, influence the sense of duty, the sense of beauty, the sense of utility, *the sense of devotional or ritualistic fitness*, and (even) the scientific sense of truth' (Veblen 1899, p. 116, emphasis added). As this passage makes abundantly clear, there is no basis for supposing Veblen would ever have argued with the proposition that material items may possess 'various and complex social meanings' however, in his mind those meanings were of no relevance to an *economic* theory of the consumption process.

In light of the foregoing, I take it as established that purchased goods and services may possess symbolic significance for a wide variety of social and cultural phenomena. But I strongly question whether there is anything in the 'new' anthropology of material culture that is fundamentally inconsistent with Veblen's assertion that emulation infuses consumption usage.

3   THE RISE OF POSTMODERN CONSUMERISM

A question of particular interest to contemporary consumption theorists is why the consumer culture emerged in the first place, that is, why today people seem to have an insatiable desire to use more and more produced goods and services in meeting their needs. Celia Lury has divided the perspectives on this question into those that reflect a production-led standpoint and those that associate the phenomenon with an expressive impulse inherent in 'human nature.' Let us first review the production-led interpretation.

Stuart Ewen (1976) has argued that until sometime early in the present century, most individuals in this country derived their 'consciousness' — their sense of self, their aspirations, and so on — primarily from community life and their roles and activities within the production process. However, during the 1920s there began a concerted effort by the business class — now seeking to be 'captains of consciousness' as well as captains of industry and finance — to use 'mass images' to create the consumers they needed, ones whose consciousness was centered on the consumption of mass produced products. Analyzing statements made by leading business leaders and advertising authorities, Ewen shows that it was their hope that, if appropriate images were put before them, people would become convinced that they were unhappy or uncertain about specific facets of their lives ('Do I have halitosis?'), and that they would seek to alleviate those concerns by purchasing and using produced goods and services (mouthwash). Ewen (1976) and Ewen and Ewen (1982) trace out in great detail how subtle but insidious images repeatedly put before mass audiences by means of magazine advertisements and cinema gradually succeeded in 'channeling' the desires of Americans into a coherent consumerist mentality. By the 1950s, they argue, people had become conditioned to see themselves as 'held together, solving their life's problems through the benefit of commodities' (Ewen 1976, p. 73). And, it was at this point in the nation's history, now with the reinforcement of television, that 'mass consumption erupted, for increasing numbers, into a full-blown (consumerist) style of life' (Ewen 1976, p. 208).

By this interpretation, then, consumerism *resulted from* people's repeated exposure to mass images channeling their desires into a mass form capable of being satisfied by mass production, and it was of course this development that Galbraith encapsulated into his concept of the revised sequence, which, according to Lower (1980, p. 97), added an 'important dimension' to the institutionalist theory of consumption. We have already noted Veblen's confident prediction that rising consumption levels resulting from the 'free choices' of emulation-driven individuals will not collectively raise them to a higher state of satisfaction about their material life, a prediction confirmed in the famous review article by Richard Easterlin (1972). The authors of the production-led theories take a somewhat different tack in arriving at the same conclusion — namely, that mass consumption, or consumerism, satisfies 'false needs' and hence offers little that conduces to the genuine betterment of human existence. William Leiss (1976, p. 57), for example, maintains that individuals reared within the consumerist framework develop a sense of profound confusion about their wants and objectives that is exploited by advertising. For, as we will explore further below, the central function of advertising is to manipulate the meanings of consumption activities (for example, 'in drinking beer, we show ourselves to be manly, young at heart or neighborly').[7] The net result, Leiss contends, is that individuals are manipulated into associating (falsely) the satisfaction of their real needs — *à la* Maslow's arrangement — with the acquisition of an ever-growing set of commodities.

Consumerism, however, has evolved further and taken on a somewhat new character in the twenty years since 1976. Veblen maintained that although they often go hand in hand, evidence of pecuniary prowess can be established not only through conspicuous consumption but also through conspicuous leisure. He further submitted that the relative degree of reliance on each is related to the size of the community and the mobility of its inhabitants, that is, the degree to which the community's various members will know each other's stature in the community (pecuniary prowess) prior to encountering one another. Veblen recognized that late nineteenth-century urbanization and the improved mobility afforded by transportation innovations were commonly exposing individuals to the observation of other members of the community who had no means of judging their pecuniary prowess (reputation) other than through their display of goods (and perhaps also their 'breeding') while under direct observation (Veblen 1899, p. 86). Accordingly, it was evident to him 'that the present trend of the development is in the direction of heightening the utility of conspicuous consumption as compared with leisure' (Veblen 1899, p. 87). This being the case, Veblen anticipated that within the present form of institutionalized 'human nature,' individuals would collectively seek to expand consumption as rapidly as productive capacity would allow (Veblen 1899, pp. 110–111).

It is doubtful, however, that Veblen foresaw the massive increases in output allowed by mass production organized along 'Fordist' lines and the degree to which it would become possible for an increasingly large segment of the population to participate in a high-consumption scheme of life. Neither, one suspects, did he foresee the degree to which mass production of ready-to-wear clothing, fake furs, and other items would facilitate status disguising — the display of fraudulent status symbols — and thereby undermine the utility of many expensive articles, especially clothing, as a means of signaling one's pecuniary prowess (cf. Blumberg 1974, p. 491). And just as these changes were taking root, the 'status float' phenomenon (Field 1970) — the tendency of fashionable practices to percolate upward from lower status to higher status groups — grew in significance under the impetus of the 1960s protest movements and the influence of the 1970s counter-culture movement. By the 1980s, under the full impact of these developments, the whole idea of a 'general purpose' status symbol along the lines envisioned by Veblen had arguably crumbled (Blumberg 1974, p. 493). And, supposedly, rather than orienting their activity to receive favorable attention (notoriety) from all members of community, individuals increasingly discarded 'class' as a means of defining themselves and instead embraced 'lifestyle' as the ordering principle of their lives and the 'reference group' within which they seek to validate their authenticity (status).[8]

Additional changes in consumption patterns were more directly production-led. For example, the flexible production and communication technologies developed during the 1970s and 1980s have produced a 'post-Fordist' economy bringing increased insecurity and inequality but also allowing for much greater individual variation within the 'channels of desire' conveyed through mass images;[9] as Brown (1992b, p. 391) has put it, 'massified uniformity is yielding to individualized and pluralized consumption.' Another change has been miniaturization (for example, in music systems), which has allowed for a greater variety of goods to be packed into the home. And the development of compound commodities (for example, vodka plus mixer) has allowed 'unskilled' consumers to enjoy an increased range of consumption usage. A pronounced shift from the consumption of material commodities to the consumption of 'experiential' commodities (such as cruises and trips to Disney World) has also occurred. Proponents of the production-led perspective also contend that producers have in recent years intensified their efforts to spread fashion into new domains, to effect a more rapid obsolescence of style in products, and to speed the diffusion of knowledge about (production-led) changing fashions and styles through catalogues, promotions, advertising, and other marketing techniques (Lury 1996, p. 61). Aggressive promotion of credit buying is also assigned a role (Mason 1981, p. 118).

4   VEBLEN'S POSTMODERN CHALLENGERS

Not surprisingly, the distinction between 'natural' and 'artificial' needs, as employed in Leiss's analysis, is unacceptable to many, and it has provided social theorists who are critical of the production-led interpretation with their point of entry into the debate about what all these changes signify concerning the role and meaning of consumption in contemporary social and individual life. Foremost among those critics is the French postmodern (post-Marxist?) philosopher, Jean Baudrillard (1988). Unable to find continuing relevance in Marx's emphasis of use-values rooted in 'genuine' human needs, Baudrillard starts with the claim that it is impossible to pinpoint what genuine or real needs are; *all* needs, he contends, are socially created. In his view, Marx's production-led standpoint toward commodities was appropriate for an earlier stage of capitalism, but modern capitalism has experienced a radical rupture with the past and the new stage calls for a fundamentally different analytical approach. Specifically, according to Baudrillard, the logic of production, which was Marx's focal point, has given way to the logic of signification. For, Baudrillard insists, the meanings that are now typically associated with consumption items are unrelated to their intrinsic qualities and arise instead from the application of the current 'logic of signs,' that is, from their positions in an ongoing process of signification and resignification. Thus, to illustrate, jeans might signify sexuality and Marlboro cigarettes masculinity (Lury 1996, p. 69).

The prevalence of the game of signs in contemporary life, Baudrillard insists, has ushered in a 'society of the spectacle,' itself a new historical stage (ibid). In its 'spectacle' stage, the 'game' of signification — the ongoing process of signification and resignification — arises to a significant degree out of pseudo-events created by the media, such as sporting events (the Super Bowl), scandals (who killed JFK?), and even the product use displayed in advertising ('Just do it!'). In other words, many of the important signification 'events' in an individual's experience have no fixed origins, make no reference to a prior reality, and have no sources of authority. As a result, contrary to Marx's assumption, the material objects entering into an individual's symbolic language — that is, into the current 'logic of signs' — 'not only do not signify use values but do not signify anything outside of themselves' (ibid.). In other words, Baudrillard perceives that commodities obtain their meaning solely from their position in a *self-referential* system of signifiers (Campbell 1995, p. 103). If this is true, to return to our central concern, then obviously they cannot be taken as mutually signifying one's relative 'pecuniary prowess.'

Baudrillard submits that as this new stage of capitalism has taken form, individuals have gradually become more and more enmeshed in the game of signification. This has led to a situation in which the needs, wants, and desires that individuals experience within themselves are increasingly 'surrendered' to the code. In other words, as individuals come to grasp the system within which they are functioning, they increasingly 'play' within the infinite possibilities allowed by the existing signs and thereby experience an illusory sense of self-determination. This means that material objects come to be understood as elements through which they are able to freely define themselves.

Colin Campbell (1987), a sociologist, has offered up a different, but similarly non-production-led interpretation of consumption's symbolic meaning. Campbell proceeds from the hedonistic assumption that people have an intrinsic desire for pleasure. In his view, the rampant hedonism evident in consumerist culture has not been manipulated into existence but instead represents a natural outgrowth of the 'emotionalist way of life' precipitated by Protestantism's emphasis on the charitable feelings of pity and empathy. Expressed again and again, those emotions came to generate pleasurable sensations of their own (as opposed to simply being means of displaying one's virtue). Individuals seeking similar pleasures, Campbell argues, sought them not in actual physical activity but within the art of daydreaming. And thereby, via the imagination, pleasure became a potential ingredient of all experience. In this manner, the pursuit of Protestant virtue was ultimately transformed into a romantic longing, and imagery became the very 'substance' of activities (Lury 1996, pp. 72–73). Or to put it somewhat differently, through the imagination individuals became the *creators* of their own pleasurable environment. Longing actually to realize the pleasures already enjoyed in the imagination, they strive in actuality to create the imagined environment or experiences, or even to become the *other* occupying the imagination. But, the actual pleasures never live up to the imagined, producing an endless cycle of new fantasies and unrealized aspirations for pleasure. Hence we have the an endless quest for novelty, that is, an alternative impetus in 'human nature' to that provided by Veblen for the ceaseless searching out of new consumption activities symptomatic of modern consumerism (Lury 1996, p. 73). And, significantly, what this means is that for Campbell, as for Baudrillard, material objects derive their meaning solely from their relation to the 'self-expressing-itself' through their use.

A complicating feature of modern consumption is the existence of youth subcultures and their effect upon what might be called the culture of youth. Veblen never had much to say about youth as a distinct segment of the consumer population. Indeed, it was not until the post-war period that 'youth' became a clearly defined social category and the basis of common identification in terms of standards of taste distinct from those of the rest of society (Lury 1996, p. 194). There appear to be three overriding characteristics of youth cultures. They are cultures of *leisure* rather than work; within them, social relationships are organized around the *peer group* rather than on an individual basis; and their members evince an overriding concern with *style* (Lury 1996, p. 196). Within youth subcultures struggles over the control of meaning in dress, demeanor, music and language are particularly intense. This suggests that this is the domain where the 'new' consumption theory is most appropriate. The interesting question, however, and unfortunately it is one that has not yet been systematically addressed by researchers, is whether the youth culture has been absorbed into the larger society by means of the culture of youth, that is, whether youth is not itself a 'lifestyle' to which almost anyone can gain access if only they acquire the relevant knowledge (Lury 1966, p. 202).

5   ARE THE POSTMODERN THEORIES AND PECUNIARY EMULATION REALLY INCOMPATIBLE?

As noted earlier, the theories of Baudrillard and Campbell, among others, are widely understood to have displaced Veblen's theory of consumption and to disallow a meaningful role for Veblen's propensity of emulation in consumption theory. Indeed, Campbell (1995) has been explicit in submitting that Veblen's theory is inapplicable to consumption behavior in contemporary society. But is there actually a logical or evidentiary basis for making this judgment? If so, it is difficult to discern. Generally, Veblen's views are rarely set forth in any detail in the new consumption literature — indeed they may not be mentioned at all — and when they are it is only in relation to putative 'stylized facts' that are little more than caricatures. What is universally ignored is Veblen's insight that emulation may work its effect primarily at a second remove — that 'image,' 'fantasy self,' and so on, are constituted by means of consumption expenditures that may give vent to invidious expensiveness without (necessarily) an awareness that this is the case.

    It is important to keep in mind that Veblen's theory is dismissed by its detractors not as a result of a careful but futile search to discern its predicted manifestation, but by noting the infelicity of its central constructs within a different system of theoretically-grounded meanings — which, themselves, may in actuality be purely speculative. Yet, if one utilizes the system of meanings forwarded in *Leisure Class*, even a casual assessment of present day consumption practices would appear to confirm (if superficially) that 'pecuniary emulation' — with its centerpiece, the invidious waste of time and/or wealth — is a prominent feature of contemporary 'postmodern' consumption processes. Weddings and funerals, for example, appear to provide compelling confirmation that honorifically demonstrating one's 'power to waste' is still a central feature of the various rituals by which life's passage is marked. Within the recreational realm, emulatory consumption would appear to explain why golfers have in recent years eagerly purchased ever more expensive golf equipment (for example, titanium alloy 'woods') with what are for the average player very marginal performance advantages. The popularity of Ralph Lauren clothing adorned with the trademark polo pony would similarly appear to be evidence that people are not only willing but eager to pay 'extra' for clothing that, in addition to its intrinsic value as apparel, provides them with a conspicuous, culturally recognized sign that they are 'classy.' The rapid spread of ever-more expensive 'fully-loaded' sports utility vehicles would appear 'impersonally' to constitute strong evidence of that same 'propensity.' The high rate of home ownership would appear to signify that there is indeed a 'conventional' (and honorific) scheme of life aspired to by all. And, of course, the activities of primary interest to many contemporary 'lifestyle' groupings (say, triathletes, travelers, or the 'piercing culture') would appear to be nothing other than 'identity' achieved through pure emulatory waste. If it is indeed true that individuals have ceased to be preoccupied with how they present themselves to the community at large and instead focus on their status within lifestyle groupings, then clearly Veblen was less than prescient in confidently predicting the increased relative 'utility' to the individual of conspicuous leisure. But it should not be overlooked that within many 'lifestyle' groupings (say, triathletes or surfers) a high level of performance is itself objective evidence that one has previously 'wasted' enormous blocks of time (in training or practicing), thereby diminishing the need to rely on conspicuous consumption to gain stature in the eyes of the other members of one's 'tribe' (also cf. Veblen 1899, p. 97).

    In short, there is nothing about the logic of contemporary consumption theories ruling out the possibility that 'lifestyle,' 'image,' 'fantasy,' 'self-expression,' and even 'youth' are simply new grooves for the expression of man's propensity for emulation, for emulatory waste. Indeed, if Scott Lash and John Urry (1987) are on the mark, this is precisely the case. For, they argue, one of modern-day 'unorganized capitalism's' important features is the widespread use of 'images' as expressive frameworks within which goods are consumed almost solely 'for their symbolic power to invidious distinctions' (quoted in Brown 1992b, p. 393) .

For the Veblenian theory to hold there must be a discernible 'leisure class' presenting the community with its standard of pecuniary reputability. An important element of the 'new' perspective on consumption is its emphasis on the increasingly central role of the 'art-culture system' (Lury 1996, p. 53) — visual art, literature, music, radio, films, TV — in shaping the images of the self-seeking-expression so central to the new interpretations of commodity usage. According to Featherstone, for example, the influence of the art-culture system has led to the 'aestheticization of everyday life,' wherein individuals pursue fantasies that involve an imitation of the lifestyles associated with artistic subcultures (Lury 1996, p. 74) — and also for many, I would add, of prominent sports figures. Thus, within the interpretations of behavior forwarded by Baudrillard and Campbell, Madonna or Michael Jordan wannabes, for example, are not seeking to imitate their social 'reference group' but Madonna herself or Jordan (McIntyre 1992, p. 52).[10]

Americans have gradually formed the habit of assessing their own consumption usage by means of a direct comparison with the fully-honorific 'leisure class' life, and the less-honorific 'middle class' life, presented to them via mass media and made visible in the activities of the 'unproductive' but 'prowess possessing' super-ordinate celebrity figures that the mass media have created. And if this is indeed the case, there would appear to be complete harmony between the new consumption theories' emphasis on the 'art-culture system' in shaping the fantasies and aspirations of subordinate members of the community and Veblen's emphasis on the role of the leisure class in doing the same. Certainly, none of the new theorists have explained why there is not.

An important element of the new theories is its de-emphasis on class in favor of aspiration centered categories — image, lifestyle, and so on. As illustrated by the following passage taken from Brown's superb synthetic statement of 'postmodern' consumption processes, economic and ascriptive class is increasingly being seen as an incidental factor in consumption behavior:

> Just because someone is a wage-worker says very little about the person today; likewise, just because someone wears a baseball cap, or has a nose ring, or is gay, or listens to country and western music tells us little about his/her politics or his/her occupation, class position, etc. Lifestyle pluralizing is increasing, in other words, and so is social heterogeneity (Brown 1992b, p. 393).

However, it does not take a highly developed 'skeptical bent' to suspect that 'lifestyle pluralization' and 'social heterogeneity' is in no way inconsistent with emulatory waste and that 'class' may indeed continue to work its sway through these phenomena. To illustrate, even though an employer or CEO may be seen in public wearing, say, a 'Braves' baseball cap identical to the one worn by his employee, when they independently happen to attend the same Braves game in Atlanta Stadium, one strongly suspects that their class status foreshadows significant differences in their actual consumption activities. For example, the employer or CEO will likely sit with other 'reputable' members of society in one of the luxurious 'sky boxes' ringing the upper tiers of the stadium and sip scotch or expensive wine as the game progresses, as meanwhile the worker is crammed into a general admission seat and swills watery beer. And while both may wear a 'Head' ski cap and similarly enjoy a skiing excursion or two during the winter months, the wage worker will most likely utilize a nearby facility easily reachable by car, possibly rent (!) his skis, and, surrounded by legions of impatient and irritated fellow enthusiasts, wait long hours in overcrowded lift lines (and then display his 'lift tags' on his jacket for the rest of the winter), as meanwhile his employer is skiing on his own skis — the finest available — at an exclusive, uncrowded Aspen resort, hobnobbing with the 'beautiful people,' and sleeping in a $300 per night luxury hotel.[11] In short, even though certain 'expressive' elements of their 'lifestyles' or 'images' may coincide, this development in no way renders inoperative Veblen's generalization that their actual consumption usage will incorporate grossly different degrees of emulatory waste.

In point of fact, market research continues to show that ascriptive or social class (which incorporates the Veblenian idea that 'honorable' employment is a dominant determinant of social status) is fundamental to understanding consumption patterns. Indeed, the noted student of social class, sociologist Richard P. Coleman (1983, p. 269), has emphasized that to understand consumption 'life style should not replace social class, but exist in combination with it.' Drawing upon recent research on class divisions in the United States, Coleman (1983) contends that there are three fundamental class categories in American society, the 'Upper Americans' (about 15 percent of the population), the 'Middle Americans' (about 65–70 percent), and the 'Lower Americans' (15–20 percent). Included in the broad category of 'Middle Americans' are the 'middle class of educated but average pay white-collar workers and their (educated and more affluent) wage-worker friends' and a 'working class' of more poorly-educated or 'average-pay' blue-collar workers. According to Coleman, each major class category has its own discrete value systems and also its own distinctive consumption practices.

Not surprisingly, the income levels of subdivisions within different classes overlap somewhat (so that well-paid blue-collar workers, for example, may earn more than poorly paid professionals) — that is, class and income are not highly correlated. One could take this as an indication that 'pecuniary prowess' and status are not highly correlated and hence that Veblen was wrong (Campbell 1987, pp. 49ff.) This inference is unwarranted, however, due to Veblen's careful association of high status with the ability to abstain from 'dishonorable' employment as well as the ability to display one's power to waste wealth. Moreover, Veblen did not claim that the propensity for conspicuous waste is a function only of income. The degree and character of contact with the 'better' classes is also an important factor[12] — indeed, Veblen never even considered the proposition that high honor could accrue to those in low status (productive) employment.   Significantly, without mentioning Veblen, Coleman emphasized that 'social status derives, in its root, more from occupational differentiation than from income' (Coleman 1983, p. 273.)   In fact, Coleman adds, social class is virtually always the controlling factor in deciding upon how to use additional household income, and vice versa.

Given the subject at hand, Coleman's explanation of consumption patterns within each major class category is particularly interesting:

> The 'over-privileged' families in each social class are those with money left over (*after the class-standard package of shelter,*[13] *clothing, and transportation* has been acquired) for the forms of 'better living' that families of their class prefer; the 'class-average' families are those in the middle of the class income range who can therefore afford the kind of house, car, apparel, food, furniture, and appliances *expected at their status level.* The 'underprivileged' are those who, while not truly poor (except, of course, in the lower class) can consider themselves in difficult straits, given what is expected from people of their status in the way of social participation and projected standard of living. Many of their consumer choices amount to scrimping, saving, and sacrificing *in order to make proper appearances where these really count* (Coleman 1983, p. 274, emphasis added).

Is there anything here that Veblen could not have written himself?

Coleman's findings, then, would appear to establish that theorists of the 'new' consumer society may be rushing it by concluding that class is no longer an important distinction underlying consumption usage. Of course, Coleman's generalizations are drawn from research findings that are now 20 years or more out of date and hence may not fully apply to the yet emerging 'postmodern' economy. Unfortunately, other than the research reported upon by Richard Easterlin confirming Veblen's predictions about the futility of pursuing greater general happiness through economic growth, virtually no systematic research has been undertaken to test whether the manifestations of emulation required by Veblen's theory are in fact pervasive features of 'postmodern' consumption processes. And that one study, Roger Mason's (1981) extensive study of conspicuous consumption in modern societies is equally dated. Nonetheless, it is worth noting that even though Mason concluded that 'pure' conspicuous consumption is rarely encountered today, status and prestige considerations 'still play a significant part in shaping preferences' (Mason 1981, p. viii). He suggested that the phenomenon of class-based store selection provides a compelling illustration of the fact that status considerations play an important role in shopping behavior (Mason 1981, p. 122). Mason found considerable support for Veblen's thesis that 'conspicuous materialism' manifests itself among all social and economic classes in 'more traditional societies' but found that it does not appear to be 'particularly important amongst the very rich[14] and in the blue-collar working class groups found in modern post-Veblen industrialized nations' (Mason 1981, p. 137), as Coleman averred. It bears repetition, however, that the Veblenian framework does not require that conspicuous waste will be prominent (particularly important) in the consumption patterns prevailing among working class consumers, given their lower means and the rapid multiplication of needed 'tools' (say, refrigerators) introduced into the scheme of life during the twentieth century. All that Veblen mandated was that under the canon of 'pecuniary reputability' the members of each class would seek to 'live up to the conventional standard of decency in the amount and grade of goods consumed' (Veblen 1899, p. 102), including their 'prescriptive expensiveness' (Veblen 1899, p. 115), and perhaps even a little more (cf. Veblen 1899, pp. 103–104). In short, there is nothing about Mason's results that is inconsistent with my Veblenian interpretation of Coleman's generalizations about the significance of class to consumption behavior.

6   EMULATION IS UNREFUTED, BUT DOES THAT MATTER?

It will surely be granted by even his strongest proponents that Veblen's discussion of consumption's symbolic function was incomplete in that he failed to emphasize adequately that 'fullness' in the life process of a *social animal* is not merely a technological matter of discovering better tools. However, as explained earlier, this 'criticism' is really external to Veblen's own endeavor and, in terms of that endeavor, in no way subverts the fitness of his 'model.' Veblen's enthusiasts will also surely grant that contemporary consumerism evidences features that differentiate it sharply from the consumption process Veblen observed in his own day (as Galbraith had recognized shortly after WW II), and presumably there is no one among them who will refuse to grant — as advertising clearly confirms — that from a functional point of view the 'new' consumption theories provide scholars with substantive insights into the role of purchased goods and services in the conduct of individual life. And it is noteworthy that Campbell's theory of imaginative hedonism does appear at first glance to meet Veblen's test that a satisfactory evolutionary theory must account for change in terms of the process itself.

Significantly, the 'new' consumption theories are now being interpreted not only by social theorists but by *economists* interested in the 'logic' of contemporary consumption processes as providing sufficient grounds for disregarding Veblen's ideas entirely. Richard McIntyre (1992, pp. 52, 57), for example, recently submitted that Baudrillard's 'philosophy of self-fulfillment' has displaced Veblen's basic idea 'of competition in consumption' and that the 'new reality' is 'a world in which individuals are defined neither as workers (thus Marx is also obsolete) nor as conspicuous consumers, but as fulfillers of their human potential through the commodity system.' Even more recently, Metin Cosgel (1997, pp. 154, 158–159) dismissed Veblen's standpoint as 'modernist'[15] and submitted that Baudrillard's signification interpretation — to which Cosgel added his own twist that it is the role of institutions to provide individuals with templates for 'encoding' and 'decoding' the messages communicated through the use of specific material items (cf. Cosgel 1997, pp. 163–166) — is much superior.

Yet, the foregoing has shown that there is nothing in Veblen's consumption theory, as Veblen propounded it, that is fundamentally incompatible with the 'new' theories. Indeed, it is probably fair to say that the critics of Veblen uniformly displace him not by citing relevant evidence or by pointing to logical flaws but by attacking a straw man. For example, the 'new' consumption theories all find the meaning of consumption activities to be signified by their function in satisfying the felt desires of individuals or in their role in facilitating their intrinsic need for self-expression. But Veblen did not accept the proposition that behavior (consumption decisions) can be accounted for by tracing it to individual inclinations. Those inclinations may provide the impetus for activity, but, he insisted, it is institutions from which they obtain behavioral content — and, of course, without that insight there would be no institutional economics. In Veblen's consumption theory, emulation provides the impetus for action, but the 'canon of conspicuous waste' controls its expression. Such control need not be direct, however, for as Veblen saw things, the institution of conspicuous waste — the reflexive approbation accorded expenditure without serviceability — subconsciously permeates *all* the standards of judgement that individuals consciously utilize to make consumption decisions. Yet, not a single critic has recognized that subtlety and dealt with it. A similar situation exists in regard to Veblen's contention that, in regard to specific consumption usage, the 'leisure class' has a selective rather than a generative function in the consumption process. And, similarly, that the maintenance of one's honor through an adequate display of 'prowess' — of pecuniary waste — is of greatest importance to his conception of emulation, not 'keeping up with the Joneses' in regard to specific usage. Again, none of the 'new' theories explain why these features are *not* characteristic of postmodern consumption processes.

Even a casual glance will confirm that 'waste,' as Veblen conceived it, is rampant within postmodern consumerism. But it is a profound question whether the diminution of emulatory waste connects with our age's sense of what matters most, of what is 'forward.' Rick Tilman (1992, p. 224), arguably the present era's foremost authority on Veblen's thought, submits that 'Veblen assumed that the prime values of life are critical intelligence, proficiency of workmanship, and altruism.' That is, making and efficaciously using better 'tools' (technology) was 'forward' for Veblen; this was the 'social value principle' giving significance to the analysis Veblen forwarded in *Leisure Class* as well as the remainder of his work. However, as evidenced by McIntyre's pronouncements, *self-actualization as an individual*, not good workmanship per se, is the dominant ethos or social value principle of *this* age — the 'age of Maslow.' And, surely, that implicit social value principle has also profoundly affected what appeals to institutional economists as 'common sense.' Indeed, it may well be that Karl Polanyi, with his social value principle of security within community, or John R. Commons, with his social value principle of equational justice (Ramstad 1995), speaks more directly to the concerns of this age than 'instrumental efficacy.' In any case, it is an urgent task for those who do believe that the reduction of emulatory waste is the (or, at least, a) central issue with which 'postmodern' man must grapple to restate their case in forceful and convincing terms that accommodates the new role of consumption in individual life and the 'common sense' fitted to a consumerist existence.

To answer the questions posed at the outset. No, Veblen has not been shown to have been wrong. Yes, pecuniary emulation, as Veblen conceived it, by all signs continues to be a central element of human nature. And yes, as Veblen proposed, our 'need' for status — as we pursue 'youthfulness,' 'health,' 'self-realization,' our 'fantasy self,' or whatever else the 'new' consumption theorists detect to motivate individual conduct — could surely be accommodated with far less 'waste' of human productive effort than it presently entails. But, acceptance of and opposition to Veblen's evolutionary theory of the consumption process — with its centerpiece, the 'propensity for (pecuniary) emulation' — has never had much to do with its scientific warrant and everything to do with ideology, that is, social value principles.[16] Its detractors today have not shown it to be 'wrong,' for when viewed through the lens provided by Veblen's denotative scheme of meanings, its operation can easily be detected wherever one glances. Similarly, those within institutional economics who no longer appear enthusiastic about Veblen's consumption theory have never explained precisely why they find it not to be compelling. Mitchell no doubt accentuated the real reason Veblen's ideas are compelling to such a small audience. Despite its empirical warrant, unless it is represented in a manner fitted to the values embraced by the new 'postmodern' consumerist generation, it is likely that Veblen's theory of pecuniary emulation will soon be within institutional economics what it has for the most part already become within the broader intellectual community — a historical footnote. That is, passé.

NOTES

1. Veblen has occasionally been charged with reading present behavior into the past. See Tilman (1992, p. 223).
2. This generalization is based on my own impressionist review and assessment of all articles published in the *Journal of Economic Issues* from 1972 forward. As noted, Brown and Stanfield are exceptions, as is David Hamilton (see Hamilton 1973, 1987, 1989).
3. In his exhaustive analysis of the objections to Veblen's ideas raised by critics, Rick Tilman has shown that virtually all of the prominent critics failed to engage Veblen on his own ground, that is, to identify logical inconsistencies or to rebut his concepts on empirical grounds (see Tilman 1992, p. 282). My intent, in contrast, is to remain within Veblen's system of meanings and to assess, as imperfectly as it will be done, whether the 'contemporary' theories of consumption nullify Veblen's propensity for emulation and hence his general standpoint toward the consumption process.
4. Both of these meanings, to illustrate, are captured in the widespread practice in the United States of males presenting their fiancées with diamond engagement rings (type 2 emulation) of an 'appropriate' (or larger) carat size (type 1 emulation).
5. By 'non-serviceability,' Veblen meant that no generic human end (one whose 'value' to the ongoing life process cannot be understood independently of the agent's subjective framework) is furthered (Veblen 1899, pp. 98–100).

6. For example, a fork is arguably functional as an eating implement. However, the practice of silver plating them is not. Neither is the practice of imprinting the fork handle with an elaborate design.
7. Raymond Williams as quoted in Lury (1996, p. 63).
8. 'Lifestyle . . . as a mode of consumption, or attitude to consuming, . . . refers to the ways in which people seek to display their individuality and their sense of style through the choice of a particular range of goods and their subsequent customizing or personalizing of these goods. As a member of a particular lifestyle grouping, the individual actively uses consumer goods — clothes, the home, furnishing, interior decor, car, holidays, food and drink, as well as cultural goods such as music, film and art — in ways which indicate that grouping's taste or sense of style' (Lury 1996, p. 80).
9. However, one should not forget that as a consequence of an extensive 'McDonaldization' (Ritzer 1996) of the service and retail sectors, there is now much greater standardization within the variety that is available.
10. And, coming full circle, here we see from a production-led-standpoint the logic of the 'I am Tiger Woods' commercials that Nike has recently developed.
11. These examples illustrate what Fred Hirsch (1976) has termed 'positional goods' and hence are not confirmatory of Veblen's emulation. They are offered simply to suggest that 'class,' both economic and ascriptive, continues to play a central role in explaining contemporary consumption patterns.
12. For example, Veblen (1899, p. 114) decreed that, due to the frequency of their contact with the well-to-do, 'there is no class of the community that spends a larger proportion of its substance in conspicuous waste' than (modestly paid) academics.
13. 'Class identification and status aspirations govern neighborhood choice, then pocketbook power dictates which house or apartment' (Coleman 1983, p. 275).
14. A quick reading of the first chapter of *Barbarians at the Gate* (Burrough and Helyar 1990), in which R.J.R. Reynolds CEO Ross Johnson's 'lifestyle' is recounted, would suggest that this conclusion needs to be very highly qualified.
15. Interestingly, Dugger and Waller (1996, p. 182) have argued that already early in this century, 'Veblen was moving into post-modernism.' It would go far beyond the scope of this chapter to establish the grounds for my agreement with Dugger and Waller and my strong belief that Cosgel is simply wrong in this assessment. Essentially, the mistake lies in not fully grasping the conception of human nature serving as a foundation for Veblen's work.
16. The reader is again referred to Tilman (1992) for the evidentiary foundation of this truism.

REFERENCES

Baudrillard, Jean (1988), *Selected Writings,* edited with an introduction by Mark Poster, Stanford, CA: Stanford University Press.

Blumberg, Paul (1974), 'The Decline and Fall of the Status Symbol: Some thoughts on Status in a Post-Industrial Society', *Social Problems,* **21**, April, 480–498.

Brown, Doug (1991), 'An Institutionalist Look at Postmodernism', *Journal of Economic Issues,* **25**-December, 1089–1104.

Brown, Doug (1992a), 'Institutionalism and the Postmodern Politics of Social Change', *Journal of Economic Issues,* **26**, June, 545–552.

Brown, Doug (1992b), 'Doing Social Economics in a Postmodern World', *Review of Social Economy,* **50**, Winter, 383–403.

Burrough, Bryan and John Helyar, (1990), *Barbarians at the Gate: The Fall of RJR Nabisco*, New York: Harper & Row.

Campbell, Colin (1987), *The Romantic Ethic and the Spirit of Modern Consumerism*, New York: Basil Blackwell.

Campbell, Colin (1985), 'Theories of Consumption', in *Acknowledging Consumption: A Review of New Studies*, edited by Daniel Miller, 56-72, London: Routledge.

Coleman, Richard P. (1983), 'The Continuing Significance of Social Class to Marketing', *Journal of Consumer Research* **10**, December, 265–280.

Coleman, Richard P. (1995), 'The Sociology of Consumption', in *Acknowledging Consumption: A Review of New Studies*, edited by Daniel Miller, 96–126, London and New York: Routledge.

Cosgel, Metin (1997), 'Consumption Institutions', *Review of Social Economy*, **55**, Summer, 153–171.

Douglas, Mary and Baron Isherwood (1979), *The World of Goods: Towards an Anthropology of Consumption*, London: Allen Lane.

Dugger, William M. and William Waller (1996), 'Radical Institutinalism: From Technological to Democratic Instrumentalism', *Review of Social Economy*, **54**, Summer, 169–189.

Easterlin, Richard A. (1972), 'Does Economic Growth Improve the Human Lot?', in *Nations and Households in Economic Growth: Essays in Honor of Moses Abramovitz*, edited by Paul A. David and Melvin W. Reder. Stanford, Calif.: Stanford University Press.

Ewen, Stuart (1976), *Captains of Consciousness: Advertising and the Social Roots of the Consumer Culture*, New York: McGraw-Hill Book Company.

Ewen, Stuart and Elizabeth Ewen (1982), *Channels of Desire: Mass Images and the Shaping of American Consciousness*, New York: McGraw-Hill Book Company.

Field, George A. (1970), 'The Status Float Phenomenon: The Upward Diffusion of Innovation', *Business Horizons*, **13**, August, 45–52.

Galbraith, John Kenneth (1958), *The Affluent Society*, Boston: Houghton Mifflin.

Haight, Alan Day (1997), 'Padded Prowess: A Veblenian Interpretation of the Long Hours of Salaried Workers', *Journal of Economic Issues*, **31**, March, 29–38.

Hamilton, David (1962), *The Consumer in Our Economy*, Boston: Houghton Mifflin Company.

Hamilton, David (1973), 'What Has Evolutionary Economics to Contribute to Consumption Theory?', *Journal of Economic Issues*, **7**, June, 197–207.

Hamilton, David (1987), 'Institutional Economics and Consumption', *Journal of Economic Issues*, **21**, December, 1531–1554.

Hamilton, David (1989), 'Thorstein Veblen As The First Professor of Marketing Science', *Journal of Economic Issues*, **23**, December, 1097–1103.

Hirsch, Fred (1976), *Social Limits to Growth*, Cambridge, MA: Harvard University Press.

Lash, Scott and John Urry (1987), *The End of Organized Capitalism*, Madison WI: University of Wisconsin Press.

Leiss, William (1976), *The Limits to Satisfaction: An Essay on the Problems of Needs and Commodities*, Toronto: University of Toronto Press.

Leiss, William, Stephan Kline, and Sut Jhally (1990), *Social Communication in Advertising: Persons, Products and Images of Well-Being*, Rev. Ed. Scarborough, Ontario: Nelson Canada.

Lower, Milton D. (1980), 'The Evolution of the Institutionalist Theory of Consumption', in *Institutional Economics: Essays in Honor of Allan G. Gruchy*, edited by John Adams, 82–104. Boston/The Hague/London: Martinus Nijhoff Publishing.

Lury, Celia (1996), *Consumer Culture*, New Brunswick, NJ: Rutgers University Press.

Mason, Roger (1981), *Conspicuous Consumption: A Study of Exceptional Consumer Behavior*, New York: St. Martin's Press.

McCracken, Grant (1988), *Culture and Consumption: New Approaches to the Symbolic Character of Consumer Goods and Activities*, Bloomington, IN: Indiana University Press.

McFarland, Floyd B. (1991), *Economic Philosophy and American Problems: Classical Mechanism, Marxist Dialectic, and Cultural Evolution*, Savage, MD: Rowman & Littlefield Publishers, Inc.

McIntyre, Richard (1992), 'Consumption in Contemporary Capitalism: Beyond Marx and Veblen', *Review of Social Economy*, **50**, Spring, 50–57.

Ramstad, Yngve (1995), '"Commons" Puzzling Inconsequentiality as an Economic Theorist', *Journal of Economic Issues*, **29**, December, 991–1012.

Resnick, Stephen A. and Richard D. Wolff (1987), *Knowledge and Class: A Marxian Critique of Political Economy*, Chicago: The University of Chicago Press.

Ritzer, George (1996), *The McDonaldization of Society*, Rev. ed. Thousand Oaks, CA: Pine Forge Press.

Sahlins, Marshall D. (1976), *Culture and Practical Reason*, Chicago: University of Chicago Press.

Stanfield, J. Ron and Jacqueline B. Stanfield (1980), 'Consumption in Contemporary Capitalism: The Backward Art of Living', *Journal of Economic Issues*, **14**, June, 437–451.

Tilman, Rick (1985), 'The Utopian Vision of Edward Bellamy and Thorstein Veblen', *Journal of Economic Issues*, **19**, December, 879–898.

Tilman, Rick (1992), *Thorstein Veblen and His Critics, 1891–1963*, Princeton, NJ: Princeton University Press.

Veblen, Thorstein (1899), *The Theory of the Leisure Class: An Economic Study of Institutions*, New York: B.W. Huebsch.

Veblen, Thorstein (1919[1898]), 'Why is Economics not an Evolutionary Science?', in *The Place of Science in Modern Civilization and Other Essays*, 56–81, New York: B.W. Huebsch.

2. The Politics of Consumption and Desire

William Waller and Linda Robertson

1 INTRODUCTION

The centennial of Thorstein Veblen's classic, *The Theory of the Leisure Class* presents a challenge to those who argue for Veblen's continuing relevance. The title itself seems to ground the work in its historical moment. The historical significance also struck cultural critics most favorable to his work, who praised it for the contribution it made to defining an emerging American consciousness as 'American' (Howells 1899a, 1899b; Ward 1900; and Kazin 1942).

Similar considerations have consistently led mainstream economists to dismiss *The Theory of the Leisure Class* as not economic theory at all but social satire, a genre always tied to, if not trapped in and dated by, the time in which it was written. Even institutionalists largely focus on its contributions to an alternative to neoclassical theories of consumption (Kyrk 1923 and Hamilton 1962, 1973, 1987, 1989).

Our analysis will similarly address Veblen as a theorist of consumption, particularly in the sense that he offers an alternative to neoclassical consumption theory. But we argue for a consideration of the historical context which Veblen's work addresses because a failure to do so obscures the most significant aspect of Veblen's contribution. Veblen not only pointed out that the economic order depends upon the *social* construction of wants, needs, and desires; he also examined the *social* mechanisms by which they were constructed. In this undertaking, he joined with contemporary writers, religious leaders, political leaders, and academicians in challenging the justifications of the Social Darwinists for the naturalness of social inequities. It is important to retrieve this aspect of Veblen's endeavor for a number of reasons. Without the context provided by the challenge to Social Darwinism, it is difficult to answer those who dismiss

Veblen as engaged in a mere satire of social manners. Moreover, the justifications of the Social Darwinists for the naturalness of social inequities have re-emerged with the breakdown of the Cold War consensus, and once again have been used to legitimate an economic order based upon individual rapacity and social indifference. This makes it all the more important to retrieve and reconsider the attack on Social Darwinism mounted by Veblen and his contemporaries.

An understanding of the historical realities Veblen contemplated is essential to grasping the fundamental principles underlying his theory of consumption, which is, we will argue, the demand that the individual lives vicariously, constructing his or her identity out of the effort to conform to the standards of consumption set by his or her status group. Absent an understanding of that principle, and of its dynamic influence on individual lives, *The Theory of the Leisure Class* can seem merely outmoded, that Veblen presupposed the 'leisure class' would continue to thrive and set the standards for American taste.

Veblen's anatomy of consumption in *The Leisure Class* is one that points toward a social order that devotes considerable time and energy to constructing the desire for what we will call living life as the figment of someone else's imagination. Veblen does not deal exclusively with the leisure class of America's Gilded Age. His argument is that social dominance was gained early in the history of civilization by those interested more in exploit than industry, who valued the display of surplus goods acquired through exploitation or outright theft. The institutions and cultural forms which grew up to support — or dress up — this fundamental social reality have changed through time. The United States, lacking in the pomp of royalty, the legitimizing structures of aristocratic birth, or the ceremonial aesthetics of an Official State Religion was unique in the history of civilization, and therefore was an obvious testing ground for the ingenuity required to invent social forms and institutions useful for rewarding the impulse to exploit. What Veblen asks us to examine is how, in the absence of traditional social institutions and forms, the cultural mainstays of conspicuous consumption and invidious comparison are nevertheless sponsored and sustained.

We will argue that the social influence which has replaced the leisure class is marketing, and what it produces. Marketing produces most obviously advertising; but these two forces are not incidental to popular culture; in a very real sense, popular culture is overly determined by marketing forces and the desire to find suitable venues for advertising. Advertisers want to attach their brand names to celebrities, films, television programs, magazines, sports events, and entertainment events that reflect and reproduce the vision of society most amenable to the marketing needs of those who manufacture consumer goods. Identity groups within consumer culture are increasingly both defined and constructed by marketers seeking to target highly differentiated groups within society, while either ignoring or actively discouraging those who do not meet the profile of the targeted group. It is a form of marketing which depends upon the construction of desire from invidious comparisons demanded by the conspicuous consumption of goods marked as exclusive to a particular group.

By demonstrating at the turn of the century how the leisure class and its corollary institutions generated both the cultural values and cultural forms underpinning the economic order, Veblen made it possible to understand at the end of the century the necessary interrelatedness of the following: marketing, advertising, the manufacture of surplus consumer goods, the production of culture, the definition of human beings as motivated by pleasure-seeking self-interest, and the justification of social inequities as evidence not of unreasonable exploit but of a natural order to things which favors moral virtue over laxity and degeneracy.

The Theory of the Leisure Class provides an economic theory which cannot be extricated from a grasp of historical forces, cultural forms, and social theory. Far from offering a limited satire of manners, or simply a theory of consumption, Veblen sets forth a highly inclusive theory for understanding the economic order and its consequences for the structuring of society and the individual.

Our argument in support of this view falls into two obvious sections. The first considers Veblen in his historical context because: (1) a review of why neoclassical economists dismissed Veblen is important not only because it reveals how Veblen's work provided an alternative to consumption theories, but also as a reminder of how early Veblen's work was misconstrued, thereby freeing neoclassical economists from having to take his insights seriously; (2) an understanding of the assault mounted by Veblen's contemporaries against Social Darwinism not only clarifies Veblen's purpose, but also illustrates why *The Theory of the Leisure Class* cannot be understood as merely a satire of manners; (3) an understanding of contemporary criticism of the leisure class and its demoralizing influence helps to place Veblen's criticism in context and deepens the understanding of his argument that the economic order relies upon a particular form of self-alienation, which is the desire to live life vicariously. To illustrate this point, we will draw upon two novels by Veblen's contemporary, the novelist and social reformer, Edith Wharton in her *The House of Mirth* and *The Age of Innocence*.

The second section considers the continuing relevance of *The Theory of the Leisure Class* for understanding: (1) the significance of the resurgence of Social Darwinist thinking; (2) reliance of marketers on a self-alienation based upon constructed desires; (3) the role of both the government and the market in constructing, at various points in this century, the cultural myths of 'homogeneity' and 'difference,' and the role of these myths in producing a consumer culture and the commodification of individuals.

In our exploration, we will identify the elements of Veblen's analysis that we think are important for reconstructing if not a Veblenian at least a Veblenesque analysis for these times and our current cultural context.

2 THE THEORY OF THE LEISURE CLASS : AN ALTERNATIVE THEORY OF CONSUMPTION MISCONSTRUED AS SOCIAL SATIRE

In *The Theory of the Leisure Class*, Veblen argues that in the United States, at the close of the nineteenth century, pecuniary emulation was the motive for consumption. Put in its simplest form people made their consumption decisions, choices and purchases based on norms of consumption appropriate for a specific reference group. The relevant reference group for a consumer was determined by their level of income. Society was stratified on the basis of income. The goal of consumption was to fit into the appropriate reference group in a way considered respectable and proper. There was no disrepute associated with moving up in status as long as the person does not put on airs to a status level that they could not maintain. The greatest social disaster for a person is to fall in status, to be unable to consume in the fashion appropriate for their reference group. However, these norms were unspoken, at least in terms of explicitly maintaining a status system based on explicitly invidious distinctions. The culture of the nineteenth century would not permit such clearly articulated social norms.

The non-explicit character of the connection between status (and the power, authority, and discretion that accompanied it) and income level had two very important consequences. A person had to make their status known to the community to maintain their relative position within it. This led Veblen to identify the techniques for putting one's financial wherewithal in evidence, namely conspicuous consumption and conspicuous leisure. This by itself would be sufficient if the culture were willing to tolerate as legitimate a society where raw financial power could be exercised at will. This, however, conflicted with American creation myths of a society of free, ungraded people, consequently a cultural myth was also required to legitimize this system. That legitimization was easily borrowed from the European context. The privilege of elites derived from their natural superiority, thus their consumption decisions were derived from their intrinsically refined tastes, superior sensibilities, and genteel origins. The American elite set the standards for the income strata below it. But this system could not be justified on the basis of divine plan as in medieval theology; instead, the elites' superior qualities allowed them to rise to the top as a result of a Social Darwinian selection process. Thus an inevitable and impersonal, but natural social process, conferred this status, prestige and privilege. And thus the power of elites was legitimized and justified on these grounds and transformed socially from arbitrary power to authority (or legitimized power and discretion).

These two consequences, making your status known and legitimizing the system of status, come together to form an important element of the aspect of Veblen's theory referred to as the pecuniary canons of taste. And as an explanation of static consumption behavior it is adequate. But consumption behavior is not static and, moreover, American culture in Veblen's time mitigated against such a view of consumption. In a culture where social status is alterable, if social advancement is held out as a genuine possibility for all people, then the stability of the social order Veblen describes will require constant change in the pecuniary canons of taste. Veblen thus had to explain the dynamic characteristics of the system.

The decreasing costs of items of consumption, increased technology, achievement of scale economies, and the accompanying increase in labor productivity meant that the goods and leisure activities consumed by the elite would become attainable to those in income strata beneath them. Moreover, the cultural mythology encourages those in lower income strata to imitate those in the higher strata. Thus, to maintain their relative position the elite not only had to continue their current level of consumption but expand it. And this became an imperative for everyone in the income strata below the elite to similarly increase their level of consumption while continuing to maintain the prior level. This gives Veblen's theory profound macroeconomic significance.

Veblen's analysis, taken as a whole, identifies an entire culture driven by consumption. Since the industrial economy about which Veblen was writing had little difficulty providing not only the fundamental biological maintenance needs of the population but indeed generated an unprecedented surplus, much if not the majority of the consumption items met the needs of maintaining the invidious distinctions required by the status system. But the status system required that the level and the amount of conspicuous consumption and leisure had to constantly increase. Thus the social order required ever increasing levels of superfluous consumption simply to maintain itself.

Veblen's analysis of consumption is the subject of *The Theory of the Leisure Class*, which was dismissed by neoclassical economists as not economic theory, but social satire. The inability particularly among economists to understand Veblen's alternative theory of consumption, which we have explored elsewhere in considerable detail (Waller and Robertson 1990), is related in an important way to the neoclassical theory of consumption. The neoclassical theory developed from the classic liberal perspective on human nature where individuals are fully formed atomistic individuals who, through the construction or acceptance of a pre-existing social contract, come together to form society. Neoclassical economics has little use for cultural norms or conventions because the needs, wants and desires that the atomistic individual pursues as the *raison d'être* for economic activity are taken as exogenously given. They are primary data, the content of which cannot be explored from within the theoretical edifice of neoclassical economics. Individuals are simply assumed to have needs, wants and desires that make up the content of what they consider their self-interest, which they pursue incessantly employing a pecuniary version of Bentham's calculus of happiness. This is usually expressed in the following way. Each self-interested atomistic individual pursues his/her unlimited wants and desires, which is expressed as maximizing their subjective utility, by consuming as much as they can given the constraint imposed by their finite incomes.

The flaws in the neoclassical framework illustrate both the strengths of Veblen's approach and why he could not be understood as a theorist by neoclassical economists. Neoclassical economics assumes consumption is an important social construction with tremendous normative significance in our culture. Indeed, it has attained almost the status of religious truth. But, the explanation that consumption is based solely on matters of individual choice, unaffected by any factor except income, flies in the face of reality as most of us experience it; and is completely contrary to the understanding of consumption among those most dependent on that activity, namely, businesses who spend enormous amounts of money trying to shape the needs, wants and desires of consumers which the theory takes as exogenous.

In neoclassical theory the needs, wants and desires of consumers are taken as expressions of their subjective valuation of the goods and services they wish to consume and the activities in which they engage. Emerging from the classical liberal position, these preferences are seen as an intrinsic part of the individual's unique human nature. Thus any attempt to compare them is impossible. And more important, any attempt to assess, restrict or change them is seen as a violation of individual freedom. Thus any systematic attempt by society to regulate individual acts of consumption, no matter how harmful or base, is treated as a fundamental violation of human rights. This has created a powerful social prescription that government has little or no business in regulating what individuals can and cannot consume.

Oddly, except that we are already acculturated to treat it as natural, attempts by firms to alter and structure our needs, wants and desires, by which we mean concerted attempts to structure our preferences, are completely acceptable as a further expression of individual freedoms associated with classical liberalism.   Hence, enormous industries specializing in the construction of needs, wants and desires have arisen to persuade us that the products, candidates, services, or ideas they purvey are what we, in our subjective heart of hearts really want.   Moreover, they understand their task as the construction of need, want and desire, not merely its arousal from dormancy.   Thus, as David Hamilton has noted, Veblen was in many ways both consumer culture's most trenchant critic and the first professor of marketing.

Veblen's theory of consumption in *The Theory of the Leisure Class* is derived from a cultural analysis of consumption behavior embedded, rationalized and legitimized within the larger symbolic system of the culture he is writing about. The neoclassical theory of consumption is not cultural in its understanding of human consumption behavior and it legitimizes consumption on grounds different from the Social Darwinian justification to which Veblen was responding. But to see this we need to move forward in our analysis.

All major commentators have noted the sharp satirical character of Veblen's description of the leisure class's behavior. And clearly Veblen's examples, drawn from the excesses of leisure class behavior of his time as well as European precedents that he thought contributed to its legitimacy, are intended to make his argument and deflate the dignity associated with many pretensions of the elite, the affluent and the aspiring social climber. But we also know that Veblen chafed under the suggestion that the purpose of the book was satirical. The question we need to address is why did Veblen choose such a conspicuously ironic rhetorical approach for his presentation. This entails a more pointed question, namely; is Veblen's *The Theory of the Leisure Class* as satirical as it is read to be by contemporary audiences? Howell's categorization of Veblen's *The Theory of the Leisure Class* as part of the realism movement in literature and Alfred Kazin's characterization of his work as contributing to an American voice and literary consciousness seem to suggest that, while certainly no one would accuse Veblen of being overly solemn, the satire and irony emerged from the actual behavior of elites. Veblen's presentation may be a more accurate perception, or at least a more accurate portrayal of the perception, of leisure class behavior of his period than we usually suppose.

3 *THE THEORY OF THE LEISURE CLASS* AND THE ASSAULT ON SOCIAL DARWINISM

Social Darwinism was used to legitimate as 'necessary' or 'natural' the social inequities attendant upon the advent of industrialization and capitalism; its tenets were applied against efforts at social reform as if such intervention would violate a natural law. William Graham Sumner, in *What Social Classes Owe to Each Other* (1911[1883]) argued that the economic order called for a Calvinistic devotion to thrift and hard work. The economy naturally encouraged the development of personal character while punishing those whom Sumner called 'negligent, shiftless, inefficient, silly, and imprudent' (Hofstadter, 1955 p. 10). Veblen's *The Theory of the Leisure Class* in the words of Richard Hofstadter 'flatly contradicted' Sumner, with whom Veblen studied as a graduate student at Yale, particularly on the point of the equation between natural selection and accumulated wealth, or between the accumulation of wealth and the development of virtue.

The arguments of the Social Darwinists invited skeptics and detractors into making comparisons between the ideal specimen of a human being which, according to the notion of survival of the fittest ought to have landed at the top of the heap, and the flesh and blood members of the social elites. The gap between the expectation and the reality provoked sharp social satire in those most familiar with the leisure class, either as outside observers of their manners and mores in the case of Veblen (at least as portrayed by Dorfman), or as an insider. This was Edith Wharton's special perspective. Born into the leisure class, she went into self-imposed exile in Paris to escape the stultifying effects of a class she regarded as utterly lacking in either initiative, a sense of civic responsibility, or cultivated taste.

Veblen and Wharton were part of a broadly-based intellectual movement engaged in refuting the opportunistic determinism of the Social Darwinists, an effort which included Progressives, Pragmatists, reform-minded Christian leaders, Marxists, socialists, and feminists. As a result of this campaign, by 1934 Henry A. Wallace could speak of 'the overwhelming realization that mankind has such mental and spiritual powers and such control over nature that the doctrine of the struggle for existence is definitely outmoded and replaced by the higher law of cooperation.'

In her portrayal of Lily Bart in *The House of Mirth*, Wharton echoes most directly Charlotte Perkins Gilman in pointing to the significant distortion of personality and character caused by requiring women to rely upon sexual attraction as the sole means of survival, a necessity forced upon them by having to depend upon men for their food, clothing and shelter. Wharton's friend, the British intellectual Violet Paget, wrote both the introduction to and a highly favorable review of Gilman's *Women and Economics*, under the name Vernon Lee. Lee's review appeared in the same issue of *The North American Review* as Wharton's review of three plays about Francesca da Rimini. Gilman acknowledged her intellectual debt to Thorstein Veblen, even though she also took issue with some of his conclusions (Joslin 1991, p. 53; Lee 1902, pp.71-90 ; Gilman 1994[1898]).

An example of these combined influences is found in the scene when, during a sleepless night, Lily Bart wrestles with the temptation to use blackmail to regain her social position. She recognizes that she cannot remake herself to become a 'worker among workers, and let the world of luxury and pleasure sweep by her unregarded.' The narrator presents Lily's case to the reader as if giving a natural history lecture on a particularly rarefied specimen under examination. Arguing that Lily was 'less to blame than she believed,' the voice of the narrator declares archly and objectively:

> Inherited tendencies had combined with early training to make her the highly specialized product she was: an organism as helpless out of its narrow range as the sea-anemone torn from the rock. She had been fashioned to adorn and delight: to what other end does nature round the rose-leaf and paint the hummingbird's breast? (p. 289).

The obviousness of where the analogy breaks down — it is society, not nature that has fashioned Lily — holds as well for Veblen's equally astute and more consistent use, as an instrument of irony, of the same pseudo-scientific objectivity embraced by the Social Darwinists. In the case of both Veblen and Wharton, the social satire went to a deeper point, opening to view the interrelatedness of the culture, individual identity, and the economy. The satire may function as the surgeon's knife, but it is the anatomy lesson about the culture that is the ultimate aim.

4   VEBLEN, WHARTON, AND THE CULTURE OF EMULATION

Wharton is an important writer to read in conjunction with Veblen because her characters and conflicts illuminate the scene Veblen draws with broad strokes. Wharton is particularly worthwhile for tallying the human cost required to sustain the leisure class; indeed, she herself said that the only justification for writing about such a trivial group was to demonstrate what was driven out or destroyed by it.

The most important demand made upon members of the class is to live vicariously. This is the fundamental insight underlying Veblen's argument that the driving force behind a consumer economy is conspicuous consumption. It is an economic order in which goods are valued because of what they signify to others about the owner's status. A capacity for emulation — or imitation — is therefore the essential virtue; how one is perceived or understood is the key to fashioning one's own identity in a manner that assures either continuing status, or the ability to move up in status. The outward signs of consumption, down to the smallest detail, become the terms by which one is judged by others, and placed within the status system.

In his attentiveness to conspicuous consumption and pecuniary emulation, Veblen discusses the projected image of the self as the essential corollary of the consumer economy. Garry Wills in *John Wayne's America: The Politics of Celebrity* says of Wayne that he created a 'self' so real to others that he could disappear into it, as he did. He finally became what he had projected on the screen — a hollow triumph, for what was he but the figment of other people's imaginations? (p. 27)

The politics of celebrity is the lynch pin of the consumer economy. The manufacture of enviable identities promotes the desire for emulation. The fundamental requirement is that one must be seen by others as possessed of the appropriate status signs and symbols in order to have social value or efficacy. The ideal definition of the participant in the consumer economy is one that entails self-commodification, or the hollow triumph of becoming the figment of other people's imaginations.

Edith Wharton's novels provide a masterful insight into how the social elites forged their identities from the axes of property, the market, and the family. Social reproduction is tied to biological reproduction as surely as the tides to the moon, with the consequent need for a thorough management and surveillance of not only behavior but of identity itself. Courtship and marriage are closely monitored and hemmed in by social ritual because sustaining wealth, and hence security, are entirely dependent upon both inherited wealth and a system of investments made on the basis of the mutual trust derived from a vast network of interlocking family ties. Genealogy coupled with the outward signs of status and conspicuous waste are therefore the most important codes for determining the most significant economic choices.

Wharton's novels provide a clearer picture of the interrelatedness of family, sexuality, psychological identity, and the economic order than does Veblen's *The Theory of the Leisure Class*. While both Veblen and Wharton are singing from the same page in the choir book, Wharton's work more insistently tallies the suffocating constraints participation in the leisure class placed upon the potential range of human development. Veblen provides an historically important analysis of the commodification of women as trophy brides; Wharton paints the complete portrait by examining the demand for self-negation that this status entailed, and the ostracism, exile, or self-destruction that comes as a consequence either of resisting the role or of playing it too well. Veblen notes the necessity among men of sustaining a high degree of mindless social conformity; Wharton reveals the personal cost to the male psyche of participating in what amounts to an endless and passionless charade, the ultimate aim of which amounts to little more than biological and financial reproduction. Veblen views the leisure class as embracing all of the wealthy elites. Wharton casts a more discriminating eye, noticing the differences that distinguish the propertied class, the financiers and capitalists upon whom they depend, and the *parvenu* class created by the advent of the mass production of consumer goods. Wharton is able to identify in the rarefied atmosphere of the extremely wealthy those who establish the canons of taste and conduct, those who seek to emulate them, and those who threaten the established social order because they are possessed of newly-made wealth but disregard feudal norms and values associated with the inherited wealth of the propertied class, particularly those related to marriage and progeny.

In *The House of Mirth*, Wharton traces Lily Bart's fall from status and ultimately class until she dies in despair from an apparently accidental, self-administered dose of sleeping medication. *The House of Mirth* can be read at one level as an attack upon the commodification of women in a patriarchal society. The only assets Lily can be said to truly possess are her great physical beauty and an unsullied reputation. She needs both in order to obtain a financial position within her social caste. She loses her reputation because of her economic dependence, her need to keep up appearances without the means to do so. This dependence opens her to the raw realities of her social setting. Her sexual identity as either a mistress or a wife is the condition not simply for her material comfort and status, but for her survival.

The House of Mirth pushes the analysis of class beyond the confines of the conventional melodramatic plot because of Wharton's insight into the psychological alienation which the leisure class imposes upon those who participate in it or who aspire to. Lily Bart is quite willing to play by the rules of the game. In her pursuit of a wealthy match, Lily understands marriage primarily in terms of status within her caste. While Lily is ostensibly a willing player in the marriage game, it is not circumstances that prevent her from realizing her ambition, it is her own unwillingness to follow through with any courtship; her consistent undermining of her own schemes. This quality is what saves the novel from being merely melodramatic. Lily has been conditioned from earliest childhood to regard herself as her sole asset, a commodity to be exchanged for security and status; so conditioned that she is alienated from her own impulses toward genuine passion, committed love, and a healthy self-regard. Yet these impulses consistently rise up to thwart the other Lily, the Lily constructed in the image of her mother's ambitions and the values most sacred to her class. No sooner does she reel in a likely candidate in whom she has set her hook than she casts him aside, or more tellingly, she commits an act which she knows will be disaffecting in her suitor's eye, as if willing him to reject her, when the motive resides with her. But while she can never manage to bring herself to enter into the marketplace for which her whole life had seemed to prepare and suit her, she also cannot openly resist it, cannot give in to the urgings of her heart and mind.

In the final scene of the novel, as Lily's life ebbs from her, Wharton includes an incongruous detail, one which some critics find troubling. As she slips under the influence of the sleeping draught, Lily hallucinates that she is holding an infant, the child of her working-class friend, Nettie Struthers. 'She did not know how it had come there, but she felt no great surprise at the fact, only a gentle penetrating thrill of warmth and pleasure' (p. 310). The child and the comfort Lily draws from it can be understood as a caving in to conventional assumptions about unfulfilled womanhood, that Lily would have been all right had she settled for husband, hearth, and family. But Wharton was keenly aware of the social stereotypes about women and gave herself over to resisting them; and she herself was childless. At one level, it seems entirely reasonable to make the point that what Lily had lacked throughout her life was a suitable human object for her love, her desires having been misdirected toward the outward signs of consumption — jewels, dresses, large homes, and the like. It also seems entirely reasonable to argue, as has been the case, that the last scene is Wharton's own declaration of independence from the constraints of her class, her demonstration of her intention to embrace her own creative impulses and motives, to become an artist and not be defined by the humdrum roles of society wife, to make of her books her children.

But there is an additional consideration which accords with the arc that Lily's life traces, and it is that in the last moments of her life, Lily becomes self-regarding of her own needs, becomes as it were a mother to herself, acknowledging her self-worth sufficiently to protect herself. As she drifts into sleep, she thinks to herself:

> She did not quite remember what it was that she had been afraid to meet, but the uncertainty no longer troubled her. She had been unhappy, and now she was happy — she had felt herself alone, and now the sense of loneliness had vanished (*The House of Mirth*, p. 310).

It is entirely consistent with the representation of the predatory social order as Wharton depicts it that the moment when Lily accepts responsibility for herself, and regards herself as worthy of her self-regard and protection, she also ceases to exist. There is no room afforded to one who seeks to protect and nurture her 'real' self when confronted with the constraints of the 'actual' world. To realize one might be that person, is to make it impossible to live as if one were the figment of someone else's imagination. Lily Bart is a hothouse flower; she cannot survive outside the confines and demands of the caste in which she was raised. The demand that she live vicariously, suiting herself to the existence constructed for her by others, cannot be met if she holds herself in sufficient regard. The moment she projects herself as both mother and child, as both sustaining herself and as being worthy of asking it of herself, she can no longer exist within the limits that have conditioned her entire existence.

The psychological cost of living vicariously is not assigned solely to women. Although the cost is greatest to Lily Bart, Wharton represents its suffocating demand on the masculine psyche as well. The cost to men is most fully developed in Newland Archer, the central character in Wharton's *The Age of Innocence*. In this novel, Wharton explicitly states the conflict between the 'real' and 'actual' life that implicitly informs the earlier *The House of Mirth*. Early in *The House of Mirth*, the narrator comments on the innerworkings of the leisure class. 'They all lived in a kind of hieroglyphic world, where the real thing was never said or done or even thought, but only represented by a set of arbitrary signs' (p. 44). In Archer, the reader is asked to recognize the struggle of the awakening self against the suffocating confines of class and convention. Of all the characters in the novel, it is Archer who is well read and cultivated. Engaged to Meg Welland, Archer falls passionately in love with her cousin, Ellen Olenska. In his idealized vision of her as the unattainable woman, he 'built up within himself a kind of sanctuary' which became,

> The scene of his real life, of his only rational activities; thither he brought the books he read, the ideas and feelings which nourished him, his judgments and visions. Outside it, in the scene of his actual life, he moved with a growing sense of unreality and insufficiency, blundering against familiar prejudices and traditional points of view (*The Age of Innocence*, Wharton 1992[1920]).

Ultimately, Archer lacks both the will and the imagination to pursue his love for the Countess Olenska, even when the social barriers to their liaison drop away years later. In Archer's lassitude and conformity to class, Wharton traces how the forces needed to sustain the economic order of property, investment, and finance suppressed those aspects of social life necessary to a truly civilized society: self-expression, use of the creative imagination, a sense of civic responsibility, personal initiative, and a political conscience. Assuring the strength and continuity of the economic order is inextricably dependent upon the institutions and cultural norms for controlling sexuality and procreation (engagement, marriage, childbearing, adultery, divorce) as well as to those necessary for sustaining approved and exclusive kinship relationships through the institutional solidarity of the family.

Wharton's novels, because her vision of the leisure class complements Veblen's analysis, help place Veblen historically, and confirm his singular contribution to conceptualizing the social dynamics that drive the economic order. Considered in its historical context, it is more difficult to mistake Veblen's intention in *The Theory of the Leisure Class* as beginning and ending with social satire and easier to grasp the quality of his economic analysis. Wharton's work also helps to clarify Veblen's purpose. Neither Veblen nor Wharton were addressing a narrowly-defined academic audience for the purpose of attaining status and recognition. Both sought to shape the understanding of their age; both engaged in the production of knowledge about the pressing issues of their time. Their efforts contributed to a change in social philosophy from the prevalent strains of Social Darwinism. Understood in the same context as Wharton, *The Theory of the Leisure Class* is more obviously a revelation of the distorting influence of consumer culture on the individual, a rebuke to neoclassical reductionism about human nature.

An understanding of the intellectual concerns of Veblen's contemporaries clarifies both the nature and purpose of *The Theory of the Leisure Class*. While the arguments of the Social Darwinists legitimizing the upper classes invited a level of satire from their detractors, the barbs were not an end in themselves; rather, satirizing the pseudo-scientific objective style used by Social Darwinists while offering a clear depiction of the mores of the upper class were part of a larger effort to undermine the dominance of social darwinism and the politics it supported. Veblen's *The Theory of the Leisure Class* certainly contributed to this effort; as with Gilman, he focused his critical lens on the economic order and its influence on the construction of character. His special contribution was to offer a theory of consumption which made the economic order responsible for the structuring of individual motives around issues of envy and emulation.

5   THE RESURGENCE OF SOCIAL DARWINISM TO SUPPORT FREE MARKET CAPITALISM

In the waning years of the century, we are witnessing again a widening of the gap between the rich and the poor, and a revival among politicians, economists, and academics in the social sciences of the strains of social thought that resonate most obviously with Social Darwinism. Its echoes can be heard in the mantra of the Free Market; in the promulgation of the idea that capitalism properly practiced builds character and civic virtue, and in the corollary argument that the problem of the inner cities is not poverty but immorality and an unwillingness to work; in the proposals of the Contract with America; in Charles Murray's *The Bell Curve* (Herrnstein and Murray 1994); and even in the silliness of Newt Gingrich's assertion to college students that the reason men fight wars is that they like to roll around in the mud, while women do not.

This line of thinking is not confronted by an equally prevalent response or by a wide range of responses, either of which approach would contribute at the very least to debunking the myth that such claims reiterate the equivalent of natural law and at best to a healthy debate about the social philosophy and vision that ought to guide policy. Given the low ebb in public discourse about social philosophy, it is worthwhile to recall not only that writers and thinkers at the turn of the century thought it natural to enter such a debate, but also to examine how Veblen and Wharton countered the Social Darwinism of their age by turning their attention to the social dynamics of wealth and describing what they saw.

6   CONSUMPTION AND THE CULTURE OF EMULATION

Veblen, with his insight into the fundamental motives of an economic order built upon conformity, envy and emulation, and Wharton, with her insight into the psychological costs of those demands, anticipated the dynamics of the consumer economy at the close of the century; an economy which relies upon the same motives even in the absence of a leisure class to set the standards of taste, consumption, and behavior. As Tiger Woods rose to prominence, Nike (who is one of his sponsors) produced an ad in which children of all races and ages were made to say 'I'm Tiger Woods.' The word 'Nike' was not mentioned or used. The aim of the ad was to reinforce the desirability of living life vicariously, of identifying with or seeing oneself with another person, or way of living. Since it was not so long ago that the newspapers carried stories of young people shooting each other over a pair of Nike Air Jordan's, with attendant criticism of Nike's advertising campaigns aimed at arousing intense longing for his shoes, it is perhaps not surprising that Nike chose to downplay its sponsorship of the ad. On the other hand, advertisers now construct ads with the intention of engaging the audience in helping to construct the meaning, to participate by filling in the syntactic gaps, the absences. To do that, audiences have to be very well informed about the dominant iconography of their popular culture; or, said another way, they have to be educated participants in the politics of celebrity, and in the hieroglyphics of the signs and symbols of status.

Tiger Woods as a model to young people who want to play golf, as a symbol for the nation of an idealized vision of race relations based on merit and not prejudice, is appropriated to the selling not simply of golf shoes, but of a positive feeling about Nike and the Nike swoosh. He becomes the figment of someone else's imagination, a commodified image used in turn to commodify those who admire him.

Veblen's *The Theory of the Leisure Class* provides a systematic analysis of the necessary demand for constructing one's identity as an image; for living as it were vicariously through the symbols of consumption and waste that defines one in terms of status. Wharton provides the insight into the sacrifice of individual identity required in order to live life in the vicarious manner demanded by the desire to conform to caste. Neither would agree that the accumulation of wealth contributes to competence, virtue, or personal initiative. In Veblen's analysis, it requires cultivation of the same talents one notices when watching a documentary of hunting carnivores or raptors; in Wharton's vision of things, it stifles any creative, useful, or imaginative impulse.

In an age when the attention has shifted from the accumulation of wealth to consumer demand and consumer confidence as the benchmarks for judging the health not only of the economy but of the society in general, their conclusions are especially valuable for pointing out the fundamental need in such an economy to induce individuals to desire to present themselves as figments of someone else's imagination, while at the same time imagining they are inventing themselves as unique, self-actualizing individuals who are pursuing their own inner desires.

7 VEBLEN AND CONTEMPORARY CONSUMPTION

David Hamilton's work, mentioned earlier, suggests that Veblen's theory has contemporary significance. But John Kenneth Galbraith's analysis of the revised sequence (1967; see dependence effect in Galbraith 1958) also suggests something more than simple emulation of the leisure class. Galbraith's analysis adds the conscious construction of desire from commercial enterprise itself.

In Veblen's analysis consumption behavior is the result of meeting norms and standards of reference groups. Each reference group is part of a social hierarchy of reference groups ranked on the basis of income. The pecuniary canons of taste and decency are dictated by the elite strata of this hierarchy and this system is legitimized by a Social Darwinian presupposition of the meritorious character of those occupying the highest strata. Thus norms and standards of consumption are constructed in a rather singular way that presumes everyone who is of significance is included within this status system. The social myth of America as a great homogenizing melting pot where people of very different origins are constructed into a single society reinforced such a singular status system.

Both Veblen and particularly Wharton were writing about a system that was ending. *The Age of Innocence* described the era ended by World War I and that same period is of pivotal significance for consumption theory. This is because the science of public relations and advertising as we know it in the modern era emerged from the propaganda campaigns of World War I. What was learned from these propaganda campaigns were the techniques for selling to a mass consumer market a product they did not want and which would be deadly to them if used as directed, that is, World War I. The flexibility and malleability of the images and myths so constructed created the art of using the culture's symbolic system to convince, persuade, motivate and mobilize the population.

These techniques were rapidly turned to commercial account in peace time. In the post-war period, the interest in selling to a mass market led to the production of popular cultural forms that represented the American population as homogeneous and homogenized.   Ozzie and Harriet portrayed the all-American family. Their life style was portrayed as the norm. It is this normal middle class existence that is to be emulated. Such programming thus provided a format for marketing appliances, cleaning supplies, and services. Juliet Schor's (1992) analysis of the speed up in housekeeping shows the ever-increasing standards of cleanliness required to sustain a minimally decent standard of living. Notice no elite social group is necessary to set the new standards. All that is required is the constant insistence of the necessity, normality and need for ever higher standards of housekeeping reinforced by fictional television characters, television commercials and women's magazines. These formats are over-determined by the needs of marketers who seek out the venues that most reflect the aims and values their advertising clients seek to promote.

By the 1960s Americans were forced to confront the mythical character of their supposed homogeneity. Many groups of people who could not identify with the mythical American mainstream began to insist on social recognition of their civil rights and basic humanity in opposition to the status of invisibility assigned them within American society. The demands of women and minorities to be recognized carries with it a radical potential to transform the social order. These influences clearly shaped both programming and advertising, as the political climate always does. Beginning in the 1970s, there was a corollary emphasis on 'difference' arising from the political right, one which benefited from social divisions along racial lines, and from promoting conflict between the middle and lower classes. In addition, the new technologies of cable and satellite transmissions meant the loss of what had been a 'mass audience' and the rise of highly segmented markets, which advertisers sought to target in ever more discriminating segments, and which depend upon not only defining target audiences, but making them feel they are an elite, that 'others' cannot participate — and by actively discouraging those who do not fit the demographer's profile. Advertising became more focused. Demographic targeting become the most important element of a successful advertising campaign. Veblen's mechanisms of emulation and vicarious living remain important. The reference group is no longer the leisure class, but instead a totally constructed reference group — constructed by the advertisers (Turow 1997, pp. 37–57).

Since there is no real class that stands in an elite position to arbitrate conformity with norms and standards of respectable life each person is placed in a position of tremendous uncertainty. All of us have many different social roles and advertisers have segmented and targeted each one. In order to fit in, to be comfortable, we must conspicuously consume in a manner appropriate for the social roles we occupy.

Each small myth sets a standard to be emulated by some segment of the population. In a society of people with multiple and fragmented identities, the multiplicity of such efforts directed at them insure that some standards will not be met. The myth of individual choice deflects significant political recognition that goods mediate desires, and are not in and of themselves objects of desire. Thus the failure to realize one's desires through consumption is perceived as personal rather than as an aspect of the economic order.

Ron and Jacqueline Stanfield (1980, 1995) have addressed the significance of the alienating character of human lives reduced to a vicarious life mediated and experienced through the social symbolism of goods and services. They identify the sacrifice of self-realization, inattention to nurturing family lives, and the loss of both civic identification and community life as results of the commodification of life. In an interesting twist on Marx's notion of commodity fetishism, where alienated workers attempt to recapture the life lost in the capitalist production processes through the acquisition and consumption of goods, they identify the emptiness left when individuals attempt to re-embed fragmented lives through consumption. In the process it is not the commodity that is fetishized but the people themselves.

Through consumption we can identify ourselves as being like those symbolically constructed beings in advertising. We can live their mythical lives or at least be a part of it as a larger social phenomena. We are commodified — sold to the advertiser. Furthermore, we are fetishized. Consider any issue of *Vogue* magazine, there will be a series of photographs of models wearing new designer clothes. The models will be of the body type currently favored by fashion designers. The photographs will be viewed by an almost exclusively-female audience. Yet the models will be posed in order to appeal to the gaze of a man. Thus the female reader of *Vogue* must look at the photograph and imagine herself as wearing the clothes for the purpose of being viewed by an imagined male. The women who read *Vogue* are expected to (and presumably do) fetishize themselves as they read the magazine (Jhally 1990).

In these times then, consumption is still driven by emulation and vicarious living as suggested by Veblen. The revised sequence identified by Galbraith shows how commerce drives the construction of vicarious desires and encourages lives mediated by goods and services as signifiers of cultural meaning. Stanfield and Stanfield argue convincingly that lives thus constructed and mediated are alienating and destructive. We argue that the fragmented identities and multiplicity of social roles typical of contemporary American lives insures a high degree of failure to live up to the emulative myths constructed by advertising and accepted as societal norms. The short-lived character of contemporary cultural myths combined with the highly targeted, symbolically charged, and flexible images and narratives appropriated by commercial propagandists (referred to as advertisers) allows for constant change thus feeding the need of a consumer economy for ever more consumption to sustain it.

Finally we note that the myth of individual choice, remains extremely potent in our society (Feiner 1995). Regardless of the individual damage or social pathology that results, commercial activity is absolved from any role in the construction of consumer behavior. As teenage girls waste away from dietary disorders, and young children kill one another over Air Jordan shoes or Oakland Raiders jackets, we calmly nod and put our trash in lemon scented trash bags, while neoclassical economists tell us that commercial society is the source of civic virtue.

REFERENCES

Dorfman, Joseph (1934), *Thorstein Veblen and His America,* New York: Viking Press.

Feiner, Susan (1995), 'Reading Neoclassical Economics: Toward an Erotic Economy of Sharing', in *Out of the Margin: Feminist Perspectives on Economics*, E. Kuiper and Jolande Sap (ed), New York: Routledge.

Hamilton, David (1962), *The Consumer in Our Economy,* Boston: Houghton Mifflin.

Hamilton, David (1973), 'What Has Evolutionary Economics to Contribute to Consumption Theory?', *Journal of Economic Issues,* **18**, 197–207.

Hamilton, David (1987), 'Thorstein Veblen as the First Professor of Marketing', *Journal of Economic Issues,* **23**, 1097–1103.

Hamilton, David (1989), 'Institutional Economics and Consumption', *Journal of Economic Issues,* **21**, 1531–1553.

Herrnstein, Richard and Charles Murray (1994), *The Bell Curve: Intelligence and Class in American life,* New York: Free Press.

Hofstadter, Richard (1955), *Social Darwinism in American Thought,* Boston: The Beacon Press.

Howells, William Dean (1899), 'An Opportunity for American Fiction', *Literature,* **16**, April, 361–362.

Howells, William Dean (1899), 'An Opportunity for American Fiction', *Literature,*. **17**, May, 385–386.

Galbraith, John Kenneth (1958), *The Affluent Society,* Boston: Houghton Mifflin.

Galbraith, John Kenneth (1967), *The New Industrial State,* Boston: Houghton Mifflin.

Gilman, Charlotte Perkins (1994[1898]), *Women and Economics: The Economic Relation Between Women and Men,* Amherst, NY: Prometheus Books.

Jhally, Sut (1990), *The Codes of Advertising; Fetishism and the Political Economy of Meaning in the Consumer Society,* New York: Routledge.

Joslin, Katherine (1991), *Edith Wharton,* New York: St. Martins Press.

Kazin, Alfred (1942), *On Native Grounds,* New York: Reynal and Hitchcock.

Kyrk, Hazel (1923), *A Theory of Consumption,* Boston: Houghton Mifflin.

Lee, Vernon (pseud.) (1902), 'The Economic Dependence of Women', (Review of Gilman, Women and Economics), *The North American Review,* 71–90.

Schor, Juliet B. (1992), *The Overworked American,* New York: Basic Books.

Stanfield, J. Ronald (1994), 'Learning from Japan about the Nurturance Gap in America', *Review of Social Economy,* **52**, 2–19.

Stanfield, J. Ronald (1996), *John Kenneth Galbraith,* New York: St. Martin's Press.

Stanfield, J. Ronald and Jacqueline B. Stanfield (1980), 'Consumption in Contemporary Capitalism: The Backward Art of Living', *Journal of Economic Issues,* **14**, June, 437–450.

Stanfield, J. Ronald (1995), 'Where Has Love Gone? Reciprocity and the Nurturance Gap', *International Association for Feminist Economics,* Washington, DC.

Sumner, William Graham (1911[1883]), *What Social Classes Owe to Each Other,* New York: Harper & Brothers

Turow, Joseph (1997), *Breaking up America: Advertisers and the New Media World,* Chicago: University of Chicago Press.

Veblen, Thorstein (1934[1899]), *The Theory of the Leisure Class,* New York: Modern Library.

Waller, William and Linda Robertson, (1990), 'Why Johnny (Ph.D., Economics) Can't Read: A Rhetorical Analysis of Thorstein Veblen and a Response to Donald McCloskey's Rhetoric of Economics', *Journal of Economic Issues,* **24**, 4-December, 1027–1044.

Waller, William and Linda Robertson (1997) 'Jo's Hair and Mrs. Beaufort's Emerald Necklace: Alternative Discourse of Value and Exchange in Women's Narratives of Wealth and Power', *Annual Meeting of the Association for Evolutionary Economics,* New Orleans, January.

Ward, Lester (1900), 'Review of The Theory of the Leisure Class', *American Journal of Sociology,* **5**, May, 829–837.

Wharton, Edith (1985[1905]), *The House of Mirth,* New York: Penguin.

Wharton, Edith (1992[1920]), *The Age of Innocence,* New York: Collier Books.

Wills, Garry (1997), *John Wayne's America: The Politics of Celebrity,* New York: Simon and Schuster.

3. Be All You Can Be: Invidious Self-Development and its Social Imperative

Doug Brown

1 INTRODUCTION

Veblen wrote *The Theory of the Leisure Class* for the twentieth century. It spoke prophetically of the rise of consumerism, of the emergence of suburban 'middle-class America,' and to the 'lifestyles of the rich and famous.' 'Conspicuous consumption' became a household word. Most who grew up within the middle-class, consumerist culture after World War II, also grew up with a set of values emphasizing the need to perform to one's maximum capacities and talents. We were told to 'be all you can be'; to actualize yourself; to 'make something of yourself.'

For us the twentieth century is not only about pecuniary success as Veblen understood it in *The Theory of the Leisure Class*, but about individual and personal success in general. Each generation was instructed that there may be more to life than money, but there's not more to life than 'being all you can be.' 'Just go out and be all you can be.' In rereading *The Theory of the Leisure Class* what stands out is the fact that one can virtually substitute individual achievement for Veblen's notion of pecuniary achievement. Now at the close of the twentieth century it strikes me that status and prestige are still bestowed on those who achieve financial success, but more importantly it goes to those who achieve as much self-realization success as possible.

The following remarks have to do with how 'self-development' (self-realization; self-actualization) has become a new and all-inclusive measure of esteem and reputability, that although not replacing Veblenian pecuniary prowess has become a more universal index. What I am suggesting is a particular interpretation of some obvious observations about the reality of self-development. I have not attempted to prove that self-development, as as I have defined it, is important. That much should be obvious to all of us. But my interpretation of its significance is debatable.

Veblen talks about esteem, honorific behavior, reputability, invidious distinction, status emulation and comparison, and about prowess. He says that the market economy is driven by the desire of people, both business and working class, to achieve esteem and status, and that this need is manifested in a pecuniary fashion. What I suggest is that today society grants status and prestige to more than just financial success. We also place a high value on one's observable degree of self-success in general. We measure people by the degree of their self-development, in other words. People in general are measured by their achievements. Moreover, self-development has become an imperative that is socially, morally, and economically imposed on us. In this respect the social imperative of self-development is similar to Marcuse's concept of the 'performance principle' in *Eros and Civilization* (Marcuse 1955). 'Performance' is what matters most.

The point is that if you do not 'make something' of yourself, then you are a 'loser' or a 'slacker.' The rewards, the status, the praise, and the money generally go to those who are ambitious, self-directed, 'driven,' and focused. To those who achieve and accomplish all that they can go the honors and the esteem; those who fall behind in the competitive self-development struggle are the slackers, and the slackers usually suffer both social and economic hardship.

Not only does it pay to be goal-driven but, moreover, basic material and economic insecurity force it upon us. The ticket to financial security for most of us in the competitive struggle is through self-development. To avoid alienating labor, dead-end jobs, and to 'advance,' we must acquire more skills and develop our talents. And by 'self-development' I include the entire range of personal-growth activities including career advancement and credentials, self-help personal growth skills, job-training, and skill-development of any non-pecuniary form, like the arts and athletics.

We grow up in a world in which if we want to 'get ahead' or avoid economic hardship, then we must develop our skills and capabilities to the maximum. In other words, we have to try to be all we can be, because if we do not we suffer not only the loss of social esteem but end up with low-wage, insecure jobs.

Capitalism is an economy that drives us to actualize ourselves just as it drives business to maximize profits. We are driven by the lure of money and status and the fear of economic hardship. So in the competitive struggle it is insecurity that causes businesses to grow, and likewise it is insecurity that causes individuals to grow! Either you grow or you 'waste your life.' What's true for firms is true for the individual players. This does not mean that businesses intentionally create a climate that nurtures self-development. They generally do not. In fact it is because the climate is so alienating and insecure that people either grow or lose. Whether it is personal growth or corporate growth, both are forms of compulsion that are essentially insatiable. Although we are conscious of the limits-to-growth argument in economic theory, we rarely apply the same reasoning to the process of personal growth. We frequently hear, 'you can always be more tomorrow than you are today!' So we may admit to excessive economic growth but never excessive personal growth! Yet the two are one organic and mutually-reinforcing process. The point in applying Veblen's *The Theory of the Leisure Class* to the twenty-first century is that if we want a sustainable and just world not only must we rethink economic growth but personal growth as well. This to me is a radical notion that is implicit in Veblen's sociology and economics.

In another sense the competitive struggle that businesses contend with forces them to innovate, to grow, to be all they can be. Their search for profits and success is their form of corporate self-actualization. So both firms and individuals are caught up in a self-actualization treadmill that is never-ending. Both parties suffer competitive stress and seek ways to opt out of it. Businesses seek monopoly power and government protection from competitive forces. Individuals seek means to 'drop out' if the stress gets too great. On the other hand some firms and individuals do not find the self-actualization treadmill to be excessive and, in fact, thrive on the process.

One of the major contributions that Veblen made in *The Theory of the Leisure Class* is to demonstrate the extent to which social, non-economic motives like the desires for esteem and status actually drive the economy. For example, Marx never thematically questioned why capitalists want to get rich or why they want to maximize their profits. Why does anyone ever want to get rich, for that matter? The answer was no doubt obvious for Marx, but for Veblen it was not. Most would say that greater wealth allows for greater immediate gratification. Increased wealth is thought to mean more power to do what you want when you want to do it. By contrast Veblen suggests that the non-economic motives of status and esteem may be the driving forces behind the insatiable thirst for riches and wealth. Thus we acquire wealth and success in order to impress others. The experience of the twentieth century appears to bear this out. Veblen merely points out that the age-old need for status takes on an unmistakable financial form in a 'pecuniary culture.'

What's at issue is the incentive system in capitalism. If the incentive system is based upon insatiability, whether it is wealth, profits, status, esteem, self-actualization, or self-development, then our notion of a sustainable and just world must consider this and find new incentives. It makes little sense to have an economy based upon satiability when its members have insatiable appetites for esteem and personal growth. Moreover, the incentive system is also a reward system. The rewards go to those who strive to be all they can be. If they manifest this in the economic sphere then they achieve financial rewards. If they manifest this in other spheres, like the arts, they may not be rewarded financially but receive social status and esteem. They may be 'starving artists' but are generally not considered 'losers' or 'slackers.'

Even academics and leftist intellectuals, going back at least to Marx, have a tendency to disregard financial prowess, but confer status on self-development prowess instead. After all, Marx considered socialism to be the institutional condition for the 'full and free development of the individual.' 'Full development,' for Marx, meant undoubtedly that the individual had a responsibility to be all (s)he could be. I would like to outline an argument that challenges the notion of status and prestige based upon intellectual, artistic, and all other expressions of self-development. Perhaps the entire concept of self-development and self-actualization is overrated in capitalism. The basis for this rethinking lies in Veblen's *The Theory of the Leisure Class.*

The argument is basically this. Self-development may be an acceptable concept, but it has taken on a new meaning in the last century. It is now subject to the same status considerations that Veblen examined with respect to pecuniary prowess. Just as Veblen talks about invidious and conspicuous consumption and leisure, society now validates invidious and conspicuous self-development. From Marx in the last century to fashionable self-help books on the Top Ten list today, 'be all you can be' is the moral and social maxim for achieving social esteem, status, and prestige. If you are not a self-actualizing, becoming, growing individual then you are left behind, either economically or socially. Alongside the corporate and national race for economic growth there is the internalized and individualized race for personal growth. Both are insatiable quests in which there are winners and losers; both are treadmills of productivism; both are subject to the same status-driven, competitive conditions criticized by Veblen. Just as the economy of capitalism is a 'driven' system, within it the individual is supposed to be 'driven' as well.

But is the social treadmill of self-developmentalism necessarily bad? Is it bad or wrong to be a driven, self-actualizing person, especially if it is not pecuniary prowess that one seeks? Clearly not. Yet, what about all of those who are not driven by internalized goals of self-development? What about all of the average people of the world who are not ambitious, not very 'self-development' oriented, and not particularly into the trendy scene of personal growth and self-actualization? The responsible and considerate individual whose life is not defined by his/her self-actualizing goals represents a substantial portion of humanity. The reward system tends to ignore them. Should this be the case?

This raises some tough questions. One way to get a handle on it is to make a mental distinction between 'self-development' activities and behaviors on the one hand, and 'virtuous' activities and behaviors on the other. What do we mean by 'virtuous?' These are behaviors that have to do primarily with being a responsible, honest, and caring person with respect to one's friends, family, associates, and ultimately with the world at large. They are behaviors that are not directly self-actualizing, but they are behaviors that are necessary for people to have if society is going to function properly. They are vital social behaviors that are not considered self-developing. There are many: compassion, kindness, fellow-feeling, caring and thoughtfulness, honesty, responsibility, reliability and empathy. The point is that there are many people who are basically nice folks, essentially friendly and fair, and responsible in both their personal and social relationships. They are the average folks of the world, who are decent and kind people, but may not have the self-development ambition and drive that will push them up the achievement and status ladders.

No one is simply one way or the other. Both kinds of behaviors as habits of thought and life occur simultaneously. This is not an either/or distinction. But there are those for whom personal growth, ambition, drive, self-actualization, and the entire range of status-related self-development behaviors are weak. They are virtuous folks that are not into self-development. Where, in this world of driven, invidious and conspicuous self-actualizers, does this segment of global humanity fit?

I want to argue in the following that a sustainable world requires not only a rethinking of economic growth, but a shift from a 'regime of status' based upon self-development to one that emphasizes virtue — responsible, humane living. What needs to be socially-fostered and encouraged is not so much the insatiable appetite for 'being all you can be,' but the satiable 'habits of life' of social and personal responsibility and kindness. We inhabit a world now that grants status for 'being all you can be.' It does not reward decent, human kindness in any kind of comparable way. What a sustainable twenty-first century world needs is not more self-actualization, but more responsible and kind behavior. We must push beyond an insatiable capitalism that puts the sanctity of the self first. It is more important now for a satiable self to be responsible and kind (in a world of social justice) than for an insatiable self to personally grow and develop its potentiality. The point is not to shift how we award status, that is, from self-development to virtue. The point is to go beyond the regimes of status, and socially and culturally embed virtuous living in a satiable economy.

Clearly, the idea is not to punish people for being self-actualizers. And obviously, some people choose very ambitiously to develop themselves in the direction of virtue and selfless service to others and humanity. Mahatma Gandhi comes to mind. People who want, like Gandhi, to actualize themselves for service to others are exemplary and should not be punished either. So we grant that people can be zealous self-developers of virtue; that people can focus their self-actualization on selflessness. Thus self-development and virtuous behaviors are not mutually exclusive.

But to the extent that status and reward tend to follow self-development behavior rather than responsible, human kindness, there is a problem that must be addressed if a sustainable and just world is to be obtainable for the twenty-first century. To follow this line of argument, one has to then think in terms of the differences between behaviors that are 'self-development oriented' and those that are more 'virtuous oriented,' and next recognize that the drivenness of capitalism tends to reward the former. *The Theory of the Leisure Class* causes us to envision going beyond a 'regime of status.' In doing so Veblen's reasoning requires rethinking self-development and making virtuous behavior the foundation for a sustainable economy. And it must be understood that there is no basis for increasing responsible and kind behavior without the requisite social justice. A kinder gentler world requires a socially-just world as a necessary condition. We can clarify this by examining *The Theory of the Leisure Class* in more detail.

2   VEBLEN AND TODAY'S GLOBALIZATION OF CAPITALISM

What is the present context when rereading *The Theory of the Leisure Class*? There is a structural and cultural transformation of consumer capitalism underway: globalization. And one observation is that the status-related behaviors that Veblen analysed in *The Theory of the Leisure Class* are as extreme as ever. Perhaps they are worsening. Because of television and the high-tech media, communication is better than a century ago. It is easier for groups, classes, nations, and individuals to make comparisons among each other. It is now easier to be conspicuous with any type of behavior. And the ways in which we can express invidiousness are greater. The variety of clothing, lifestyles, housing, and cars, for example, has mushroomed. It is easier to 'show off,' in other words.

Yet Tilman suggests that of Veblen's books, *The Theory of the Leisure Class* is 'perhaps the most conspicuous example of an American classic that largely lacks a scholarly apparatus' (Tilman 1992, p. 188). This clearly makes rereading it for today more difficult, but a new twist or spin can be given to an enduring 'approach' evident in Veblen's *Leisure Class*.

Status emulation and invidious comparison, through as yet an unclear but habitual and evolving fashion are observably worse. Also, this may be the worst of times for such developments. Because with the globalization of all life activities, our global ecosystem cannot sustain the continuous drain on resources resulting from invidious living and status-determined lifestyles.

The globalization of consumer culture aggravates insatiable invidious behavior. This trend not only belies greater human insecurity, but is simply too wasteful to be tolerated for another century. Veblen was aware of this possibility. 'The invidious comparison can never become so favorable to the individual making it that he would not gladly rate himself still higher relatively to his competitors in the struggle for pecuniary reputability' (Veblen 1918[1899], pp. 31–32). He then states that 'since the struggle is substantially a race for reputability on the basis of an invidious comparison, no approach to a definitive attainment is possible' (Veblen 1918[1899], p. 32). Thus:

> The presumption, therefore, is that the farther the community, especially the wealthy classes of the community, develop in wealth and mobility and in the range of their human contact, the more imperatively will the law of conspicuous waste assert itself in matters of dress, the more will the sense of beauty tend to fall into abeyance or be overborne by the canon of pecuniary reputability, the more rapidly will fashions shift and change, and the more grotesque and intolerable will be the varying styles that successively come into vogue (Veblen 1918[1899], p. 178).

Although Veblen is referring here to invidious fashion behavior, it applies generally to all expressions of status emulation. As Veblen suggests when consumer culture evolves in novel ways and goes global, the same thing happens with invidious behavior.

So the most important development with respect to a rereading of *The Theory of the Leisure Class* is the current adaptive transformation of consumer capitalism called globalization. It involves a cultural shift of the system, the high-tech driven globalization of capitalism, and a movement towards global self-regulating markets. The two revisions of Veblen's book that are suggested by globalized capitalism are: (1) conspicuous leisure and conspicuous consumption are now a subset of 'conspicuous and invidious self-development,' and (2) greater insecurity coupled with more means for self-expression are making status and invidious behaviors worse.

Globalization brings with it the above cultural changes that affect status behavior. The label, 'postmodernism,' is frequently used to describe this. Yet as Rosenthal states of postmodernism, 'when we cut through the fanfare, what this often boils down to is an affirmation of plurality and complexity, something we can all gladly endorse, but which does not seem to require the firepower of postmodernism to give it expression' (Rosenthal 1992, p. 101). The postmodern changes in capitalism are different because they have to do with the reality of high-tech living in a global system of increasingly self-regulating markets. Rosenthal is correct to say that:

> The transformations in social and economic life that underlie theories of the postmodern, such as the new economies of information, new global organizations of commodity production, the impact of new technologies on work life and the impact of just-in-time production on job security as well as commodity consumption — all of this continues to take shape around us, continues to cry out for understanding (Rosenthal 1992, p. 104).

So today, as Veblen said a century ago, we still 'live under a regime of status handed down from an earlier stage of industrial development' (Veblen 1918[1899], p. 323). Conspicuous leisure and conspicuous consumption exist today. But they are the surface of a deeper problem. The bigger problem is that of conspicuous and invidious self-development.

Conspicuous self-development is not necessarily pecuniary, but like leisure and consumption, it is a means to demonstrate prowess, to achieve esteem, honor, and reputability. As Veblen says, 'esteem is gained and dispraise is avoided by putting one's efficiency in evidence' (Veblen 1918[1899], p. 16). Although conspicuous consumption and leisure show the individual's efficiency at making money, what they are really showing is the individual's success at being an individual — a self. Conspicuous self-development shows the individual's efficiency at 'life in general.' Whether it is self-development or financial success, it is all about 'being all you can be.' The point is to put your efficiency at being all you can be in evidence. Whether it is financial or not, does not matter.

How does this relate to postmodernism and globalization? First, there are a variety of terms other than postmodernism that are in popular usage: globalization of production, flexible accumulation, the New International Economic Order, flexible specialization, post-Fordism, and just-in-time production (see Harvey 1989, 1991; Jameson 1991; Lash and Urry 1987; Lyotard 1984; MacEwan 1991). As Soja states, 'another culture of time and space seems to be taking shape in this contemporary context and it is redefining the nature and experience of everyday life in the modern world' (Soja 1989, p. 60). Harvey refers to this as a new round of 'time-space compression' (Harvey 1989).

Polanyi's notion of the 'double movement,' that is, self-regulating market forces versus the 'protective response,' is another way to understand this new economic and cultural shift to postmodern capitalism (Polanyi 1957). The nineteenth century was one of 'disembedding' of economy from society, while the twentieth century has been marked by 're-embedding' forces. Social democracy, the welfare state, negotiated contracts, and US global hegemony worked to stabilize and partly re-embed economic activity in the last half-century.

Postmodern capitalism is a term addressing the social and cultural effects of a new round of global self-regulation that is unraveling the old system. There is a new period of disembedding taking place at the global level. Postmodernism is about the breaking down of barriers that were previously part of the twentieth century protective response. Barriers that once held things together are breaking down, that is, the demise of the nuclear family and the decline of unionism. Barriers that once kept things apart are also breaking down, that is, the 'peripheralization of the core' exemplified by Los Angeles, now the 'Capitol of the Third World.'

Thus, global self-regulation, that is, disembedded market forces, induces flux, diversity, de-centeredness, complexity, and most importantly a new phase of material and psychological insecurity. The insecurity is evident in many different ways, including identity crises with kids and gangs, the growth of religious fundamentalism, the wars in Bosnia and West Africa, and the intensification of all forms of social conflict, whether it be racial, ethnic, gender, or class. There is a climate of fear and uncertainty that manifests itself in virtually every part of the world. Insecurity is not something Veblen discussed in *The Theory of the Leisure Class*. Yet perhaps it is postmodern insecurity that is aggravating invidious and emulatory behavior.

3   INVIDIOUS SELF-DEVELOPMENT

In *The Theory of the Leisure Class* Veblen is clear that expressions of invidious comparison and status emulation can change and evolve because they are habits of mind and life, which themselves can change over time. As he states, 'the propensity for emulation — for invidious comparison — is of ancient growth and is a pervading trait of human nature. It is easily called into vigorous activity in any new form, and it asserts itself with great insistence under any form under which it has once found habitual expression' (Veblen 1918[1899], p. 109; see also pp. 148, 186, 189). Thus, as societies evolve the ways in which people make status comparisons and measure their success and prowess change as well. Since Veblen wrote *The Theory of the Leisure Class* the standard of reputability, of success, and of esteem has evolved. Self-development has become a 'universal' standard for prowess and status.

Veblen focused on a pecuniary standard which still exists, but self-development is more universal and undoubtedly runs deeper in the human psyche. As a habit of thought and mind, it is at least as old as the Enlightenment. The moral maxim of 'be all you can be' is a modern concept that has evolved with the concept of the individual. The sanctity of the self, of the individual, is the basis for classical liberalism and neoclassical economics and makes little sense unless it is conceived of as a 'becoming' self that exists as potentiality. In the modern world the individual is viewed as important, with inalienable and natural rights, because the individual embodies potentiality and can aspire to perfection. Thus, we often hear that the most significant feature of being human is that 'we can always be more tomorrow than we are today.' We are special in this modernist view because we are self-actualizing beings, capable of change and growth. And it is on the basis of our different ways of actualizing ourselves that we can make status comparisons. Ultimately the degree and manner of self-development is the basis for all invidious comparisons, because we are comparing our selves with respect to some principle of achievement. So conspicuous leisure and conspicuous consumption are what Veblen considered to the main ways to demonstrate the prowess of self-achievement and development in a pecuniary society.

Conspicuous leisure, as Veblen argued for his day, was gradually giving way to conspicuous consumption (Veblen 1918[1899], p. 87). Now self-development has become the universal common denominator, and as a standard it includes both pecuniary and non-pecuniary measures.

Postmodern capitalism, as it continues to universalize and also 'multiculturalize' consumer culture, is fostering a more general expression of success and achievement used for status emulation and invidious comparison. The system is still one in which people are concerned with self-respect and esteem, and as Veblen stated, 'the usual basis of self-respect is the respect accorded by one's neighbors' (Veblen 1918[1899], p. 30). No doubt this holds true today. Additionally, respect, honor, dignity, that is, those features that are the basis for esteem, continue to be a function of socially-determined achievement and success.

As Samuels states Veblen 'believed that people were driven by habits and custom and by whatever constituted achievement in the currently reigning system of status emulation' (Samuels 1992, p. ix). Veblen states this numerous times, for example: 'in any community where such invidious comparison of persons is habitually made, visible success becomes an end sought for its own utility as a basis of esteem. Esteem is gained and dispraise is avoided by putting one's efficiency in evidence' (Veblen 1918[1899], p. 16; pp. 181, 69, 26–28).

Veblen's logic a hundred years ago was, 'I am better than you because I am more successful than you. And I am more successful than you because I have more wealth than you (pecuniary prowess). I can show you that I have more wealth and financial success by my conspicuous leisure and my conspicuous consumption. In fact I am so successful at making money that I can be wasteful with my time and money.' Thus, being 'better' is judged by one's degree of success; but success is measured by wealth, and wealth is demonstrated by conspicuous leisure and consumption.

In updating Veblen's logic for today's postmodern capitalism it might read, 'I am better than you because I am more successful than you. I am more successful than you because I have achieved more than you. I can show you this by my self-development accomplishments.' Of course, this formulation does not exclude the idea that one can demonstrate self-development by pecuniary prowess (wealth) as indicated by conspicuous leisure and consumption. But conspicuous self-development is broader and includes many expressions of personal achievement that are not pecuniary.

Veblen realizes, I think, that he may be dealing with a potential contradiction as well. On the one hand, he says that people dislike waste and continue to value serviceability and the instinct of workmanship. On the other hand, he says that they award prestige and status to the upper classes based upon the conspicuous waste visible in the lifestyles of the rich and famous (Veblen 1918[1899], pp. 94–95). How does he reconcile this? He states that conspicuous waste is something that people tend to use as an index of pecuniary success. This is esteemable because pecuniary success indicates that rich folks must have achieved substantial serviceability in the market process in order to have made all of their money.

So people, through habits of mind and life, continue to value serviceability. As Veblen says, 'the propensity for achievement and the repugnance to futility remain the underlying economic motive. The propensity changes only in the form of its expression and in the proximate objects to which it directs the man's activity' (Veblen 1918[1899], p. 33). Thus from the perspective of the lower classes the rich can be wasteful because they have first been successful at applying their instinct of workmanship towards making lots of money. Yet even with self-development we admonish people for 'wasting their potential' if we perceive that they are not ambitious and applying themselves to self-actualization.

As much as conspicuous leisure and conspicuous consumption may be or can be at odds with the instinct of workmanship, conspicuous self-development is not. Veblen states that, 'all extraneous considerations apart, those persons (adults) are but a vanishing minority today who harbor no inclination to the accomplishment of some end, or who are not impelled of their own motion to shape some object or fact or relation for human use' (Veblen, 1918[1899], p. 94). Even the leisure class appreciates the value of serviceability. Thus for Veblen, 'the line of least resistance has changed in some measure, and the energy which formerly found a vent in predatory activity, now in part takes the direction of some ostensibly useful end. Ostensibly purposeless leisure has come to be deprecated' (Veblen 1918[1899], p. 95). So self-development is actually a better index today for status-seeking because it is more inclusive than conspicuous leisure and consumption and does not embody any element of waste. Even if one's self-development embodies little serviceability for society, it still embodies the realization of one's potential for its own sake.

Unfortunately, people are increasingly insecure in postmodern capitalism, and they continue to try to be 'better than each other'. And we continue to define 'better' as being more 'productive' in terms of ambition and personal growth. Thus, 'I am better than you because I am more productive than you' is the updated version of *The Theory of the Leisure Class*. Only today the productivist standard of status and emulation is less pecuniary than in Veblen's time. Self-development is productivist but less pecuniary; on the other hand, it has a degree of serviceability that leisure and consumption do not have.

4   INVIDIOUS DISTINCTION WITH A POSTMODERN VENGEANCE

The universal status-index of self-development is in part due to the effects of the high-tech revolution and the globalization of capitalism. These changes associated with postmodern capitalism have greatly increased the means and forms for individualized self-expression. There is increased diversity for self-expression. Harvey argues that 'new technologies (particularly computer modeling) have dissolved the need to conjoin mass production with mass repetition, and permit the flexible mass production of "almost personalized products" expressive of a great variety of styles' (Harvey 1991, p. 76). This is 'mass customization' or 'social heterogeneity.' The increased diversity of self-expression that is created contributes to novel and non-pecuniary status emulation. Invidious self-development encompasses these new forms. Veblen states:

> A standard of living is of the nature of habit. The relative facility with which an advance in the standard is made means that the life process is a process of unfolding activity and that it will readily unfold in a new direction whenever and wherever the resistance to self-expression decreases (Veblen 1918[1899], p. 106).

What has happened is that postmodern capitalism has decreased 'resistance to self-expression.' Even though some self-expression is determined by income, much of it is not. America's youth, whether they are poor street kids or children of the rich, are carving out new ways to express themselves with styles and meanings unheard of twenty years ago. Wholly new and expanded realms of self-expression now lead to entirely new forms of invidious distinction.

It is easier to make your mark of distinction when the ways in which you can distinguish yourself from others are so much greater. In many respects the history of humankind since the Agricultural Revolution is the history of the multiplication of ways in which people can distinguish themselves from one another. More division of labor, greater specialization, more diverse consumer goods, greater variety in living styles — all of these contribute to making status comparisons. More diversity means more basis for comparison.

Status comparisons would not necessarily have to be made unless people were insecure with respect to their place in society and the esteem granted them from others. And the more individualistic and competitive the society becomes, the more insecure people become. So we hear, 'it is all up to you; sink or swim; make something of yourself or else.' Of course, this is precisely what drives capitalism, the carrot and the stick. Yet the carrot and stick have a lot to do with status, emulation, and the insecurity we feel when we know it is 'do or die.'

So postmodern capitalism leads to growing insecurity. Corporations, governments, and workers the world over have become increasingly insecure as they contend with global self-regulating market forces that no one seems to control. It was this type of insecurity that Polanyi believed was the motive behind the protective response of the nineteenth century. With the second disembedding that is now occurring, there is more insecurity. Confusion, anxiety, stress, identity crises, and 'decenteredness' speak to this observation. Jameson refers to this as 'psychic fragmentation' (Jameson 1991, p. 90). In 1967, Foucault summarized our postmodern condition:

We are in the epoch of simultaneity: we are in the epoch of juxtaposition, the epoch of the near and far, of the side-by-side, of the dispersed. We are at a moment, I believe, when our experience of the world is less that of a long life developing through time than that of a network that connects points and intersects with its own skein (Foucault 1986, p. 22).

Deindustrialization, globalized production, outsourcing, the Los Angeles riots of April 1992, violent ethnic conflict in Bosnia and Africa, growing poverty and inequality, the crime and violence of everyday life, the crisis of the European social democracies — all of these phenomena point toward either symptoms or causes of more insecurity and discontinuity. This is merely a partial list. No doubt we should expect even greater invidious and status-type behaviors in this period of flux and global transformation. We are in the throes of a global identity crisis, and folks are asking themselves who they are and in so doing asking themselves how they compare and measure up against others.

5   THE SOCIAL IMPERATIVE OF SELF-DEVELOPMENT

The competitive struggle and the postmodern insecurity we face make self-development more than just a moral imperative. There are winners and losers, and the more you commit to self-development of one form or another, the more likely you are to be a winner. What is the imperative? For one thing it is insatiable. As Veblen states, 'since the struggle is substantially a race for reputability on the basis of an invidious comparison, no approach to a definitive attainment is possible' (Veblen 1918[1899], p. 32).

But it has a coercive dimension as well. Veblen realized this with respect to the pecuniary struggle, and it is no different with self-development in general. He calls pecuniary emulation a 'canon of life' with a 'coercive' side to 'which men have to adapt themselves' (Veblen 1918[1899], p. 212). The 'pecuniary struggle' in which Veblen says all classes are engaged requires people to cultivate certain traits, 'tenacity of purpose' and 'consistency of aim' (Veblen 1918[1899], pp. 237–238). He then mentions that failure to become this way is like 'a hornless steer would find himself at a disadvantage in a drove of horned cattle' (Veblen 1918[1899], p. 263). So today failure to 'be all you can be' implies being a hornless steer! Well, if one rejects the social imperative, then it is either face the difficulty of finding a viable, security-and-esteem alternative, that is, be a successful drop-out, or suffer the disadvantage of being a hornless steer.

People either take the plunge and internalize the values of productivism, that is, self-motivation, self-direction, ambition, goal-drivenness, tenacity of purpose and all of the other traits found in the current list of self-help books, or they look for a social niche that allows them to opt out of the struggle as much as possible. And there are niches, of course.

But the real problem is that these are not the values that we should be talking about for a sustainable society for the twenty-first century. The people who today are not emulating productivism, but are decent, caring folks are likely to be left out of the growth-driven reward-loop. The reward and status system is in sync with a growth-driven economic system; it is not in sync with the moral and ethical values of 'virtue' — responsibility, compassion, and human kindness.

Veblen was aware of this, too. He suggests that the canons of reputability cause problems: 'its effect upon the temper of a community is of the nature of an arrested spiritual development' (Veblen 1918[1899], p. 213). Over the last 200 years since the Enlightenment and the maturation of capitalism, what it means to be human has become identified with the ability to self-actualize.

The traits of 'virtue,' that cluster of more selfless behaviors, have been downplayed. Being human now means 'be all you can be,' not selfless service to humanity. And 'selfless service to humanity' does not necessitate submission to oppression and the world's injustices. Again, Gandhi comes to mind. Veblen agrees. He says that the 'collective interest is best served by honesty, diligence, peacefulness, goodwill, an absence of self-seeking, and an habitual recognition and apprehension of causal sequence' (Veblen 1918[1899], p. 227). Although this is not an all-inclusive list of the cluster called 'virtue,' it indicates Veblen's understanding of today's problem.

6 TOWARDS A POST-INVIDIOUS SOCIETY FOR THE TWENTY-FIRST CENTURY

The reward and status system is today tied to the insatiable goal of self-development. The ambitious and productivist players are in sync with the insatiable growth-driven economy. The decent and responsible folks who are not self-actualizers are left behind in the struggle for status and esteem. Veblen also states:

The decent requirements of waste absorb the surplus energy of the population in an invidious struggle and leave no margin for the non-invidious expression of life. The canons of decent life are an elaboration of the principle of invidious comparison, and they accordingly act consistently to inhibit all non-invidious effort and to inculcate the self-regarding attitude (Veblen 1918[1899], p. 362).

What is needed is what Veblen referred to at one point as the 'non-invidious residue of the religious life.' On a note of optimism, he states:

> This non-invidious residue of the religious life, — the sense of communion with the environment, or with the generic life process, — as well as the impulse of charity or of sociability, act in a pervasive way to shape men's habits of thought for the economic purpose (Veblen 1918[1899], p. 334).

Of course, he also realizes that through institutions and habits of life and thought, the individual assimilates invidious behavior patterns as well. To practice virtue and fellow-feeling in an institutional setting based on greed and envy is difficult. 'Under any human phase of culture, other or later than the presumptive initial phase here spoken of, the gifts of good-nature, equity, and indiscriminate sympathy do not appreciably further the life of the individual,' and 'freedom from scruple, from sympathy, honesty and regard for life may, within fairly wide limits, be said to further the success of the individual in the pecuniary culture' (Veblen 1918[1899], p. 223).

Veblen's vision, as we know, was one of living aesthetically and materially in a simple but harmonious fashion with people and nature — a non-invidious lifestyle of justice and security based upon serviceability toward the life-process. In *The Theory of the Leisure Class*, Veblen favorably mentions the 'primitive phase of social development,' and suggests what is probably an optimal outcome for the twenty-first century. 'What emulation of an economic kind there is between the members of such a group will be chiefly emulation in industrial serviceability. At the same time the incentive to emulation is not strong, nor is the scope for emulation large' (Veblen 1918[1899], p. 16).

One of the most important features of the postmodern landscape that differentiates Veblen's period from our own is the global character of the life-process today. A post-invidious society and a movement beyond *The Theory of the Leisure Class* requires that the pressing issue of global insecurity be addressed. If Karl Polanyi's assessment is correct, this will require some form of democratic and just re-embedding of global economic activity — a global protective response. This implies subordination of markets and profits to assure biosphere and human security, and this can only be achieved by a socially-just redistribution of power and resources. Global security and justice is a fundamental requisite for non-invidious living — what Rifkin calls 'biosphere politics' (Rifkin 1991).

There's an additional way to consider this. There are three categories of human activity: (1) taking care of each other; (2) having fun; and (3) self-development. Whether the activities are institutionalized or personal, our lives can be sorted into one or more of the three. For example, we take care of each other by personal acts in the family, by government legislation, by being a friend, and even national defense. The ways in which we care for each other are too numerous to mention. We do it in social and institutional ways, individual ways, voluntaristic and obligatory ways. There is an enormous range of institutions and activities that relate to this. Both paid-market and unpaid-household labor falls within this category. And this class of activities can be authoritarian, consensus-based, democratic, or patriarchal. We take care of each other in diverse ways, some more humane than others, some more democratic than others.

Then there is having fun. These are activities that can be social or individual, formal or informal. But this class of activities is one that adds a sense of pleasure and joy to our lives, and is not purposive for either self-actualization or caring for others. They are the activities that we enjoy for their own sake and give us experiences of immediate gratification. They have no particular meaning other than the pleasure that we derive from doing them. They lead nowhere in particular. Of course, this is a subjective determination. What is fun for one person may not be for another.

Finally, there is the set of activities that contribute to self-development and actualization. These may be fun or they may not be. They may be meaningful and worthwhile without being fun. They lead us beyond what we are today. They involve the 'becoming,' transcendent dimension of our lives, whereas having fun is mostly immanent and involves 'being' more than 'becoming.' Clearly there are activities, like cooking a special meal for friends and family, that combine all three categories. Cooking the special dinner may be fun, contribute to taking care of others, and be a creative effort at becoming a gourmet cook.

What is the point? When we examine economic systems in terms of these three classes of activities, we can determine which kinds of activities are emphasized by each kind of system. For example, most precapitalist societies, or what Polanyi called embedded economies, were ones that emphasized taking care of each other. Taking care of each other was prioritized over having fun, while self-development was essentially an unknown concept. In feudal Europe, the lord-serf relationship and Christian institutions served for taking care of one another. Life was not supposed to be fun; having fun was downplayed in favor of salvation-through-faith. Taking care of each other imposed a set of moral and religious obligations for all members. It was both a regime of status, as

Veblen states, and a rather stale regime of taking care of each other. Having fun and developing one's potential were not part of this economy. People can find meaning and purpose, love and joy in this world, but self-development and fun were not what this system was about.

With capitalism, we leave to the market mechanism the task of taking care of each other. Taking care of one another is not a stated purpose or ideological pillar of a market economy. Along with some family nurturance and neighborly reciprocity, the market should take care of us. At least that is what classical liberalism tells us. With the invisible hand of the market doing the essential provisioning, we are free to self-develop and have fun. However, if we are having too much fun at the expense of our self-actualization, we may fall behind as slackers or maybe even losers.

The optimal situation in capitalism is to find a niche where one actually has fun developing her/himself. The problem is that not everyone seems to be able to find that niche. Most do not. College students scan the career spectrum searching for that one kind of job that reconciles fun and self-development. Career manuals such as *What Color is Your Parachute* try to help. Self-help books, career placement offices, and guidance counselors are there to help individuals find that one niche where one can demonstrate ambition and enthusiasm simultaneously. Yet most people of the world are not affluent enough to even get to the search. Clearly, to pose the question, 'what do I want to be,' and then to hear the response, 'just be all you can be,' requires a minimum level of living unaffordable to many, if not most.

But the point is that the focus of our lives is not on taking care of each other. We leave that to the market. What the market compels us to do is develop our skills and talents in an effort to obtain security, meaning, and purpose. The individual, that is, the self, is the object of capitalism. It allows one that space to have fun and to self-develop, which has proved over time to be of great value. But it does not emphasize taking care of each other. It does not set this as its purpose. Taking care of each other is not a thematic goal of capitalism.

Most likely, having fun and self-development would be considered the main intentions of the system. With the carrot and stick approach, it fosters self-development and likewise punishes excessive fun. If all people want to do is have fun, it is better to be rich first. Others will end up as slackers and losers.

The status system grants little recognition to those who put taking care of others first in their lives. The status system is not directed toward that cluster of behaviors associated with other-regarding and fellow-feeling. Nor is status systematically awarded to having fun either — except to the extent that a common reward for self-development success and financial prowess is the indulgence of immediate gratification at the consumerist smorgasbord. Status flows to the over-achievers, the workaholics, and the successful self-actualizers.

For a sustainable society in the twenty-first century, the emphasis that capitalism awards to having fun and self-development must be redirected. The reward and incentive system must be shifted from self-development to taking care of each other. This can no longer be left to the invisible hand of the market, particularly if some type of stationary-state economy is established. People have to think in terms of, and be rewarded more for, caring for each other. Self-development need not be discouraged, but neither should it be the basis for measuring one's worth. Having fun? Clearly, this is part of what we consider to be fully human. It should not be discouraged either. Most people do not want a return to the dire and dreary lives of feudal Europe.

An economy focused on taking care of each other and having fun is an economy most suited to a sustainable post-invidious world. Self-development can be left to the individual, but should not be a social and moral imperative as it is today. The cluster of behaviors of 'virtue' are mostly linked to taking care of each other, and it is these values and behaviors that are essential. An economic arrangement that is focused on virtue rather than self-development is one that focuses on taking care of each other.

So sustainability implies a reversal of priorities relative to today. Instead of relying on the invisible hand and the imperative of self-development to assure our future, perhaps we should consciously use the visible hand of virtue, emphasize these traits, and assert taking care of each other rather than self-development as the top priority. How important is 'being all you can be?' My rereading of Veblen would no doubt relegate it to third in a sustainable and just economy. Today it is number one.

Nothing I have mentioned suggests a particular path to a post-invidious society. Supporting democratic and popular empowerment movements, working toward broader coalitions between progressive and leftist groups, fighting environmental and social injustice; these are the means we have. Rethinking the value of 'be all you can be' and re-orienting it towards virtue and social responsibility is also important. Growth of the economy, the corporation, the state, and no less, growth of the individual will not sustain the earth. Possibly if the individual grows in selflessness, as Gandhi hoped, progress can be made. Only this type of self-development makes sense; otherwise a shift from self-development to virtue needs to take place. If this can be part of a majoritarian movement for global peace and justice, a sustainable society has a chance.

One additional caution about a post-invidious society should be mentioned after rereading *The Theory of the Leisure Class*. There is a sense that, for Veblen, non-invidious living means homogenous living. Yet the notion that 'I am better than you' is not the same as 'I am different than you.' 'Different' is good; 'better' is invidious.

Diversity is a basic feature of both postmodern capitalism and invidious self-development. The globalization of production and the new 'regime of flexible specialization' have increased the means by which people can define themselves differently from one another. This simultaneously allows for more diverse expressions of both invidious and non-invidious self-development. Diversity is an essential feature of self-development in general. Just as we do not want to eliminate leisure and consumption, but only the invidious character of them, neither do we want to eliminate self-development. A post-invidious society is, therefore, one that continues to value diversity and pluralism along with the simplicity and functionalism of Veblenian aesthetics. A simple world of pluralism, justice, and security is merely another way to describe a post-invidious society. What is clear now is that the 'majoritarian democratic movement' that we hope to contribute to and see develop will have to be global in size and scope.

REFERENCES

Foucault, Michel (1986), 'Of Other Spaces', *Diacritics, 16*, Spring, 1, 22–26.
Harvey, David (1989), *The Condition of Postmodernity: An Enquiry into the Origins of Cultural Change,* Cambridge, MA: Basil Blackwell.
Harvey, David (1991), 'Flexibility: Threat or Opportunity', *Socialist Review, 21*, 1, 65–78.
Jameson, Fredric (1991), *Postmodernism: Or the Cultural Logic of Late Capitalism,* Durham, NC: Duke University Press.
Lash, Scott, and John Urry (1987), *The End of Organized Capitalism,* Madison: University of Wisconsin Press.
Lyotard, Jean-Francois (1984), *The Postmodern Condition: A Report on Knowledge,* Minneapolis: University of Minnesota Press.
MacEwan, Arthur (1991), 'What's New about the "New International Economy"?', *Socialist Review, 21*, 3–4, 111–132.
Marcuse, Herbert (1955), *Eros and Civilization,* New York: Beacon Press.
Polanyi, Karl (1957), *The Great Transformation: The Political and Economic Origins of Our Time,* Boston: Beacon Press.
Rifkin, Jeremy (1991), *Biosphere Politics: A Cultural Odyssey from the Middle Ages to the New Age,* New York: Harper Collins.
Rosenthal, Michael (1992), 'What was Postmodernism?', *Socialist Review, 22*, 3, 83–106.
Samuels, Warren (1992), preface in *Thorstein Veblen and His Critics, 1891–1963: Conservative, Liberal, and Radical Perspectives,* i-xix, Princeton: Princeton University Press.

Soja, Edward (1989), *Postmodern Geographies,* New York: Verso.
Tilman, Rick (1992), *Thorstein Veblen and His Critics, 1891–1963: Conservative, Liberal, and Radical Perspectives,* Princeton: Princeton University Press.
Veblen, Thorstein (1918[1899]), *The Theory of the Leisure Class,* New York: Viking Press.

PART II

What is the Leisure Class Up To?

4. Thorstein Veblen and the Upper Class

William M. Dugger

1 INTRODUCTION

Thorstein Veblen's treatment of the upper class in society is uniquely creative and highly relevant to the global economy of the twenty-first century. In *The Theory of the Leisure Class*, Veblen explained that the upper class is a predatory structure. The upper class did not contribute to society; it preyed upon society. Veblen was profoundly critical of the upper class, finding in it no redeeming features at all. In this, he differed from all other major social thinkers, except for the anarchists. Leading anarchists, such as Emma Goldman and Peter Kropotkin, shared his basic stance toward the upper class. None of them, however, developed a critical theory of the upper class that became as widely read and discussed as Veblen's *The Theory of the Leisure Class*. Veblen's critical theory of the upper class is his most uniquely creative and relevant contribution to social theory. Unfortunately, this feature of his thought is seldom emphasized. It will be here.

When it comes to a Veblenian understanding of the upper class, most social thinkers just do not get it. Conservative thinkers do not get it because they generally celebrate the greatness of their societies and are seldom critical of their own upper class, usually finding it functional and quite worthy of praise. Joseph Schumpeter's celebration of entrepreneurs is an example. Veblen, however, found nothing celebratory or functional in the upper class.

Even Karl Marx argued in *The Communist Manifesto* that the upper class was functional, in a dialectical sense. It accumulated capital and it helped forge the conditions that would bring about a transformation of capitalism into something better. So the upper class, Marx theorized, performed a dialectical function and was possessed of a kind of social value. Its effect, ultimately, would be positive. Veblen however, did not agree and he denied any social value, dialectical or otherwise, to the upper class. In the American case, formerly isolated communities were brought together by nineteenth century improvements in communication and transportation and by the Civil War. This national unification allowed Veblen to observe for himself the opening up of a vast hinterland to a status panic. Veblen moved freely between the milieus of the rural farm, the country town, and the big American city. Veblen saw that the American case involved a dominant leisure class. So, national unification encouraged conspicuous consumption and leisure far more than thrift and entrepreneurship. Ida Tarbell referred to this national unification as the nationalization of the American economy. It is from this nationalization, to use Tarbell's term, that Veblen drew his *The Theory of the Leisure Class*. That book, drawn from the nationalization of the American economy in the nineteenth century, serves as a mini-preview of the globalization of the planetary economy in the twenty-first century.

But first we must explain how Veblen's treatment of the upper class in *The Theory of the Leisure Class* differs from most social theories. This will involve a quick description of traditional treatments of the upper class, the functional theories of conservatives and the dialectical theories of early Marxists, and it will involve a contrasting description of Veblen's treatment of the upper class.

2   TRADITIONAL TREATMENTS OF THE UPPER CLASS

Conservative treatments of the upper class come in many varieties and space does not permit a thorough survey of them all. Instead, focus will be on the strand of economically conservative thought headed up by Adam Smith. Joseph Schumpeter's theory of the entrepreneur will serve as a twentieth century representative of the Adam Smith strand. Schumpeter's theory is not only widely known and accepted in conservative circles, it also provides stark contrasts with Veblen's theory (Schumpeter, 1961).

Schumpeter theorizes that the upper class is functional. This is not to say that the members of the upper class intend to benefit society. They are not altruists. But it is to say that they intend to benefit themselves and by doing so they also end up benefiting their society. Schumpeter explains that their intent is to build personal dynasties, to conquer, and to create. But the unintended effects of their actions drive their economy to develop (Schumpeter 1961, pp. 93–94). The members of the Schumpeterian upper class are entrepreneurs and the basic entrepreneurial function they perform is that of innovation. Their innovation drives economic development, benefiting society in general.

Innovation itself involves several different sorts of changes, and the entrepreneur implements these changes against considerable social resistance. The changes include introducing a new good, introducing a new method of production or distribution, opening a new market, 'conquest' of a new source of supply, and carrying out a new organization or a reorganization (Schumpeter 1961, pp. 65–66). These innovations are implemented in the self-interest of the entrepreneur, but the entrepreneur does not carry them out through a purely rational process of decision-making because such a process is not really possible when change is being introduced (Schumpeter 1961, pp. 79–86).

While the class function theory of Schumpeter relies on the processes of innovation and economic competition to connect the narrow interest of the upper class to the broad interest of society, the early class contradiction theory of Marx relies on the processes of exploitation and dialectical transformation to do so. With Marx we do find the critical concept of exploitation replacing the celebratory concept of innovation. Nevertheless, we also find traces of a final or ultimate beneficence obtained, albeit dialectically, between the pursuit of the narrow interest of the bourgeoisie and the effect that pursuit has on the broader interest of society. In both of these non-Veblenian theories, when members of the upper class pursue their own self-interest, ultimately the unintended effect on society is deemed to be good.

Although Marx argued that the bourgeoisie exploited the working class in its pursuit of profit, the bourgeoisie's pursuit of profit had a dialectical effect on society as a whole (negation of the negation, in dialectics). In a moving passage from *The Communist Manifesto*, Marx stated:

> The bourgeoisie, during its rule of scarce one hundred years, has created more massive and more colossal productive forces than have all preceding generations together. Subjection of Nature's forces to man, machinery, application of chemistry to industry and agriculture, steam-navigation, railways, electric telegraphs, clearing of whole continents for cultivation, canalization of rivers, whole populations conjured out of the ground — what earlier century had even a presentiment that such productive forces slumbered in the lap of social labor? (Marx 1988, p. 59).

So the selfish pursuit of profit by the capitalists had the unintended effects of improving numerous aspects of social and economic life. Furthermore, the selfish pursuit of profit by the capitalists is leading, dialectically, to a destruction of capitalism itself. Marx argued:

Modern bourgeois society with its relations of production, of exchange and of property, a society that has conjured up such gigantic means of production and of exchange, is like the sorcerer, who is no longer able to control the powers of the nether world whom he has called up by his spells. For many a decade past the history of industry and commerce is but the history of the revolt of modern productive forces against modern conditions of production, against the property relations that are the conditions for the existence of the bourgeoisie and of its rule (Marx 1988, p. 60).

The selfish actions of the capitalists were having the selfless effect of preparing the world for their own exit.

The conservative treatment of Schumpeter and the early radical treatment of Marx share a common thread in their strand of thought. Follow the thread back in time, and you find Adam Smith's famous statement of the invisible hand leading the individual capitalist's selfish use of their own capital to serve the public interest:

He intends only his own gain, and he is in this, as in many other cases, led by an invisible hand to promote an end which was no part of his intention. Nor is it always the worse for the society that it was no part of it. By pursuing his own interest he frequently promotes that of the society more effectually than when he really intends to promote it.(Smith 1986, p. 265).

The common thread leading from Smith through the early Marx and through all of Schumpeter is belief in the social beneficence and importance of the unintended effects of human actions. In particular, both Adam Smith and his followers, including Joseph Schumpeter, and Karl Marx and some of his followers emphasized that selfish actions frequently have unselfish effects. In his strand of thought, Adam Smith theorized that self-serving, entrepreneurial acts are guided by an invisible hand to have unintended, social-serving effects. In Adam Smith the selfish act had a socially beneficial result through the workings of competition. In *The Communist Manifesto,* Karl Marx also argued that the intended, self-serving acts of capitalists have unintended, social-serving effects.

However, there are two major differences between the two. First, while Adam Smith saw the beneficial effects coming about because of competition; Karl Marx saw the beneficial effects coming about because of the workings of dialectics. Second, while the followers of Adam Smith have continued to this day to believe in the unintended beneficial effects of selfish actions, this belief has been modified and/or dropped by many of the followers of Karl Marx. A further comment on Marx and Marxism is required for clarity. As it has developed and matured, Marxism has moved away from dialectics and has moved closer to Veblen's analysis of the upper class. Even Marx himself came to rely on Hegelian dialectics more as a beginning vocabulary of terms than as a definitive analytical framework.

3 VEBLEN'S TREATMENT OF THE UPPER CLASS

Veblen did not use this common thread of unintended beneficial effects when he began weaving his own strand of thought. Veblen's emphasis on opaque cause and effect allowed no place for invisible hand and dialectical contradiction.

Veblen argued that the upper class was predatory in intent and harmful in effect. He did not argue that its role was beneficial to society, either directly or indirectly, intentional or unintentional. Instead, he explained at length that the actions of the upper class had deleterious effects on society. Veblen did not accidentally overlook the unintended effects of the selfish acts of the upper class. He was not ignorant, for he read widely in several languages and was an astute observer of both the high and the low. He also lived in small town, rural farming community and big city; on the east and west coasts, and in the middle of the United States. (Diggins 1978; Dorfman 1972; Tilman 1992).

Veblen did not ignore the unintended effects of the selfish acts that were alleged to benefit society. He addressed them directly and forcefully, not only in *The Theory of the Leisure Class*, but in virtually all of his subsequent books as well. (This commemorative volume and my chapter in it, however, are limited to discussion of *The Theory of the Leisure Class*.) Veblen thoroughly discredited each case of unintended beneficial effect. His debunking is devastating.

Although devastating to much of conservative economic theory, Veblen's theory has always lacked a certain cachet. The reason is simple. He did not unearth or discover some obscure 'scientific' phenomenon. Instead, he dealt with observations of the life process, common to us all. What he did not do was unearth or discover (or more precisely, invent?) the unintended beneficial effects of selfish actions. Doing so would have lent a pseudo-sophisticated aura to his theory; would have given it the authority of science, the quality of seeing through the veil of common appearances down to the alleged fundamentals of enduring truth. Forsaking the conservative establishment's seal of approval, Veblen argued that the upper class pursued leisure, not work; engaged in consumption, not accumulation; and was socially conservative, not socially progressive.

The title for his first book is quite appropriate, for in it Veblen explained that the upper class was not a productive class. It did not value work. It valued leisure. And 'leisure,' explained Veblen, 'does not connote indolence or quiescence. What it connotes is non-productive consumption of time. Time is consumed non-productively: (1) from a sense of the unworthiness of productive work, and (2) as an evidence of pecuniary ability to afford a life of idleness' (Veblen 1953[1899], p. 46).

Emulation spreads leisure class values and meanings throughout the underlying population. Under the influence of the predatory leisure class, productive work is denigrated. Veblen argued that 'labor comes to be associated in men's habits of thought with weakness and subjection to a master' (Veblen 1953[1899], p. 39). Under the baneful influence of the leisure class, work is unworthy and should be avoided by all right-thinking folks. Furthermore, its avoidance should be put in evidence at every opportunity, in order to demonstrate personal worthiness and autonomy and in order to dispel suspicions of weakness and subjection.

To the extent that a culture becomes dominated by these kinds of leisure class values and meanings, the members of that culture find it difficult to voluntarily and happily devote themselves to productive work. Causing such difficulty for members of society is dysfunctional and has no unintended, beneficial effects on society as a whole. When individual members of a society find it difficult to devote themselves to productive work, the work needed for social provisioning is bound to suffer. But when one individual member of that society's leisure class demonstrates his great worthiness by showing off his leisure, that member still raises his social status. So self-interest is raised and social interest is lowered; invisible hands, unintended effects, and deeper truths not withstanding. When the self-interest of a member of the upper class is raised at the expense of the broader social interest, the relationship between the class and the society is not functional and not dialectical, but dysfunctional and predatory.

Veblen emphasized, with good reason, that one of the conditions required for the emergence of a leisure class was an economy that generated a significant surplus above the subsistence level. Without the surplus, either the leisure class could not emerge to prey upon the underlying population, or the predation would threaten the continued survival of the underlying population. The other condition required for the emergence of a leisure class was the existence of a 'predatory habit of life,' meaning, to Veblen, 'habituation to the infliction of injury by force and stratagem' (Veblen 1953[1899], p. 25). If society managed to inculcate in its youth industrious attitudes favorable to hard work and social service, it did so in spite of the pernicious effects of the leisure class.

The upper class, Veblen explained, engaged in conspicuous consumption, not capital accumulation. He did not refer to its members as 'capitalists,' so he did not imply that their intended or unintended social function was capital accumulation. The leisure class deprecated frugality and the resulting gradual accumulation of useful things. It celebrated prodigality and the display of lavish expenditure. If society managed to use its economic surplus to accumulate useful tools and equipment in farm and factory, it did so in spite of the leisure class and its conspicuous consumption.

Emulation, 'the stimulus of an invidious comparison which prompts us to outdo those with whom we are in the habit of classing ourselves, is the driving force behind conspicuous consumption' (Veblen 1953[1899], p. 81). To protect their good repute, emulation continuously drives consumers to engage in higher levels of spending. Veblen explained, 'the standard of expenditure which commonly guides our efforts is not the average, ordinary expenditure already achieved; it is an idea of consumption that lies just beyond our reach, or to reach which requires some strain' (Veblen 1953[1899], p. 81). This emulative drive leads to ever-higher levels of wastefulness. 'In order to be reputable, it must be wasteful' (Veblen 1953[1899], p. 77).

The upper class, Veblen's leisure class, did not facilitate capital accumulation — not directly or indirectly, not intentionally or unintentionally, not in the present or in the future. Capital accumulation from the leisure class, no way, no how. However, this is not to deny that capital accumulation has occurred and continues to occur. Nor is this to deny that its occurrence was and will continue to be credited to the account of the upper class. After all, the members of that class possess whole forests of paper that have been worked up by lawyers, accountants, and financiers into Federal Reserves Notes, property deeds, stock certificates, corporate debentures, and such. These papers 'prove' the pecuniary worthiness of the upper class members who hold them. Veblen did not deny any of these opaque facts. Instead, he emphasized them. (For a Veblenian account of saving and investing, see Neale 1991.)

Schumpeter thought that the upper class entrepreneurs were innovative, not conservative. The entrepreneurs introduced new products, new processes, new combinations, and new technology. They did so against the resistance of the rest of society. The entrepreneurs, then, promoted social progress. Their creative destruction developed the economy and society, argued Schumpeter. Veblen knew different. The upper class, the leisure class, Veblen explained, was conservative and had conservative effects on society as a whole. The emulative drive to engage in ever more conspicuous consumption had a particularly retarding result:

The result is that the requirements of pecuniary reputability tend: (1) to leave but a scanty subsistence minimum available for other than conspicuous consumption, and (2) to absorb any surplus energy which may be available after the bare physical necessities of life have been provided for. The outcome of the whole is a strengthening of the general conservative attitude of the community. The institution of a leisure class hinders cultural development immediately: (1) by the inertia proper to the class itself; (2) through its prescriptive example of conspicuous waste and of conservatism; (3) indirectly through that system of unequal distribution of wealth and sustenance on which the institution itself rests (Veblen 1953[1899], p. 141).

Veblen did not confuse innovation in consumer fads or financial speculations as promoting social progress. Instead, such activities waste resources and retard progress in 'physical comfort and fullness of life' (Veblen 1953[1899], p. 141).

4 VEBLEN'S RELEVANCE

Veblen's theory of the upper class was constructed from his observations of the nationalization (unification) of the United States economy in the nineteenth century. Several elements of his theory are relevant to the globalization of the planetary economy in the twenty-first century. Of course, wide allowances and special adaptations must be made in Veblen for differences in (1) processes, (2) contexts, (3) institutions, and (4) technologies.

(1) The different processes involved, nationalization versus globalization, bring in issues of national sovereignty under global unification that are much more fundamental than issues of federal and state sovereignty under national unification.

(2) The differences in the contexts, one nation's economy in the nineteenth century versus the national economies of the whole globe in the twenty-first century, bring in enormous problems of factor mobility and immobility. Capital has become mobile, while labor is still far less so.

(3) Different institutions are also involved — the International Monetary Fund, World Bank, and World Trade Organization are the leading institutions in globalization and cannot easily be understood in terms of nineteenth century American institutions. The USA did not even have the Federal Reserve System until the twentieth century.

(4) We are not even sure of the technologies that will affect the twenty-first century. But we can be sure that communication, transportation, entertainment, and much else will be very different.

In spite of all these differences, Veblen is still relevant. Of the utmost relevance is Veblen's debunking of an important element of mainstream economic theory — he devastated the doctrine of the unintended beneficial effects of selfish upper class actions. In the context of market systems, Veblen's debunking goes to the very heart of the case for laissez-faire. Society cannot simply leave the market economy alone, relying on the unintended effects of the actions of selfish capitalist/entrepreneurs to distribute benefits widely amongst the members of the underlying population.

When the United States economy was nationalized (unified) after the Civil War, society relied far less on laissez-faire than is commonly understood (Tarbell 1936; also, for the pre-war period, Bourgin 1989). Even so, nationalization resulted in enormous conflict and waste, caused largely by the spread throughout the great hinterland of leisure class activities, values, and meanings and it all culminated in the tawdriness of the gilded age.

While the nation was being unified and the leisure class was spreading its baneful effects across the hinterland of former frontiersmen, indigenous Americans, and farmers, industrialization was also sweeping across the economy. All the changes going forth make it hard to separate out the effects of each process that was shaping the nation. Nevertheless, Veblen clearly understood that the construction of the American agricultural and industrial colossus was not due to the hard work of the leisure class; was not due to the saving and capital accumulation of the conspicuous consumers; and was not due to the encouragement given social innovation by the socially conservative leisure class. In each instance, Veblen explained that the leisure class contribution was in the opposite direction.

The upper class will claim credit for whatever progress the human species manages to make in the twenty-first century. But, if the Veblenian vision is relevant, none of that progress will be due to the upper class, the leisure class. Progress will take place in spite of the leisure class, not because of it. This is a simple insight. Lots of simple folks suspected it in the nineteenth and twentieth centuries, but were then dissuaded from it by conservative intellectuals defending the status quo. Getting back to that simple insight requires Veblen's help in digging us out from underneath the crushing doctrine of the unintended beneficial effects of selfish actions. Once dug out from underneath this buncombe, it becomes easy to see that the globalization of the leisure class in the twenty-first century will cause economic waste and social conservatism, not economic efficiency and social adaptability.

As the leisure class becomes global, institutionalized waste will become global. Waste will rise to unprecedented, undreamed of, unimaginable levels. Both conspicuous leisure and conspicuous consumption will spread and intensify far beyond the United States, Canada, Australia, New Zealand, Europe, and Japan. The waste will be astonishing, in spite of continued global poverty and in spite of spreading environmental destruction. Globalization will intensify emulation and waste for the same reasons that nationalization did so. Nationalization exposed emulating individuals to far more stimulation as they met far more people to try to impress. Improved transportation and communication systems in the nineteenth century and on the national level made the stage on which emulation and waste took place a far larger one. As a result, they accelerated. Globalization will do the same, only more so. The improved transportation and communication systems, of course, will be of the twenty-first century and will be on the global level. So the stage will become as large as the whole globe.

Conspicuous leisure: enormous amounts of human effort will be wasted with the global spread and intensification of conspicuous leisure. This does not mean people will be idle. It means that people all over the globe will be caught up in an emulative drive to devote ever more of their time to unproductive activities that demonstrate their worthiness, through their demonstrated exemption from work.

Globalization means that the members of a particular nation's leisure class no longer compete on the narrow, national stage. Their competition to demonstrate their exemption from work must become global. They must try to impress a far wider and more skeptical audience with higher standards. Global emulators compete on Asian, Australian, Polynesian, European, and American stages where far more exemption from work than ever before is required to make the needed impression. The global stimulus to conspicuous leisure is already leading to a new kind of frenzied leisure, the outlines of which can just be discerned on some of the stages. One can already observe the globalized standards of conspicuous leisure in the frenzies of such playgrounds as Bangkok, Rio de Janeiro, and Acapulco. In the twenty-first century, an increasingly exhausted leisure class will press down much harder on the underlying populations and on environmental resources to finance the intensification of conspicuous leisure brought about by the globalization of the competition.

Conspicuous consumption: globalization will also speed up the wastefulness of conspicuous consumption, adding to the pressure on underlying populations and on environmental resources. New entertainment technologies seem to be particularly important in the globalization of conspicuous consumption. United States films and television programming increasingly spread the consumption standards of the American upper class into the villages of the world. Invidious distinctions have soured the lives of many of us, exposed as we have been to the personal snobbery of our local and national leisure class. In the twenty-first century, however, snobbery will be increasingly high-tech. New global entertainment technologies already have made invidious distinctions more personal and more pervasive as television and film have pushed more and more of us to measure up against the higher consumption standards of our television favorites and movie heroines. To the extent that television programming and films intrude more and more into our lives, whether we live in village or city, our consumption standards will be influenced by what we see there. To the invidious distinctions of person to person comparison will be added the invidious distinctions of comparison with high-tech images. The pressure to consume conspicuously will intensify. We will not only have to keep up with the Joneses, but also with the images of the Joneses.

Globalization will intensify the pressures of predation exerted by the leisure class on the rest of the population and on the environment. Those pressures include the support of more conspicuous leisure and more conspicuous consumption. These Veblenian forces of predation do not preclude the possibility of growth, narrowly and traditionally defined. On the contrary, these Veblenian forces may very well take place alongside an acceleration of the growth of GGP (Gross Global Product, the global equivalent of GNP, Gross National Product). The emerging global leisure class will, no doubt, claim credit for such growth. It will be argued that the members of the global upper class have abstained from consumption and their resulting saving has financed a wonderful accumulation of capital benefiting us all. It will also be argued that members of the upper class have worked hard innovating, bringing in new technologies against the recalcitrant conservatism of the rest of the population.

If Veblen's *The Theory of the Leisure Class* is correct, the arguments will be false. The narrowly measured growth that may take place in the globalizing twenty-first century will do so in spite of the efforts of the leisure class, not because of those efforts. Furthermore, neither the underlying human population of the globe nor the environmental system of the globe will benefit in proportion to the growth. The values and meanings of the global leisure class will further denigrate the working life that most of us pursue. The values and the meanings of the global leisure class will spread more envy and discontent among most of us who cannot keep up with them. And, the pressure to support the burden of waste will intensify the reckless abuse of the environment. The allegedly beneficial, unintended effects of the selfish actions of the leisure class will not mitigate the harm. To mitigate the harm will take a globalization of democracy and its social control of predatory human actions.

REFERENCES

Bourgin, Frank (1989), *The Great Challenge,* New York: Harper & Row.

Diggins, John P. (1978), *The Bard of Savagery,* New York: Seabury Press.

Dorfman, Joseph (1972), *Thorstein Veblen and His America,* 7th ed., Clifton, New Jersey: Augustus M. Kelley.

Marx, Karl (1988), *The Communist Manifesto,* Edited by Frederic L. Bender, New York: W. W. Norton.

Neale, Walter C. (1991), 'Who Saves? The Rich, the Penniless, and Everyone Else', *Journal of Economic Issues,* **25**, December, 1160–1166.

Schumpeter, Joseph A. (1961), *The Theory of Economic Development,* Translated by Redvers Opie, New York: Oxford University Press.

Smith, Adam (1986), 'The Wealth of Nations', In Robert L. Heilbroner, ed. *The Essential Adam Smith,* New York: W.W. Norton, 149–320.

Tarbell, Ida M. (1936), *The Nationalizing of Business, 1878–1898,* Originally published in New York by the Macmillan Company, Reprinted Chicago: Quadrangle Books, 1971.

Tilman, Rick (1992), *Thorstein Veblen and His Critics,* Princeton, New Jersey: Princeton University Press.

Veblen, Thorstein (1953[1899]), *The Theory of the Leisure Class,* New York: New American Library.

5. Executive Consumption: Not Conspicuous, but still Invidious

William Hildred

1 INTRODUCTION

An American tourist created a small international incident when a security guard asked her to leave Harrods, London's premier shopping center. The stated reason for her ejection was her being inappropriately dressed. She countered that her similarly dressed mother was not thrown out of the establishment, suggesting instead that discrimination against portly women (size 18) was the root of the situation. Her conclusive evidence of discriminatory purpose was that she had spent $2,000 on varied merchandise, and 'was wearing a $3,000 Cartier watch, a $600 Italian designer handbag, $100 brown leggings, and a $200 white shirt' (Lederer 1997). Several dozen pre-qualified bidders spent over $3.5 million for castoff clothing from the closets of the former Princess of Wales (Chang and Seligmann 1997).

Officials of Citizens Utilities, provider of gas, electricity, and water services to communities across the nation, asked the Corporation Commission of Arizona to include in its rate base the expense of maintaining an office for a retired executive, the costs of several pieces of expensive artwork, and two luxury automobiles. Also presented as legitimate costs of providing utility services to its customers were director's fees for both the CEO and his wife, and expenditures for international travel (Smith 1996).

What do these phenomena have in common? What interpretation of their significance is warranted? Nearly every university student coping with Principles of Microeconomics will see examples of constrained maximization. Shoppers and bidders are attending to their preexisting utility functions, exercising consumer sovereignty with incomes obtained through efficient market processes. The utility firm's officers are pursuing profit maximization (for the eventual good of society, whether intended or

85

not) by ensuring that all costs of their services are covered by the allowable price.

This does not ring true to those who follow in Veblen's tradition. He would see the Harrods shopper's affectation of costly attire as the visible display of personal worthiness to associate with the better social strata. Slathering over the once-worn gowns of an ex-princess is emulation carried to absurd extremes. Public utility executives are less interested in the price and serviceability of their product than in the comfort and pageantry of their work life.

Veblen's continuing relevance is due to his showing the necessity of going behind neoclassical assumptions, first with his incisive examination of consumer belief and behavior in 'America the Commercial', and his subsequent setting forth of a mode of analysis to aid in detection of the service rendered by chicanery by business. This chapter interprets several social phenomena in the manner of Veblen, beginning with the presentation of contemporary evidence that reveals the enduring errors of the dominant economic theory. These errors concern the importance and formation of tastes, the rectitude of modes of acquiring income, the processes of determining costs of production, and the plausibility of achieving efficiency under extant market structure. The chapter also introduces a phenomenon of which Veblen could not have been aware, its evolution having occurred in large part since his death. This phenomenon is dubbed 'Stealth Consumption,' being largely invisible to all but those who are able to exercise it in varying degrees, but yet subject to emulation and invidious comparison within the favored group. The ideological residue of the foundation of conservative political preference, known to economists as neoclassical theory, will be clear.

2   CONTEMPORARY EXTRAVAGANCES

Readers of the business section and society pages of the average metropolitan daily newspaper often get breathless glimpses of life at the top. The following review of typical reports recalls Veblen's portrayal of conspicuous consumption. Flagrant waste and communal detriment are major elements in its practice, even as ordinary consumers take cues from their social and financial betters in deciding upon objects of their desire. It is here called 'waste' because this expenditure does not serve human life or human well-being on the whole, not because it is waste or misdirection of effort or expenditure from the standpoint of the individual consumer who chooses it (Veblen 1953[1899], p. 78).

The astute man('s) functioning is not a furtherance of the generic life process. At its best, in its direct economic bearing, it is a conversion of the economic substance of the collectivity to a growth alien to the collective life process — very much after the analogy of what in medicine would be called a benign tumor, with some tendency to transgress the uncertain line that divides the benign from the malign growths (Veblen 1953[1899], p. 195)

Royal status — European, Arabian and Asian alike — usually confers wealth sufficient to set those so chosen far apart from the simply wealthy. The duties of monarchs of all ages and genders begin with establishing their uniqueness among humankind by proper display of that wealth.

For example, among the elect a wife of the king of Saudi Arabia and her retinue of 300 flew to Phoenix, Arizona, for neurological treatment. The expected three weeks of confinement ultimately became four months, during which a hospital floor of 28 rooms was reserved for her care. Aides not needed at all times found shelter on entire floors at two luxury resort-hotels. For the remainder of her 22-month recovery following release from the hospital, the group rented six houses at a cost of $30,000 to $50,000 per month and more than 50 cars (Snyder and Beard 1996).

Finally, aristocracies of humans and sheep occasionally combine in new ways. In the case of the sheep, special care and feeding of 600 selectively-bred animals included indoor living and protection from dirt by being clothed in a special jacket. From 190 of these, the owners selected the best wool and bundled it in a 255 pound bale that sold for $924,000 at auction, with a Japanese firm outbidding an Italian company. The winner expected to use about $30,000 worth of wool in each of 30 suits, affordable by the human aristocracy ('Pedigree Sheep's "Golden Fleece" Nets $924,000').

Purchasing power less than royal but decisively grand puts some families among the preferred clientele of the Peninsula Suites in Hong Kong. After a recent renovation, the hotel includes two-story suites renting for $4,820 per day ('Kowloon Hotel Towers in Opulence'), and such families could appreciate the value of a $500,000 charge for a parking space (Shephard 1994).

Nieman Marcus, the famous Dallas department store, offered in its 1996 Christmas catalog: a dog house, which although not to scale, was a model of St. Peter's Basilica ($9,400); a children's Japanese-home playhouse ($10,000); and a customized house trailer ($195,000) (Kaul 1996). Robb's Reports, also a catalog for the refined subscriber (income over $750,000, net worth $3 million), made available for 1996 Christmas giving: a Manhattan penthouse ($35 million); a Bentley auto ($324,500); a wooden bathtub ($34,000); and — one that Veblen would savor — a walking stick ($795). Among the more distinctive gift combinations for the owner of a large, 250 acre homestead, a customized golf course and clubhouse ($15 million); and a Cartier wrist watch that keeps both time and golf scores, actuated by buttons of emerald, sapphire, and ruby set in 18-karat gold and complemented by 342 diamonds ($79,300) (Goodykoontz 1996).

For the less affluent golfer, an opportunity to elude January cold in the United States and play golf in selected tropical locations was offered by Concorde Golf Tours. The trip was open to 78 people, whose $49,000 payments would give them 22 days of flying on the Concorde to play golf and see sights in Brazil, Tahiti, Thailand, India, and the United Arab Emirates (Western 1997).

People with more money than time to shop for gifts have recourse to 'personal shoppers' employed by fashionable retailers. One such aide provides services to women who spend between $50,000 and $400,000 on each year's wardrobes. In appreciation for his performance, he was honored on his thirtieth birthday, presented with a first-class flight from New York to Los Angeles, a suite at the Bel Air, and a limousine to deliver him to festivities costing others $10,000 per plate (Whitaker 1997).

'Investors' with more money than sense can be viewed at classic-car auctions. In 1996, a high point of an auction in Phoenix was reached when an owner announced that the $212,000 bid for his merchandise was too meager, but bidding was stalled. The owner asked the auctioneer to forego his $15,000 commission; a coin was tossed over the proposal and the owner won (Golfen 1996).

Respite from the demanding role of creating jobs for the masses can itself entail significant effort. Fortunately, the entrepreneurial spirit has moved an Idaho man to compile a newsletter by which his $300,000 median income subscribers can locate suitable relaxation. Selections in 1996 included a month-long global tour for $38,500, a private villa in Bali for $965 per night, a double room at London's Savoy Hotel for $480 or the Ritz in Paris for $800 per night, or an 11-day Mediterranean cruise in a suite of 1,000 square feet including bedroom with queen bed, living room with private verandah, and marble bathroom for $14,395, or around-the-world on the Queen Elizabeth II for $100,000 (Jackson 1996).

Alternatively, with adequate means, one might purchase a simple family yacht. The capital gains tax cut of 1981 stimulated such purchases, rather than the promised surge of productive investment, to the extent that long-distance telephone providers on the East and West coasts found it necessary to create two new area codes to handle the volume of calls from ocean-going craft (Phillips 1990, p. 44).

Hereditary monarchs probably do not seek out these treasures. More likely, customers for these products are akin to the economic royalists decried by Franklin Roosevelt, who now consume as royalists with their highly developed incomes. Within their ranks today is a new genus of pecuniary captaincy, whose forte may be creating giant corporations to produce useful products in the manner of Carnegie, but also involves manipulation of ownership claims to control and exploit the assets of firms largely built by others. In either case, their gargantuan remuneration does not stem from masterful deployment of productive resources, but from a rising stock market. This is apparent in the financial pages of the newspaper, not in the textbooks of neoclassical economics.

3   COMPENSATION OF CORPORATE EXECUTIVES

Much celebrated in the business press as the archetype of the successful American business leader is the recent Chairman and CEO of Sunbeam Corporation, Albert Dunlap — not unwillingly nicknamed 'Chainsaw Al' for his thorough stable-cleaning at every institution he is called to lead. In 1996, his salary related compensation amounted to $576,974. Accompanying this pittance was the award of a million restricted shares in Sunbeam worth $12.5 million, and options on 2.5 million shares worth perhaps $13 million ('Sunbeam Chief's Pay Soars'). A larger compensation package was claimed by a CEO more revered by his employees, Andrew Grove of Intel. He attained this result with salary and other direct compensation approaching $800,000, and a bonus of $2.6 million. The major element in his success was his decision to buy a million shares of Intel stock at prices from under $7 to over $61 per share, as permitted in previously granted option agreements. The aggregate value of this action was estimated to be about $95 million, since the market price of the stock rose during the year from $50 to $137. The company also gave him 72,000 new stock options to prepare yet more fully for the future (Kalish 1997). The largest 'bonus' went to Lawrence Goss of Green Tree Financial Corporation. His salary was only $433,000, but added to this was $102 million, including $95 million in stock (Walsh 1997).

One designer of executive compensation packages asserts that profits, not stock prices, trigger incentive awards (Pearlstein 1997), but he does not sing the praise of profits in a large choir. In the business press, unfortunately for teachers of economics, profit is not held to be the appropriate performance standard for corporate leaders. One finds nearly complete assent to the idea that the standard is the price of the company's stock and its increase. Thus stock incentive rewards of options and long-term 'incentives' increased from 1989's 31 percent of CEO's compensation to 43 percent in 1995, as salaries fell from 37 percent to 27 percent of the compensation package during the same period (Blanton 1997).

Finally, the hiring of key executives seems always to look ahead to the time of separation. As the executive genius goes forth to the simpler life of retirement or to rescue yet other struggling corporations, we may presume that anxiety for the future is not a common affliction, for suitable departure pay is available in the initial or expiring contract. This too is often in the form of stock. One of the more lavish models of this generosity was reported to the Securities and Exchange Commission by the Walt Disney Company in 1997. President Michael Ovitz's exit was eased by provision for cash and stock options worth $76 million to $130 million, despite his performance in office for only 14 months, 'generally considered to have been undistinguished if not disastrous' (Usborne 1997, p. E2). In answer to such criticism, Ovitz is reported to have stated, 'I just made a smart deal for myself. This is America. This isn't the Soviet Union. It's the supply and demand of the marketplace' (Grover 1997, p. 41).

It follows, then, that as major incentive of riches from stock speculation should determine executive compensation, so should it influence the outlook of members of corporate boards, who determine the compensation of the executives. In 1995, the National Association of Corporate Directors announced that directors,

> Should be paid primarily in company stock rather than cash and perks, and they should be required to own large amounts of stock. Unfortunately, the association found that growing numbers of directors are voting themselves valuable benefits, such as life insurance and pensions, that aren't tied to company performance (Brown 1995, p. D3).

Only weeks before, an 'investor' responded to an article on executive compensation in a national business weekly with the observation that:

> Many in the finance industry would argue that the only meaningful way to judge company performance is based on the returns provided to shareholders, and that it is in fact dangerous to judge the performance of companies based on traditional accounting measures such as return on equity. The reason this practice is dangerous is that accounting measures fail to consistently indicate the actual health and value of companies (Lukasik 1995, p. 52).

The view that the majority of Americans are now providing for the future by becoming owners of American Business, and so will benefit from the diligence of top executives in the casino of Wall Street, while comforting to these executives and their stock traders, is not credible. Ten percent of

Americans owned 75 percent of all investment assets in 1989 (Henwood 1996, p. 6). Although 36 million (37 percent of all) households 'hold' stock, 5 percent own 77 percent of equity holdings (individually held shares, defined contribution pension plans, IRAs, Keoghs, 401Ks, and mutual funds). Of individually owned stocks, 1/2 percent hold 59 percent (Kuttner 1996, p. 73).

The story has just begun. Beyond the direct provision of spendable, speculative income, the high officials of corporate America are guaranteed additional real income in the form of luxurious consumption that is only occasionally remarked upon, and does not depend on stock market trends This consumption is obtained as a cost of running the business, and like the most advanced military Stealth aircraft, is invisible under the appropriate conditions.

4   STEALTH COMPENSATION

A recent dramatic case involved J. Peter Grace, revered by 'fiscal conservatives' in politics for his merciless exposure of waste in government, investigated and publicized over many years through his organization, Citizens Against Government Waste. Recent events suggest the possibility that the intimate knowledge that guided his searches was acquired through personal practice of the art of dubious spending in the company that bears his family name. His removal as head of the company followed revelations that he had spent 'millions of dollars in company money for private security guards, nursing care, and a private apartment' (Wilson 1995, p. D1). A stockholder's lawsuit might eventually have revealed these activities, but a power struggle within the inner circle was more assuredly effective; without it, he might have continued for many more years to support his personal consumption by charges to company accounts.

His case is unique only for its irony. Indeed, it is quite reasonable to suspect that every business provides opportunities for personal consumption that are considered in law or custom to be the cost of getting the product in the hands of the consumer, from the small shopkeeper to the mightiest corporate mogul. Let us continue the examination of this situation with several examples from the public record and others in the form of 'ideal type' composite examples, some slightly modified to disguise the identity of the protagonists.

The Small Entrepreneur

After many years of saving and working in a large bureaucratic organization, Ted's dream of operating his own restaurant, and getting rich, was suddenly possible as a company failed and offered its assets for sale at a price that he could afford. One of the inducements was the seller's revelation that the business produced somewhat more profit than was reported to the tax authorities; proof was provided in the form of a copy of the 'real' account books. Weeks of cleaning, seeking out agreeable suppliers, standing for health inspections, hiring cooks, servers, and cleanup people preceded the grand opening day. These days signaled an endless future of fourteen-hour drudgery, as the enterprise required more nurturing than anticipated. Despite the work load, he was his own boss and some benefits were now open to him that were not thinkable while in the employ of others. Among these were providing jobs and learning opportunities to his own children and their extended-family cousins, taking meals on the job, and buying a computer with Internet access for the business, and for the educational advancement of the younger generation when the business purpose has been served for the day.

Later, as the business prospered, the opportunity arose to buy a van, for deliveries, of course, but also handy for occasional family outings. Also, he could buy health care and dental insurance for some of the younger ones who had not been previously fortunate in this matter. He gave discounts to several members of the business community, and in turn bought their merchandise at reduced prices. He joined several business groups, and pleasantly found that their conventions were always held in desirable locations. At business expense, he and his wife — conveniently designated as an officer of the firm — attended the meetings, and remained for a few extra days of leisure beyond the convention dates. As a non-cash bonus, the entrepreneur also was assured of public gratitude for creating jobs, an accomplishment that obliged the community to applaud expression in the local newspaper of his understanding of the dangers of government meddling that disrupts the smooth execution of entrepreneurial decisions. In this ritual, the entrepreneur was supported by attestation of the soundness of his ontology in the lecture halls and scholarly documents of professors of business who had read some of the writing of Joseph Schumpeter on the social virtues of entrepreneurship.

The Bureaucrat

A department head of a wholesale hardware regional office was excessively preoccupied with business matters. 'Excessively' meant that the obligations imposed by his employer were requiring too much attention; his wife's fortieth birthday loomed and he, along with several relatives, had decided that a cruise around the isles of Greece would be a perfect celebration of her passage into mid-life. Assuring himself that the work for which he is paid will be better accomplished if he did not have to attend to all the arrangements for the trip, he hosted lunch for the head of the firm's travel office and asked that some help be rendered. The travel officer made all arrangements, including reservations for air travel, a land package, and two weeks aboard a luxurious vessel for the department head and his wife, plus 30 other friends and relatives who paid their own expenses. Some 80 hours of travel office employees' time was used in making the arrangements; since no account was established for accumulating the expenses of this activity, they were charged to overhead or other accounts, and passed in that way into the elevated prices of nuts and bolts that appear in small but expensive packages at discount stores and supermarkets.

Like Ted, his employment provides opportunities for subsidized leisure in the form of conventions, golf, and sundry parties; his menu was more substantial than Ted's.

The Financial Manipulator

The entire top management of a financial institution of modest size found that harmonious collaboration on the job was seldom complicated by mistrust of others in the group, for they were all relatives, sons and sons-in-law, abetted by one or two daughters, of the founding genius. His reported salary was several million dollars, and with that of the inbred group amounted to tens of millions annually. The family enjoyed travel to European and Caribbean destinations as a group, on company aircraft large enough to accommodate them, their grandchildren, and an occasional United States Senator and spouse.

In time, he might have lusted for a larger craft, such as the $35 million Gulfstream V, cruising at nearly 600 mph over 7,500 miles with 19 passengers (Field 1997). If times were really good, he could aim for a Boeing 737, modified for conference rooms and offices, bath and shower, and a fitness area ('An Updraft For Corporate Jets'). Whichever craft he selected, he might hope to park it among the 1500 others at the Super Bowl, and attend at the expense of the Host Committee (Western 1996). The Arizona legislature helped many executives in this matter, appropriating $2 million to help organize the 1996 event. With this and other moneys, the Host Committee sent CEOs of the Fortune 500 gifts of paperweights ($21,000), complementary admission to area golf resorts, invitations to a country club reception hosted by the governor of the state, to a party before the game, and to a golf tournament. In addition, 25 lucky CEOs received tickets to the football game. In justification of this generosity, boosters pointed out that '59 percent of the people who attend a Super Bowl are decision makers at their companies' (Reagor 1996, p. E1). Not all who failed to get free tickets were dismayed. 'Nearly all of corporate America is here (and) thirty-five percent attend the game on corporate expense accounts' (Bland and Van der Werf 1996, p. SB1).

The costs of the family's jaunts were allocated to central office administration, along with the fees charged by auditors who certify that the wealth displayed in the palatial furnishings of the clan headquarters has been obtained legally. Thus armed, sellers of the firm's 'securities' (unkindly called junk bonds by some) found a ready market among the elderly whose Social Security and Medicare sustenance required augmentation. Within a few years the paper empire collapsed, destroying the livelihood of the elderly savers. For the securities fraud, the patriarch, who viewed 'regulations as challenges to his creativity rather than expressions of public policy' spent the next several years in federal prison (Mayer 1990, p. 169).

The Public Utility Deceiver

Citizens Utilities Company provided gas, electricity, and water services across the nation, including the State of Arizona, where the rates charged for these services were determined by the Corporation Commission. In rate filings over several years, the company repeatedly sought to inflate its rate base and allowable expenses, persisting even after the requests were denied, including: (1) artwork for the Connecticut headquarters building; (2) furniture and equipment for an office for a retired executive; (3) other office equipment and machines; (4) structures and improvements; and (5) two Cadillac automobiles. In a water rate filing, the rounded amounts sought for the rate base were: (1) $182,000; (2) $4,900; (3) $10,700; (4) $208,700; (5) $73,200.

Most of these items were also loaded with a charge for depreciation expense, in total exceeding $211,000. Other expenses resisted by the Corporation Commission included a rent charge for an empty building ($74,400); abnormally large payments for temporary help ($332,000); abnormally high consultants' fees ($317,000); salary, benefits, and supplies for an executive chef's work ($40,600); company car expense ($9,600); videos for officers ($76,000); special corporate events ($43,000); wellness and company sports programs ($59,000); physical examinations for executives ($3,500); community relations and contributions ($255,000);

and miscellaneous ($102,000). Two European members of the board of directors received travel reimbursement exceeding $66,000, and unspecified directors were reimbursed for legal expense of $35,000. Direct benefits to the CEO's family included his salary of $1,065,000 and directors fees to him of $28,000 and to his wife of $25,000, plus his $50,000 expense account, $12,000 for the premium payment on a life insurance policy, and international air travel and hotel expenses of $57,000. This CEO was also indispensable to other firms. He simultaneously obtained salaries from Citizens and from Century Communication Corporation, where he was Chairman of the Board and CEO (Smith 1996).

The Top Don

The RJR Nabisco story is often cited as the epitome of lavish corporate living. Whether or not corporate executives know of more outlandish operations, the general public, including movie-going non-readers who saw the movie 'Barbarians at the Gate,' probably knows of no more egregious case. It may be a source of inspiration for lesser CEOs.

In short, following the merger of RJR and Nabisco, Ross Johnson emerged as CEO of the combination. Like a godfather, he ordered substantial pay increases for his loyal executives; 31 divided $14.2 million among them, not exactly mind-boggling. The Stealth Consumption is notable, though. The head of the tobacco-business part of the firm had a stretch limousine; the chauffeur was paid $50,000 annually. Johnson added to his utility function with 24 club memberships; another chose a $75,000 Mercedes for his company car. Lower level managers were allowed one club membership and a $28,000 car. Air transportation was emphasized. Ten aircraft and 36 pilots were part of the overhead cost structure. Johnson's fascination with athletes and other celebrities led him to use these aircraft to support his social life among them, often putting the planes at their disposal. To be sure, they used them only on company business, easily assumed as they were paid for ill-defined public relations tasks. Each year Don Meredith received $500,000, Frank Gifford $413,000; golfing buddies Ben Crenshaw ($400,000) and Fuzzy Zoeller ($300,000) stood in the monetary shadow of Jack Nicklaus ($1,000,000). O.J. Simpson may have resented his only getting $250,000, for he often missed the engagements for which he was paid. The aircraft fleet was attractive to the members of the Board of Directors; Johnson gave them free access, not restricted to business purposes. He also raised their annual compensation to $50,000 and devised other ways to reward compliant behavior, such as giving $2 million to Juanita Kreps to endow two chairs at Duke University.

Finally, Johnson supported the prosperity of architectural, construction, and interior design businesses in the region. A new hangar for his air force was accompanied by an office building graced by a three-story atrium, $600,000 in furniture, $100,000 in art, and $250,000 worth of landscaping. In the headquarters building in Atlanta, he accented antiques from China ($100,000 for a lacquered screen from the eighteenth century and two newer $16,000 vases) and France ($30,000 each for two chairs and cabinets). Other pieces included porcelain dessert services worth $40,000, porcelain china costing $20,000, and a $50,000 Persian rug (Burrough and Helyar 1991, pp. 92–97).

5   EXAMINATION OF THE MYTHS

De gustibus non inquirandum; this dogma of neoclassical economics has always been rejected by followers of Veblen, both for its crippling effect on understanding the behavior of buyers in market exchanges and for its subversive result in supporting belief in the existence of consumer sovereignty.

Veblen would have examined today's extravagances with insistence on recognition of the hierarchical order of spenders, with each stratum taking its spending inspiration from those above it. Estates, castles, and homes of the elite are viewable from a distance by members of the lower orders, but along with their travel and toys, are more surely envied by those within the same general range of the pecking order. The invidious purpose is served within that venue.

As to the behavior of more ordinary spenders, the development of highly potent advertising and marketing technique has assured survival and intensification of the emulative urge. As normal members of modern acquisitive society tutored by television, young people begin to imbibe the required habits of invidious contrast before they speak or walk. They have their own infant fragrances and bottom-wipes, to launch them early on proper appreciation of the finer things (Wood 1994). The environment of formal schooling inculcates herd behavior of many kinds, not least in the matter of physical appearance; currently, emphasis is on oversized clothing inscribed with names of idolized athletic figures and teams. Immersion in the cult of celebrity, including that of the multimillionaire athlete, inures even the preschooler to gross inequality and fosters ignorance of the nature of socially useful behavior and employment. Accordingly, the value systems of post-pubescent citizens are fully formed as to the propriety of every manner of foolish outlay, even as it exceeds their realistic aspiration by hundreds or thousands of times.

The situation is not discordant because of supporting socialization in correct beliefs about the origins of incomes. To secure the deadness of minds and consciences, youth in many states are required to endure a high-school 'economics' course presented by the football coach, who has not heard of John Bates Clark, but teaches that the natural order delivers up incomes according to one's contributions to the processes of market exchange. Thus, those who spend lavishly do so deservedly.

In cognate fashion, university professors of economics carry through the indoctrination with the teaching that business firms are the agents by which our society provides for its livelihood; that in the hope of getting profits, these entities obtain resources at their opportunity cost, and use them to make goods and services at least cost and lowest price. The special social role and status of the entrepreneur is notable here. The entrepreneur is credited not only with creating the dynamism of the market system, but also justifies the portion of the firm's revenues that go to profit. That which is a cost is a necessary and legitimate deduction from revenue when calculating profit, and a necessary and legitimate addition to price when calculating the value of the product. Economists teach the young from the first week that 'normal' profit is a cost and is the deserved compensation for the entrepreneurial function.

However, 'cost' is a social construct (Hildred and Watkins 1996). The rulings of regulatory agencies that bear on the issue of allowable costs of providing utility services suggest insight to more general practices by which costs are identified or defined. Public utilities reveal the lowest order of corporate stealth consumption, in that they must receive approval for compensation and other outlays in the forum of public regulation. The distinctive quality of the regulatory decision in many of these matters, exemplified above in the salary of Citizens Utility's CEO, consultants, and temporary workers, was that the requested expenditure is beyond the normal bounds, suggesting a question about the nature of the normal. The regulatory agency's focus on the egregious implies that all that is allowed is acceptable under ordinary standards. What is, then, the normal compensation of these executives, so commonplace that it does not excite the curiosity of staff and consultants? Since the generosity of compensation of executives in unregulated firms is probably greater, a minimum level of such expenditure is suggested from the record of treatment of the regulated firms.

Regarding custom and legality in compensation portfolios, it seems also that the stock option is desirable compensation because the associated complexity of financial reports is a useful means of deluding shareholders

(Blanton 1997). Also, tax law provides additional advantage, the stock option is deductible for tax purposes, but need not be revealed in the annual report to stockholders as an expense. This arithmetic happily increases the reported profit, when advantageous evidence of the extraordinary competence of the executives is needed (Gordon 1997).

Other kinds of 'long-term compensation' also owe their existence to sympathetic writers of tax law. The deal is simple:

> Rather than take all their pay and pay taxes on it, executives let the company hold on to some. The company invests the money, and the executives do not pay taxes on any of it until they take the money years later.
>   It sounds like the IRA or 401(k) used by tens of millions of Americans. Except this deal excludes the rank and file and has special benefits: there are no government limits on how much can be put away, and many top executives have put away millions. A lot of companies guarantee them high interest rates on the money and throw in a matching contribution (Drew and Johnston 1996, p. A11).

In this arrangement, whether in the form of stock options or other instrumentalities, shareholders need not be informed (Drew and Johnston 1996).

Thus, we discern a ranking of stealth compensation, each level with its own justifications. The small shopkeeper converts personal consumption into business expense, but with some difficulty, as the borderline of the illegal is approached or as the presence of competitors makes it difficult to boost product prices sufficiently. In this, though, the activity is entrepreneurial and the money that remains is justified profit. Middle managers in the corporate enterprise may use company resources for personal benefit, from keeping an adequate stock of office supplies at home, to having access to wellness centers and other corporate facilities that are legitimized as objects of expenditures by corporate authorizers. In the role of middle manager, though, one is simply an employee, not an entrepreneur, and consequently suffers the inglorious status of the bureaucrat, albeit not as lowly as the public-servant bureaucrat. Compliant corporate boards of directors recognize that top managers such as themselves, perhaps having risen to the pinnacle through the ranks of the bureaucrats, upon arrival are endowed with the potency of entrepreneur, and are allowed to assert the associated prerogatives in full. This level of authority includes full conversion of specified personal benefit into recognized cost and an element of the price of the product of the firm. As to the determination of income through productive behavior, we must note that although stock options are touted as a method to reward performance, the cause and effect connection is doubtful because many, and unknown, influences other than profit are at work in determining stock prices, and the reward often seems to flow regardless of performance. Graef Crystal, whose highly paid talents as a compensation consultant have been turned, since his formal retirement, to criticism of 'excessive' compensation, comments:

> If you read these reports from the directors, when things are going well, it's always because of the brilliance of the CEO. But on the downside, it's those damn politicians in Washington or its (sic) Wall Street or it's the drop in oil prices — somehow it's always someone else's fault (Pearlstein 1997, p. E1).

In the face of evidence about the importance of stock-market rewards for the highest-paid members of the 'labor force,' there should be no quarter given those who speak of the just deserts of docile producers covering only the productivity-based costs of their commodities. At every level, costs are socially determined, both for the application of productive agents in a real function and for the comfort of managers who have the power to influence that social process, directly or indirectly.

Finally, it is necessary to examine the Veblenian function of invidiousness as an influence on the social construction of costs and the structure of compensation, as exemplified in Stealth Consumption. Invidiousness requires that consumption be viewed by someone of lesser importance, but meddling stockholders and regulators must be deflected if the Stealth Consumption is to continue. At least four modes of deception regarding managerial compensation are present. The overriding deception is that of conventional theory, which sanctifies market outcomes as efficient; John Bates Clark 'proved' that resources are compensated in accordance with their (competitive) marginal revenue product. This diverts attention of the general public from the potential of excessive compensation. Three subsidiary deceptions hide germane phenomena from stockholders or tax collectors or both. Deferred compensation is not recorded as a cost, deceiving stockholders with inflated profit data and withholding — legally, of course, because of the current structure of the law — tax revenue from government. Stock options delude stockholders and both defer and reduce tax liabilities of the favored executives. Finally, the consumption in question reduces profits, thus harming stockholders and provide an untaxed benefit to the executives.

As Veblen indicated, different circumstances and audiences decree different expressions of invidious display. In the corporate world, the culture of corporate leaders will assure that the benefits of pay and perquisites are topics of conversation on many occasions. The pecking order will be known, and this will ordinarily be sufficient. It is also likely that the expression of exploit and prowess, from which additional prestige derives, takes the form of inner-circle storytelling about gulling stockholders and frustrating tax collectors, and accomplishing the gulling and frustrating more completely and cleverly than others with whom they share the splendid segregation of the sports arena skybox. In this setting they may also rejoice collectively that the legality of their good fortune will continue, as the political influence of their class succeeded once more in preventing imposition of accounting rules that would have required the cost of stock options to be disclosed as an expense (Koretz 1996).

Neoclassical economic theory holds, usually with no mention of any empirical evidence, that the lure of large profits is essential to the preservation of entrepreneurial vitality, but that competitive markets exist in sufficient strength to reduce eventually those profits to the minimal level at which the efficiency requirements of society as a whole are attained. Since theoretical comprehension is absent regarding the behavior firms called 'oligopolistic,' especially the manner of their pricing and derivation of profit, little comment is directed to them. In a rare display of candor, Rosen admits that we know almost nothing on this matter; he does not continue to the devastating conclusion that American business is dominated by oligopoly, so he is able to continue the fiction that neoclassical theory has some cogency for policy formulation, in his case, taxation (Rosen 1995, 289).

A reasonable Veblenian insight would be that while we must remain agnostic about how prices are determined in the majority of modern business enterprises, we can be relatively confident that pricing according to marginal cost is not among the plausible explanations. Oligopolists will determine prices according to their own lights, assuredly giving considerable attention to customary costs of production, including their Stealth Consumption. As to the stock market portion of their compensation, they will do what they must and can to manipulate ownership claims by takeovers, restructurings, acquisitions and sell-offs, in that process mysteriously causing stock prices to move in directions comfortable for them. That their focus of attention is not on the production and sale of commodities useful to the life process of the community is of no concern to them, if not to the general community.

CONCLUSION

Veblen began his inquiries with rejection of crucial neoclassical assumptions. One does not understand irrational behavior by compressing it into a mold of mythical rationality, nor does the influence of tastes become comprehensible by choosing to ignore the manner of their formation. One does not understand the distribution of income by assuming that it results from blind forces of nature. One does not discern the degree of efficiency in the matter of making the community's living by assuming the salutary operation of imaginary competitive markets. In his method, these matters are appropriately objects of inquiry, not assumption. Accordingly, inquiry reveals that much consumption is harmful to the community; it allows resources to be devoted to the production of commodities whose only merit is that someone can be persuaded to purchase them, often with merely invidious intent. Inquiry reveals that the largest incomes are obtained through extortionary processes and raging speculation, and not by virtue of useful contribution to the material well-being of the community. Inquiry reveals that the dominance of the community's provisioning activities by gargantuan firms assures not efficiency, but its opposite. Thus, the unexamined premises from which neoclassical economic theory, and associated laissez faire policy predilections, derive are seen to be contravened by evidence; they remain viable only as elements of ideological obfuscation that deprive the community of warranted knowledge of its situation.

The community that understands the predatory thrust of successful businesses is in a position to understand the aid to that predation of the community's acceptance of neoclassical doctrines. That community is also able to begin questioning the desirability of current arrangements, and exploring through democratic processes the reconstruction of those arrangements for the purposes beneficial to all. Veblen's work remains one of the few constructive guides to this kind of social inquiry, and hopefully, rationality. Sadly, the pessimism for which Veblen is known seems also a major part of his legacy, one that the judicious observer of contemporary life escapes only with great difficulty.

REFERENCES

Anonymous (1987), 'High Life Afloat: Superduper Yachts', *Time*, September 7, 72–74, cited in Phillips (1990, 44.)

Anonymous (1995), 'Kowloon Hotel Towers in Opulence', *The New York Times*, printed in *The Arizona Republic*, February, T3.

Anonymous (1995), 'Pedigree Sheep's "Golden Fleece" Nets $924,000', *Associated Press*, printed in *The Arizona Republic*, January, A25.

Anonymous (1996), 'An Updraft For Corporate Jets', *Business Week*, August, 33.

Anonymous (1997), 'Sunbeam Chief's Pay Soars', *The Arizona Republic,* April, E1.

Bland, Karina and Martin Van der Werf (1996), 'Glamour, Glitz in XXXcess', *The Arizona Republic,* January, SB1.

Blanton, Kimberly (1997), 'Real Salaries of the CEOs: Stock options', *Boston Globe,* printed in *The Arizona Republic,* March, E1.

Brown, Jeff (1995), 'It's Worth Shareholder's While to See If CEO is Overpaid', *The Philadelphia Inquirer,* printed in *The Arizona Republic* June, D3.

Chang, Yahlin and Jean Seligmann (1997), 'Going, Going, Gone! Di's Defrocked', *Newsweek,* July, 47.

Burrough, Bryan and John Helyar (1991), *Barbarians at the Gate: The Fall of RJR Nabisco,* New York: Harper Collins Perennial edition.

Drew, Christopher and David Cay Johnston (1996), 'Rich Get Richer: Ploy Gives Tax Break To Execs', *The New York Times,* printed in *The Arizona Republic,* October, A11.

Field, David (1997), 'Canadian Firm Pulls Learjet Out of Sales Nose-Dive', *USA Today,* July, 4B.

Gordon, Mary (1997), 'Tax Bill Targets Stock Options As Compensation', *Associated Press,* printed in *The Arizona Republic,* April, E8.

Golfen, Bob (1996), '$15,000 Coin Flip Dazzles Auction', *The Arizona Republic,* January, D1.

Goodykoontz, Bill (1996), '"Robb" For the Rich, Not For the Poor', *The Arizona Republic,* December 23, C1.

Grover, Ronald (1997), 'Ovitz Ranting', *Business Week,* July 21, 15, 41; review of Slater, Robert. *Ovitz: The Inside Story of Hollywood's Most Controversial Power Broker,* New York: McGraw-Hill.

Henwood, Doug (1996), 'The Dow and the Joneses', *The Nation,* April 3, 6.

Hildred, William and Larry Watkins (1996), 'The Nearly Good, The Bad, and The Ugly in Cost-Effectiveness Analysis of Health Care', *Journal of Economic Issues,* **30,** September, 755–775.

Jackson, Kristin (1996), 'The Rich and Hard-To-Please Willing To Pay For Getaway', *Seattle Times,* printed in *The Arizona Republic,* February 25, T5.

Kalish, David (1997), 'Intel Chief's '96 Income Leads Pack', *Associated Press,* printed in *The Arizona Republic,* April, E1.

Kaul, Donald (1996), 'Can Wealthy Afford Higher Income Taxes? Ho! Ho! Ho! Ho! Ho!', *Tribune Media Services,* printed in *The Arizona Republic,* November, B11.

Koretz, Gene (1996), 'Keeping Options Under Wraps: Why Execs Fought FASB So Fiercely', *Business Week,* June, 26.

Kuttner, Robert (1996), 'Soaring Stocks: Are Only the Rich Getting Richer?', *Business Week,* April 28, citing James Poterba and Andrew Sawich in *Brookings Papers on Economic Activity,* **2,** 73.

Lederer, Edith (1997), 'Store, Customer in Big Dispute', *Associated Press,* printed in *The Arizona Republic,* May, A12.

Lukasik, Todd (1995), 'Readers Report', *Business Week,* May 12, 52.

Mayer, Martin (1990), *The Greatest-Ever Bank Robbery,* New York: Charles Scribner's Sons.

Pearlstein, Steven (1997), 'CEO's Get Richer as Employees Try to Stay Even', *Washington Post,* printed in *The Arizona Republic,* April 5, E1.

Phillips, Kevin (1990), *The Politics of Rich and Poor,* New York: Random House.

Reagor, Catherine (1996), 'Arizona Courts Big Business With Red Carpet', *The Arizona Republic,* January, E1.

Rosen, Harvey (1995), *Public Finance,* 4th ed., Chicago: Richard D. Irwin, Inc.

Shephard, Chuck (1994), 'News of the Weird', *The Arizona Republic,* November, C3.

Smith, Ralph (1996), 'Direct Testimony of Ralph C. Smith on Behalf of the Arizona Corporation Commission Staff', *Docket No. E–1032–95–417,* July.

Snyder, Julie and Betty Beard (1996), 'Saudis Splurged During Valley Stay', *The Arizona Republic,* July, A1, A16.

Usborne, David (1997), 'Severance Outrage is Lacking in US', *London, The Independent,* printed in *The Arizona Republic,* January, E2.

Veblen, Thorstein (1953[1899]), *The Theory of the Leisure Class,* New York: The Macmillan Company.

Walsh, Sharon (1997), 'Green Tree CEO Pockets $102 Million Bonus for '96', *The Washington Post,* printed in *The Arizona Republic,* March, E2.

Western, Ken (1996), 'Bowl Fans Bring Cash For Valley', *The Arizona Republic,* January, A1.

Western, Ken (1997), 'Ultimate Golf Junket Puts Game On Higher Plane', *The Arizona Republic,* June, A1, A7.

Whitaker, Barbara (1997), 'For Some Lucky Workers, Dream Jobs Really Come True', *The New York Times,* printed in *The Arizona Republic,* January, D1, D10.

Wilson, Catherine (1995), 'Ousted W. R. Grace Exec Given $43 Million', *Associated Press,* printed in *The Arizona Republic,* April, D1.

Wood, Dana (1994), 'Fragrance, Skin-Care Products Aimed At Young Market', *New York Times,* printed in *The Arizona Republic,* October, D1.

6. Veblen's Leisure Class Theory and Legalized Gambling: Jackpot Realism

Rick Tilman and Ruth Porter Tilman

1 INTRODUCTION

For our understanding of gambling, two traditions in the philosophy of leisure are relevant. The classical perspective dating from the Greeks, particularly Aristotle, views leisure as time free from the obligation to work. It is a condition of existence in which activity is engaged in as an end-in-itself, that is, for its own sake. Pure contemplation is thus leisure's most sublime form. In order to engage in contemplative activity, individuals must possess the ability to both reason logically, that is, generalize from the particular, and intuitively understand the good. But knowledge is to be used not for personal or material gain but for self-illumination. Its purpose is self-actualization not social aggrandizement. Thoroughly class and gender biased and supported in terms of material provisioning by slavery, this tradition of leisure has little in common with the one analysed by Thorstein Veblen in *The Theory of the Leisure Class*. Veblen wrote that leisure connoted 'non-productive consumption of time' (Veblen 1975[1899], p. 43) and believed that leisure-related resources were ordinarily employed not for contemplative purposes nor intellectual activity, but for purposes of conspicuous consumption and display, conspicuous waste and exemption from useful labor. He felt that the question to be asked regarding all expenditure is 'whether it serves directly to enhance human life on the whole — whether it furthers the life process taken impersonally' (Veblen 1975[1899], p. 99). He also writes that:

> In order to be at peace with himself the common man must be able to see in any and all human effort and human enjoyment an enhancement of life and well-being on the whole. In order to meet with unqualified approval, any economic

fact must approve itself under the test of impersonal usefulness — usefulness as seen from the point of view of the generically human, (Veblen 1975[1899], p. 98).

Legalization of gambling in Nevada by an act of the state legislature in 1931 was an important catalyst for the massive growth of the 'gaming' industry after World War II, although it existed on a substantial subterranean scale before the Depression. The city of Las Vegas, Nevada, was incorporated six years after the publication of *The Theory of the Leisure Class*, and its first hotel-casino was built twelve years after Veblen's death in 1929. As powerful as Veblen's predictive ability was, within his frames of reference, he could not have foreseen today's Las Vegas. However, gambling in its various forms dovetails into his analysis of leisure as sheer waste and futility and as often possessing emulatory significance.

Veblen suggests in his distinctive satirical prose that gambling is evidence of superstition and animism in the human community. In his time, the main forms of gambling, most of which he discusses, were church raffles, often illicit card games, horse-racing and other animal sports, and, of course, athletic events, (Veblen 1975[1899], Chapter 11). He noted that the higher leisure class found prize-fighting distasteful (Veblen 1975[1899], p. 271); something that may have changed, in view of the exorbitant ticket prices charged for championship boxing matches in Las Vegas to people who buy the best seats.

Apologists for the casino industry argue that gambling has its own 'entertainment value,' that it provides an emotionally exhilarating experience especially if one wins and, in any case, provides relief from boredom. And, from the perspective of neoclassical economics, what people do with their resources should be a private matter and not subject to critical public scrutiny or collective censure.

Now with a century since publication of *The Theory of the Leisure Class*, however, it is important to note that most states permit several forms of gambling; 46 states have charitable bingo; 43 have pari-mutuel betting; 29 have Indian gambling establishments; 13 allow casino or riverboat gambling (Internet Gambling 1997). Lotteries, which have worse odds than roulette, are run by 37 states to raise public revenue.

Historically eliminated by most states from the late nineteenth century through the first half of this century, state revenues from lotteries now often replace, but do not supplement, other revenues. In 1994, state governments took in $10 billion from lotteries. By 1996, they were bringing in $25 billion per year in the United States. In London, England, lottery revenues are helping to finance renovation of the British Museum and Library. The very presence and issue of gambling on the internet means that gambling is virtually global. Legalized gambling (and gambling addiction) spread internationally through the device of the corporation makes important the analysis of Veblen's claims about it.

C. Wright Mills, in his introduction to the 1953 edition of *The Theory of the Leisure Class*, uses the term 'crackpot realism' to describe various illusory beliefs and practices exposed by Veblen. We argue that the coexisting status of corporate 'gaming' and the epidemic of gambling addiction by governments and individuals (Las Vegasization), amounts to what Mills termed 'crackpot realism.' More to the point, we call gambling legalization 'jackpot realism,' which ignores the ugly side of the trend to the advantage of the people in power.

First, we will explicate Veblen's theory of gambling through textual exegesis of his chapter, 'The Belief in Luck,' which is sandwiched between chapters on 'Modern Survivals of Prowess' and 'Devout Observances.' Veblen's discussions in these three chapters overlap as easily and obviously as sports books with football betting and dozens of wedding chapels that pack the Las Vegas Strip. We will show the relevance of Veblen's theories to legalized gambling today, including its emulatory features. We will argue that Veblen was essentially correct in his diagnosis of its socially pathological justifications and consequences; the latter meaning that gambling 'industries' do not serve Veblen's prescribed ends of life.

2 PROWESS, BELIEF IN LUCK, AND DEVOUT OBSERVANCES

'As it finds expression in the life of the barbarian, prowess manifests itself in two main directions, — force and fraud' (Veblen 1975[1899], p. 273). Veblen's discussion of prowess ties into analysis of gambling in at least two ways. First, sports books and athletic events, for which heavy betting occur, are an inextricable aspect of our casinos and culture. Second, 'force and fraud' is not off the mark in describing the power of 'gaming' lobbyists or casino developers and the advertising used by government lottery directors and corporations to entice gamblers. Force and fraud, according to Veblen, are expressed in pecuniary occupations.

Veblen points to the egoistic role of self-aggrandizement present in sports betting when he comments that not only does the stronger side score a more signal victory, and the losing side suffer a more painful and humiliating defeat, in proportion as the pecuniary gain and loss in the wager is large (Veblen 1975[1899], p. 277). The wager is seen as 'enhancing the chances of success for the contestant on which it is laid' (Veblen 1975[1899], p. 277).

Veblen did not use the term 'gambling addiction,' but, he talks about 'the spiritual basis of the sporting man's gambling habit' (Veblen 1975[1899], p. 294). His thoughts on athletics link his theories to current trends. In the following segment from Veblen's 'Modern Survivals of Prowess' chapter, we substitute the word 'gambling' for the term 'athletic sports':

> Addiction to [gambling], not only in the way of direct participation, but also in the way of sentiment and moral support, is, in a more or less pronounced degree, a characteristic of the leisure class; and it is a trait which that class shares with the lower-class delinquents, and with such atavistic elements throughout the body of the community as are endowed with a dominant predaceous trend (Veblen 1975[1899], pp. 271–272).

In a subsequent paragraph, Veblen writes:

> The prevalence and the growth of the type of human nature of which this propensity is a characteristic feature is a matter of some consequence. It affects the economic life of the collectivity both as regards the rate of economic development and as regards the character of the results attained by the development (Veblen 1975[1899], pp. 272–273).

In 'The Belief in Luck,' Veblen links gambling with the history and prehistory of the human race and claims that it possesses transcultural significance. 'The gambling propensity is another subsidiary trait of the barbarian temperament. It is a concomitant variation of character of almost universal prevalence among sporting men and among men given to warlike and emulative activities generally' (Veblen 1975[1899], p. 276).

Veblen explained that at the root of the gambling urge was a belief in luck, that is, personal intervention on one's behalf by Divine Providence (Veblen 1975[1899], Chapter 11). According to Veblen, this provided the main psychological impetus for taking part in games of chance; yet the proclivity for gaming did not depend entirely on a belief in intervention by the Almighty. The excitement of the game itself and the cultural stimulation of the environment in which gambling takes place also lent support to the gambler's flagging spirits should he or she succumb to a losing streak.

Veblen's main point was that the gambler believes in luck and that this quasi-religious belief is what motivates the persistent bettor who may actually find it necessary to invoke the name of the Deity, or a mascot, to further his or her fortunes with the gambling apparatus. Not surprisingly, Veblen argues that these beliefs and their social consequences are not culturally isolated phenomena nor socially-encapsulated practices. Rather, they are connected with other values and processes which collectively damage the social fabric of the community. He advances an important thesis regarding gambling's social impact, 'this trait also has a direct economic value. It is recognized to be a hindrance to the highest industrial efficiency of the aggregate in any community where it prevails in an appreciable degree' (Veblen 1975[1899], p. 276).

Veblen points to the animistic and superstitious aspects of the gambler's psyche which are linked with a belief in the potential intervention of Divine Providence in the game. As he put it:

> In its simple form the belief in luck is this instinctive sense of an inscrutable teleological propensity in objects or situations. Objects or events have a propensity to eventuate in a given end, whether this end or objective point of the sequence is conceived to be fortuitously given or deliberately sought. From this simple animism the belief shades off by insensible gradations into the second, derivative form or [sporting man's] phase, which is a more or less articulate belief in an inscrutable preternatural agency (Veblen 1975[1899], p. 280).

Veblen's theory of gambling emanated from his theory of the leisure class phenomenon, yet it was also practiced by working-class delinquents who represented an arrested, that is, socially stunted stage of individual and social development. Gambling, in his view, lowered the collective industrial efficiency of the community through dissipation of its mental acuity and its physical and emotional energies. It was also objectionable because it wasted other material resources that conceivably could be put to better use. Although the animistic and superstitious proclivities of humankind have been present throughout the history and possibly much of the prehistory of the race, the pursuit of gaming reinforces and intensifies them in industrial society.

3   STATUS EMULATION IN LARGE-SCALE GAMBLING

In what follows, the gambling industry is analysed from a Veblenian perspective modified, of course, by an updating of the social environment to take account of structural tendencies and economic changes that have occurred since his lifetime. Specifically, this means using Veblen's theory of status emulation to analyse the use of economic resources in the economy and the patterns of consumption prominent among gamblers insofar as these can be shown to be linked directly with the structural imperatives of the gaming industry. Our hypothesis is the following: where legalized gambling spreads on a large scale in market economies and cultural environments roughly similar to our own, it will reproduce these same patterns. Thus, the expansion of legalized gambling in its corporate form to the Pacific rim countries, the North Atlantic community, the Commonwealth and the more advanced parts of the Third World can be expected to produce roughly similar effects to those gambling has induced in Nevada.

We now inject Veblen's ideas regarding invidious emulation as it pertains to the provision and consumption of forms of gambling. Gamblers, be they professionals, regulars at local casinos, or simply tourists casually trying their luck, are part of either status-enhancing or status-detracting emulatory processes which may expand or weaken the sense of self-worth or general esteem. The common thread for the range of gamblers is their use of leisure time that appears to an observer to be both entertainment and wasteful of resources. Assuming that losing money is less wasteful than winning, the entertainment factor and the waste factor would seem to be inversely related to one another. Although traditional one-armed bandit slot machines have been largely supplanted by games of chance in video slot machine form, the former, especially if played continuously as gambling addicts do, is an apparatus that requires waste of physical and mental resources, as well as time.

What may appear on the surface to be spontaneous self-indulgence in a frivolous game of chance by the gambler, may in reality be a serious form of emulatory rivalry. What matters is not simply winning but playing those games which are most status enhancing — sitting at the baccarat table to provide visible evidence of ability to pay is more invidious than motives for playing the nickel and quarter slot machines. It is ostentatious display of pecuniary prowess that is most likely to enhance social status. Appearances of status enhancement for the 'high rollers' are, ironically, increased especially when they lose large sums of money. The hotels in which the high rollers play will often 'comp' or compliment these gamblers with deluxe accommodations, service, and entertainment.

As important as amounts of money wagered, styles of dress that accompany betting, and sophistication of the game are, it is also the esteem of peers that matters and this may require getting on the 'bandwagon.' Playing those games most often indulged in by the group upon whose esteem one's sense of self-worth most depends affects gamblers' choices. For most players, this means joining the game(s) most appealing to companions and other players who really 'count' in the hopes of making oneself socially acceptable to them. Yet, a self-anointed elite may ultimately come to deride those mediocre and vulgar gamblers, on whose 'bandwagon' almost anyone can climb; or sneer at those whose play produces 'Veblen effects' based on price, or the amount waged. Repulsed by these philistines, the wagering 'snob' emerges as evidence of the cultural superiority of the aesthete. Bored by convention and contemptuous of both *nouveau riche* and unwashed herd, the snob distances himself from both by engaging in games of chance that only the culturally-competent can appreciate and enjoy (Liebenstein 1950).

In time, the snob may become bored with gambling snobbery or come to feel that the practice of it is not sufficiently status-enhancing. He will thus move on to what has been described as 'counter-snobbery' (Steiner and Weiss 1951). This is a more simplistic and austere life style in which gambling may be considered irrelevant or, at best, as a casual, inexpensive activity which aims only at impressing other counter-snobs with its innocuousness. The status aspirations and pretensions of other groups no longer matter — only the needs of the counter-snob for more social deference and then only from other practitioners of counter-snobbery.

Regarding most casino employment, the relative status of jobs generally correlates with the invidious hierarchy of the range of games available. Employees who rove slot machine areas providing coins are at the bottom of the invidious job ranking. Slot players are among the masses of casino gamblers, but like all gamblers, they are served 'free' drinks, and this points to one of the gender-specific casino roles. Beverage servers are traditionally female and usually must have certain physical attributes to be employed (for example, being slim with good legs) and look attractive in their often skimpy uniforms or costumes. In the patriarchal system of mega-resorts, cocktail waitresses, not unlike 'showgirls,' as casino trophies, are offered to gambling customers for vicarious consumption. The place of cocktail waitresses in the invidious employee ranking may depend on the gamblers they serve. For example, serving drinks to bingo players cannot enhance status as much as serving to poker players. The chance for making good tips, called 'tokes' in Nevada, is one factor because 'classier' gamblers will generally tip more. Cocktail waitresses have higher income and, perhaps, more invidious status among casino personnel who are traditionally women, such as 'keno girls' and 'change girls.'

Blackjack dealers make up a large proportion of workers on the casino floor. On the Las Vegas Strip, they are required to audition as part of the hiring process. Physical appearance in the dealer's uniform is a criterion for employment. Their status among the casino-floor hierarchy may be roughly the same as cocktail waitresses, and their income is also enhanced by tips. However, dealers have at least two levels of superior employees constantly watching their moves on the job. Supervising blackjack dealers are the 'pit bosses' (usually male), probably another supervisor, and experts on spotting cheaters monitoring partly hidden security cameras. Pit bosses have invidious distinction on the casino floor. Opportunities are narrow for casino workers to accrue experience in games with more limited numbers of gamblers, such as baccarat. Specially trained attendants to the most glamorous game hold a prestigious position in casino floor hierarchies. This suggests that one could develop a taxonomy of status-enhancement as it pertains to games of chance; an empirically verifiable inventory of social deference or honor using forms of wager ranging from cheap slots with lower pay-out rates to intermediate status production through blackjack ('21'), poker, craps, or roulette; and finally, to more sophisticated games of both skill and chance where the well-attired indulge themselves at baccarat.

4   GENERIC ENDS OF LIFE DEFEATED

Gambling takes place in a localized cultural setting characterized by institutionalized and legalized fraud and manufactured consensus. To illustrate, note the use of the euphemism 'gaming' as opposed to 'gambling' which serves as a symbol to divert attention from the bad odds and consequences for the gambler. Veblen says that 'collective interest is best served by honesty, diligence, peacefulness, good-will, an absence of self-seeking, and an habitual recognition and apprehension of causal sequence, without admixture of animistic belief and without a sense of dependence on any preternatural intervention in the course of events' (Veblen 1975[1899], p. 227).

Mega-resort casinos and government-run gambling were rare in Veblen's day. Games of chance, 'wagering,' as he has called it, or betting, included the church bazaar or raffle, betting on sports and games, horse and dog racing. A question for the student of legalized gambling who wishes to apply Veblen's standards to the contemporary situation is how the industry as a whole, or discrete segments of it in isolation, contribute to the growth of noninvidious community (Tool 1977). And, perhaps more important, what is the larger social and moral impact of gambling likely to be as it continues to spread?

Today, gambling and the tourism based on it have come to dominate the Nevada economy. The correlation between the spread of legalized gambling and the existence of certain socially pathological traits is remarkable and strikingly evident in the empirical studies on the subject. Although no definitive claims are made here for the existence of causal relationships, it is difficult to otherwise explain the incidence of homicide, suicide, other violence, juvenile delinquency, substance abuse, gambling addiction, obesity, broken families, mental illness, respiratory disease, and work alienation.[1] Of course, these are present without legalized gambling, but, at the very least, the work patterns and social values induced or attracted by the gaming industry exacerbate existing social problems. It is no accident that Nevada has a disproportionately high number of its residents clinically depressed, incarcerated, or on probation or parole.

To many public choice theorists and neoclassical economists of the libertarian stripe for whom consumer tastes are a given, the genesis of the gambler's revealed preferences, as expressed in the fleshpots of casino resorts, is irrelevant. For these economists, value is merely subjective preference and measurable only by price in the exchange mechanism of the market. They ignore the fact that capitalist property relations, a price system and market mechanism are part of a larger power system which benefits ownership and control groups disproportionately from the want creation that it calculatingly fosters. Large sums are expended by corporate gambling interests on political campaigns, advertising and salesmanship. If we use Veblen's 'generic ends of life' as a formal standard, the wants and desires fostered by these corporate leaders are not in the long-term 'best interest' of individuals or society.

Veblen wrote of the 'generic ends' and of 'fullness of life impersonally considered' (Veblen 1975[1899], Chapter 13). These are closely tied to the 'instincts,' or more accurately, 'proclivities' for altruism, proficiency of workmanship and critical intelligence for he believed that any viable scheme of life must be rooted in values that will sustain the community. Those values that are not community-sustaining, he referred to as 'pecuniary' and 'sporting.' It is clear that these are based primarily on the use and validation of force and fraud, especially the latter. Although Veblen's readers cannot be certain when he is engaged in speech acts with serious valuative import, he does use language and concepts that are undeniably value-laden. Indeed *The Theory of the Leisure Class* is littered with phrases such as conformity 'to the generically human canon of efficiency for some serviceable objective end' (Veblen 1975[1899], p. 259), and 'actions and conduct as conduce to the fullness of human life'(Veblen 1975[1899], p. 311).

Though defenders claim gambling provides needed public revenue and diversion from monotony, as a use of leisure time, gambling precludes enjoyment of other potentially consummatory behaviors.[2] Using Veblen's standard on leisure time experience as a means to measure 'fullness of life, impersonally considered,' it follows that gambling is developmental primarily in a pathological sense. For, given his criteria, it is neither culturally elevating, conducive to the growth of critical intelligence, likely to increase empathy or altruism, or enhance proficiency at socially useful work.

The growth of legalized gambling and dependence by state governments on games that appear to create social problems for communities have led us to adapt Mills' crackpot term. The mindset of habitual gamblers, those in the pecuniary occupations of the industry, and government leaders who condone legalization, amount to 'jackpot realism.'

NOTES

1. Because of the highly transient nature of many of the communities where gambling is pervasive, it is sometimes difficult to disaggregate pathologies that are internally generated from those imported by tourists and passersby. This analytically and heuristically significant task is not undertaken here.
2. C. Wright Mills and others often comment about the fact that few Americans read serious books, and that comic book reading by adults has been prevalent. In this same vein, unless one subscribes to 'pushpin is as good as poetry,' there is little consolation to be derived from such leisure time 'choices' as gambling.

REFERENCES

'Internet Gambling: Overview of Federal Criminal Law' (1997), *Congressional Research Service, Library of Congress, Report for Congress,* June (citing General Accounting Office).

Liebenstein, Harvey (1950), 'Bandwagon, Snob, and Veblen Effects in the Theory of Consumer's Demand', *Quarterly Journal of Economics,* **64**, May, 183–207.

Steiner, Robert L. and Joseph Weiss (1951), 'Veblen Revised in the Light of Counter-Snobbery', *Journal of Aesthetics and Art Criticism,* **9**, March, 263–68.

Tool, Marc R. (1977), 'A Social Value Theory in Neoinstitutional Economics', *Journal of Economic Issues,* **11**, 4, December, 823–846.

Veblen, Thorstein (1975[1899]), *The Theory of the Leisure Class,* New York: Augustus M. Kelley.

PART III

Veblen and the Women's Movement

7. Veblen and Feminist Economics: Valuing Women's Work in the Twenty-First Century

Janice Peterson

1 INTRODUCTION

The social and economic status of American women at the turn of the last century is one of the central themes addressed by Veblen in *The Theory of the Leisure Class*. In this work, Veblen provides a framework that has proven useful in understanding many of the economic problems faced by women in the United States during the twentieth century and anticipates many of the theoretical issues addressed in the works of contemporary feminist economists (Jennings 1993; Waddoups and Tilman 1992).

The global economy of the late 1990s differs in many ways from the economic world observed and dissected by Veblen in *The Theory of the Leisure Class*. The globalization of capitalism has transformed economic, political and social institutions in important ways, presenting women with new realities and challenges. What is Veblen's relevance today as we shift our focus away from the industrial, national economy and attempt to analyse the status of women in the context of globalization and economic restructuring?

This chapter argues that the continuing relevance of Veblen's work lies in his recognition of the fundamental economic significance of gender, a recognition still lacking in traditional economics. The economic restructuring that has accompanied the globalization of capitalism has had particularly important social and economic consequences for women. Feminist economists argue, however, that these consequences have not been adequately addressed in the economics literature because of the gender bias in traditional economic theories and the empirical methods that derive from these theories. It is argued that to understand the process of restructuring and to assess its impact on women requires the development of a 'holistic analysis in which gender is the fundamental organizing principle of the economy' (MacDonald 1995, p. 180).

Feminist concerns over the impact of economic restructuring, and the failure of traditional economics to address these concerns, point to insights of continuing relevance in *The Theory of the Leisure Class*. The first section of this chapter provides an overview of the issues and concerns raised by feminist economists regarding economic restructuring. This is followed by an examination of the relationship between gender and status found in Veblen's analysis of leisure class society, particularly his distinction between 'industrial' and 'pecuniary' employment and his analysis of women and 'vicarious leisure.' The chapter ends with observations on the contemporary relevance of the feminist insights in Veblen's work and the theoretical challenges that remain to be addressed in order to move toward the holistic economics necessary for meaningful inquiry in the next century.

2 ECONOMIC RESTRUCTURING AND WOMEN

Both the 'developed' nations of the 'North' and the 'developing' nations of the 'South' have begun to experience significant economic restructuring as they approach the twenty-first century.[1] This restructuring is attributed to a variety of forces, including increased international competition, shifts in the international division of labor and the centers of economic power, and rapid technological change. Economic restructuring has implied an increased emphasis on market forces, with national governments and international institutions (such as the IMF and World Bank) pursuing policies of trade liberalization, deregulation, privatization, and fiscal and monetary restraint (MacDonald 1995, p. 180; Aslanbeigui, Pressman and Summerfield 1994, p. 3).

The literature on economic restructuring has largely ignored gender issues and has generally focused on how the 'average person' is affected by such economic changes and 'reforms'. Yet, studies that have addressed the impact of economic restructuring on women find that these changes have generally led to 'fewer gains or greater losses for women.' In many cases women have been disproportionately affected by both the resulting negative economic trends, such as higher unemployment and poverty, as well as the loss of publicly provided social services (Aslanbeigui, Pressman and Summerfield 1994, pp. 3–5).

Feminist economists argue that it is imperative that the consequences of economic restructuring for women be adequately addressed, both for our understanding of these important economic processes and for the purposes of devising reasonable national and international economic policies. In the South, feminist economists have been particularly concerned with the impacts of structural adjustment and macroeconomic policies on women, as well as the role played by women workers in the successful industrialization processes of many nations. In the North, feminist analyses have focused on the impact of increased earnings inequality and the 'missing middle,' increased labor market 'flexibility,' and the 'feminization of labor' on the economic status of women (MacDonald 1995, p. 179–180; Mutari and Figart 1997, p. 121; Figart and Kahn 1997, p. 151).

In a recent discussion of the research challenges posed by economic restructuring, Martha MacDonald argues that traditional economics has been of limited value to analysts working to assess the impact of restructuring on women in both the North and the South. She argues that these limitations reflect the focus of traditional economics on 'the visible, male-dominated, public, cash economy, rather than the full range of human economic endeavor,' rendering invisible the work of many women (MacDonald 1995, p. 176). This not only distorts theoretical understandings, economic restructuring processes, but severely limits the empirical work that can be pursued using traditional statistical measures of economic activity.

The invisibility of women in official accounts of economic activity poses serious problems for feminist economic research. National and international economic statistics are based on the traditional — neoclassical — definition of economics which equates economic activity with production for profit in the market. Activities other than production for the market are considered peripheral and not attributed value in the economic sense. This conceptualization of the economy further devalues the work of women through its embodiment of the 'public/private dualism,' which separates the activities of the 'public sphere' (defined to include the market economy) from the activities of the 'private sphere' (defined to include the home and family). The private sphere has been defined as 'not the economy' and women have been viewed as non-economic beings because of their association with it (Jennings 1993; Waller and Jennings 1990).

The association of work and production with the market and public sphere has contributed to the under-representation of women's work in traditional economic statistics in a number of ways, including the omission of unpaid domestic labor, the under-representation of production in the subsistence and informal sectors, and the undercount of remunerative labor performed by women in the home (Peterson 1993). This under-representation of women's work contributes to distortions in accepted perceptions of women's economic roles and contributions. It reinforces the view of women as non-economic and unproductive, providing the basis for policies that ignore the needs of women and are detrimental to their social and economic well-being.

Feminist scholarship on US economic history, for example, has documented a serious undercount of women's productive efforts, including remunerative work performed in the home, in the official labor force statistics collected and published by the US Census Bureau during late-nineteenth and early-twentieth centuries (Bose 1987; Folbre and Abel 1989; Folbre 1991). This undercount of women's labor force participation exaggerated perceptions of 'female domesticity' at the turn of the century and distorted analyses of changes in women's economic behavior over time. In developing nations, the undercount of subsistence production and informal sector work has been a particularly serious problem, obscuring a great deal of critically important economic activity (Beneria 1982; Boulding 1988; Ward 1990). This has led to erroneous conclusions about the relationship between economic growth and women's economic status (Beneria 1982, p. 127) and has contributed to the inappropriate design and implementation of development projects (Newland 1980, pp. 7–11).

While the problems associated with the devaluation and invisibility of women's work are not new, feminist concerns about economic restructuring have highlighted their importance. MacDonald argues that to adequately analyse and respond to the process of economic restructuring it is necessary to broaden the analysis of economic activity and to recognize the importance of all forms of women's work — paid and unpaid, in the labor market and in the home. This requires economists to address the critical theoretical and empirical concerns associated with the measurement and valuation of women's unpaid work, as well as those associated with the analysis of intra-household decision-making and power relations, and gendered processes in the paid labor market (MacDonald 1995, p. 180). The following sections examine the relevance of Veblen's work for addressing these concerns and the development of a more holistic economics.

3 GENDER AND STATUS IN 'LEISURE CLASS' SOCIETY

Veblen treated the study of women as a central component of economic analysis and his views on women's social and economic status were an integral part of his critique of both American society and traditional economic theory (Diggins 1978, p. 146; Miller 1972, p. 78). As Daphne

Greenwood has argued, 'Thorstein Veblen dealt with the social and economic position of women as basic to the nature of the economic system. He did not view "woman's place" as a special topic to which economic theory might be applied, but as an intellectual window through which there may be deeper insights into the value systems dominant in society' (Greenwood 1984, p. 667). The importance of gender in Veblen's economic framework is illustrated by the fact that he 'placed socially constructed distinctions between men and women at the center of this first major work, *The Theory of the Leisure Class*' (Jennings 1993, p. 112).

Veblen argues that the inferior status of women has its roots in the same socioeconomic processes that led to the development of the 'leisure class,' thus placing the status of women at the heart of his analysis and critique of capitalism. He argues that the institution of leisure emerged as communities adopted a 'predatory habit of life' and technology advanced to the stage where subsistence could be obtained 'on sufficiently easy terms to admit the exemption of a considerable portion of the community from steady application to routine labor' (Veblen 1953[1899], p. 25). Leisure class communities are characterized by well-defined status hierarchies reflected in rigorously observed class distinctions. Such class distinctions are defined and maintained by distinctions between the employment considered proper for different classes. 'The upper classes were by custom exempt or excluded from industrial occupations, and are reserved for certain employment to which a degree of honor attaches' (Veblen 1953[1899], p. 21). Thus, in leisure class communities upper classes' status is determined by the activities one is able to avoid, most particularly activities of the industrial employment.

Veblen argues that the esteem, or lack thereof, associated with different employment in modern leisure class societies is a direct reflection of the distinction between 'worthy' and 'unworthy' employment found in earlier 'barbarian' cultures, a distinction based on the degree of 'exploit' involved in the activity. 'Under this ancient distinction the worthy employment are those which may be classed as exploit; unworthy are those necessary everyday employment into which no appreciable amount of exploit enters' (Veblen 1953[1899], p. 25). According to Veblen, this distinction derived from perceived differences between men and women, thus instituting an invidious distinction between male and female occupations:

In nearly all of these tribes the women are, by prescriptive custom, held to those employment out of which the industrial occupations proper develop at the next advance. The men are exempt from these vulgar employment and are reserved for war, hunting, sports, and devout observances (Veblen 1953[1899], pp. 22–23).

Thus, gender is seen to be the basis for the original division of labor and for cultural beliefs on the value associated with different employment. Work performed by women is accorded less value *because* it is performed by women.

Veblen argues that this invidious, gender-based distinction between 'worthy' and 'unworthy' employment did not disappear with the evolution of the modern capitalist era, but finds expression in the distinction between pecuniary (non-industrial) and industrial employment. The downgrading of industrial occupations and the modern 'aversion to menial employment' is a 'transmuted form of the barbarian distinction between exploit and drudgery' (Veblen 1953[1899], p. 26), and reflects the fact that this type of work was originally performed by women. Gender and class status are seen to be inextricably linked in modern society.

Thus, the distinction between industrial and pecuniary employment, which is central to Veblen's analysis and critique of capitalism, is fundamentally gendered. This analysis provides critical insights into the devaluation of women's work in the paid work force and in the home. The paid work traditionally performed by women falls, virtually by definition, into the category of industrial employment and is accorded little economic value or status. In addition, women's provisioning work in the home is no longer recognized as 'economic' as the definition of economic activity shifts from serviceability and social provisioning to competition and contest in the market place.

The cultural definition of women as 'non-economic' is also important in Veblen's analysis of vicarious leisure. With the development of leisure class society, women's economic roles become closely tied to men's social status, granting women what Veblen describes as a 'vicarious life':

> It is still felt that woman's life, in its civil, economic and social bearing, is essentially and normally a vicarious life, the merit or demerit of which is, in the nature of things, to be imputed to some other individual who stands in some relation of ownership or tutelage to the woman (Veblen 1953[1899], p. 229).

Most importantly, women become a vehicle through which men display their wealth and exhibit their ability to consume leisure vicariously through their maintenance of a wife not openly engaged in 'productive labor.' 'In modern communities which have reached the higher levels of industrial development, the upper leisure class has accumulated so great a mass of wealth as to place its women above the imputation of vulgarly productive labor' (Veblen 1953[1899], p. 106). Thus, a woman's appearance as economically unproductive becomes critical to the status of her husband or father. In addition, it becomes important to her own culturally-defined feminine identity. As Veblen states, 'the good and beautiful life then, assigns to the woman a "sphere" ancillary to the activity of the man; and it is felt that any departure from the traditions of her assigned round of duties is unwomanly' (Veblen 1953[1899], p. 230).

Veblen's analysis illustrates the importance of the 'cult of domesticity,' the nineteenth century ideology which equated women's place in the home with virtue and femininity, in casting gender roles into 'economic male' vs. 'non-economic female' terms. 'It grates painfully on our nerves to contemplate the necessity of any well-bred woman's earning a livelihood by useful work. It is not "woman's sphere." Her sphere is within the household, which she should "beautify," and of which she should be a "chief ornament"' (Veblen 1953[1899], p. 126).

The prescriptive standards for gender roles and family life embedded in this ideology were highly influential, despite the fact that this ideology never accurately reflected the lives of many women. Many men did not earn a wage sufficient to maintain wives in 'proper domesticity,' and many married women 'garnered significant income' from remunerative labor in the home (Jennings and Champlin 1994, p. 100; Folbre 1991, p. 466). But, as Veblen illustrates, the canons of social reputability, required that women's productive efforts be concealed (Jennings and Champlin 1994, p. 100).

4 FEMINIST INSIGHTS AND CHALLENGES

In *The Theory of the Leisure Class*, Veblen portrays women's position in economic society as an analytical window through which the prevailing system of status and values can be observed. He argues that in early predatory societies the contributions of women were deprecated because they lacked the requisite elements of prowess and exploit. In modern capitalist societies, the predatory and acquisitive instincts are refined and are manifested in the behavior of the pecuniary leisure class, where women are relegated to the roles of conspicuous consumption and vicarious leisure. According to Veblen, this downgrading of women's work is a reflection of the dominance of disserviceability over workmanship in modern society and is reinforced by the fundamentally-flawed emphasis on market relations in traditional economic analysis.

Veblen's analysis of the status of women contains insights for the definition of economics and the devaluation of women's work that are very consistent with the work of contemporary feminist economists. His analyses of the relationship between gender and the status of different occupations and the processes through which women have been defined as non-economic are particularly relevant to the empirical and theoretical concerns raised by feminists in discussions of economic restructuring.

As feminist concerns about economic restructuring illustrate, an adequate analysis of the status of women requires that the traditional definition of economics be replaced by a much broader vision of the economy. Veblen, like contemporary feminist economists (Nelson 1993), rejects market relations as the source of value, focusing instead on social provisioning. Veblen argued that a great deal of the market activity carried out by men is fundamentally wasteful, and illustrated how pecuniary interests often hinder or subvert actual social provisioning. He included much of women's domestic work in provisioning and recognized that women performed useful economic work in the home in addition to the wasteful activities associated with leisure class norms and required for social reputability (Jennings 1993, pp. 112–113; 1994, pp. 227–228).

Thus, Veblen's vision of the economy rejects the market/non-market, economic/non-economic distinctions that have been so critical to the devaluation of women's work in traditional economics. He rejected the traditional association of paid work in markets with 'the economy,' recognizing that real economic production can take place both in the home and in the market. In Veblen's analysis it is not where work takes place, or whether or not it is paid for, that determines the value of its economic contribution. It is the serviceability of the activity and its contribution to the provisioning process that gives an activity its designation as economic.

This has important implications for the valuing and measurement of women's unpaid work. Economic accounting systems that use the market as the basis for their definition and measurement of work and production miss the essence of economic value as Veblen defines it. A measurement scheme based on the provisioning definition of economics would include activities such as domestic labor, informal sector production and volunteer work, thus providing a much more accurate picture of both women's economic contributions and the real economy.

Feminist work on economic restructuring has also illustrated the need for a better understanding of household decision-making and labor market processes. As economic restructuring challenges the traditional division of labor and transforms the structure of work in the home and the market, new ways of analyzing these institutions are needed. Veblen's recognition of the relationship between class status and gender is critically important here and offers valuable insights for the development of new analytical tools.

Feminist economists have been particularly critical of traditional economic models of the household, which abstract from issues of patriarchal power and social norms, thus distorting women's actual experiences and providing little insight into this critically important economic unit (Ferber and Nelson 1993, pp. 6–7). Veblen's work illustrates how household decisions are driven by culturally defined (and often ceremonial) material wants and governed by the social norms associated with class status. This provides a framework for analyses that recognizes the importance of social norms and pecuniary emulation in determining household consumption patterns and gender-related work roles (Brown 1987).

The gender and class stratification identified in Veblen's distinction between pecuniary and industrial employment is also relevant to many of the contemporary labor market issues raised by feminist economists. Veblen's insights are particularly relevant to discussions of occupational segregation and pay equity policies designed to deal directly with the undervaluation of women's work.[2] Such concerns and policies have become particularly important in light of the labor market changes associated with economic restructuring (Figart and Kahn 1997; Mutari and Figart 1997).

Empirical research has demonstrated a relationship between occupational segregation and the gender-based wage gap (Figart and Lapidus 1997, pp. 188–189). It is argued that 'through the process of occupational segregation certain jobs have become identified as women's work, and these jobs pay less primarily because women do the work' (Figart and Kahn 1997, p. 17). Women are not in low-paying, low-status jobs because they choose to be, the explanation offered by traditional economics. The status of different occupations is related to the gender of the people who perform them. As Veblen argued a century ago, women's jobs pay less because women do them. Pay equity policies find theoretical support in Veblen's work.

One of the issues that presents the greatest challenge to feminists in addressing these concerns is the need to develop theories and policies that adequately reflect the diversity of women's experiences. Feminist economists have viewed the absence of women from the economics profession as one of the sources of gender bias in traditional economic theories and methods. The fact that the production of economic knowledge has historically excluded women is seen to have contributed to the lack of attention to issues of particular concern to women (Ferber and Nelson 1993, pp. 2–8). As feminist economics develops alternative approaches to economic inquiry, it is faced with the challenge of developing theories and methods that adequately reflect the experiences of all women (Seiz 1997). It has been argued that much of the work by feminist economists reflects the perspectives of white, professional women in the North, thus ignoring or downplaying the concerns of women of color and working class women in the North as well as women in the South.[3]

The lack of attention to, and in some cases inappropriate treatment of, race is particularly significant in *The Theory of the Leisure Class*. As Ann Jennings and Dell Champlin have noted, Veblen does not address American race relations in his critique of American society and his theories of cultural evolution draw on outdated, racist anthropological sources. They argue, however, that his work does not depend on these outdated sources and his method is conducive to a meaningful treatment of race through its recognition of the importance of cultural beliefs and the 'staying-power of old habits of thought' (Jennings and Champlin 1994, p. 108).

Rhonda Williams has stressed the importance of advancing a 'feminist theory that conceptualizes gender as racially constituted' (Williams 1993, p. 151). This requires a recognition of the importance of race in constructing many of the dualisms feminist economists seek to deconstruct. The public/private dualism expressed through the 'cult of domesticity' has played an important role in analyses of the devaluation of women's work. Williams stresses the importance of seeing this ideology as 'a very race-specific discourse,' that 'affirmed immigrant women's roles as wives and mothers but did not do so for African-Americans, Chinese-Americans, or women indigenous to the Americas' (Williams 1993, p. 151). Thus, while the conceptual division between the home and the economy has been important in defining traditional gender roles, it has done so in a highly 'racialized fashion' (Williams 1993, p. 151).

Addressing the implications of race and class privilege is critically important in the context of globalization and must be incorporated into the analysis of twenty-first century capitalism. The basic framework presented in Veblen's work is amenable to the incorporation of such concerns and offers possibilities for the development of a meaningful economics for the next century. Contemporary feminist economists argue that an equitable and sustainable future requires the refocusing of economic analysis and policy, placing more emphasis on the activities that sustain life and community. It is in his contributions to this endeavor that Veblen maintains his relevance.

NOTES

1. 'Economic restructuring' is a term also used to describe the changes taking place in the formerly-socialist nations where central planning is being replaced with a market economy. The processes and problems of restructuring in these economies has been found

to be similar to that in many developing countries (see Aslanbeigui, Pressman and Summerfield 1994).

2. Deborah Figart and Peggy Kahn define the concept of 'pay equity' broadly to include 'a wide range of approaches to the reevaluation of predominantly female jobs.' This includes traditional comparable worth wage reform as well as low-pay campaigns and career mobility programs (Figart and Kahn 1997, p. 18).

3. Veblen's discussion of the 'woman problem' and 'New Woman Movement' illustrates his recognition of the upper-class orientation of the women's movement at the time he wrote *The Theory of the Leisure Class* (see Veblen 1953[1899], pp. 231–232).

REFERENCES

Aslanbeigui, Nahid, Steven Pressman and Gale Summerfield (1994), *Women in the Age of Economic Transformation,* London: Routledge.

Beneria, Lourdes (1982), 'Accounting for Women's Work', in Lourdes Beneria, ed., *Women and Development,* New York: Praeger, 119–147.

Bose, Christine (1987), 'Devaluing Women's Work: The Undercount of Women's Work in 1900 and 1980', in Christine Bose, Róslyn Feldberg and Natalie Sokoloff, eds., *Hidden Aspects of Women's Work,* New York: Praeger, 95–115.

Boulding, Elise (1988), 'Measures of Women's Work in the Third World', in Mayra Buvinic, Margaret Lycett and William McGreevy, eds, *Women in Poverty in the Third World,* 286–299.

Brown, Clair (1987), 'Consumption Norms, Work Roles, and Economic Growth, 1919–80', in Clair Brown and Joseph Pechman, eds, *Gender in the Workplace,* Washington, DC: The Brookings Institution, 13–49.

Diggins, John (1978), *The Bard of Savagery,* New York: Seabury Press.

Ferber, Marianne and Julie Nelson (eds) (1993), *Beyond Economic Man: Feminist Theory and Economics,* Chicago: University of Chicago Press.

Figart, Deborah and Peggy Kahn (1997), *Contesting the Market: Pay Equity and the Politics of Economic Restructuring,* Detroit: Wayne State University Press.

Figart, Deborah and June Lapidus (1997), 'Reversing the Great U-Turn: Pay Equity, Poverty and Inequality', in Ellen Mutari, Heather Boushey and William Fraher IV, eds, *Gender and Political Economy,* Armonk, New York: M.E. Sharpe, 188–205.

Folbre, Nancy (1991), 'The Unproductive Housewife: Her Evolution in Nineteenth Century Economic Thought', *Signs,* **16,** Spring, 463–484.

Folbre, Nancy and Marjorie Abel (1989), 'Women's Work and Women's Households: Gender Bias in the US Census,' *Social Research,* **56,** Autumn, 545–569.

Greenwood, Daphne (1984), 'The Economic Significance of 'Woman's Place' in Society: A New-Institutionalist View', *Journal of Economic Issues,* **18,** 663–680.

Jennings, Ann (1993), 'Public or Private? Institutional Economics and Feminism', in Marianne Ferber and Julie Nelson, eds., *Beyond Economic Man,* Chicago: University of Chicago Press, 111–129.

Jennings, Ann (1994), 'Feminism', in Geoffrey Hodgson, Warren Samuels and Marc Tool, eds, *The Elgar Companion to Institutional and Evolutionary Economics*, Cheltenham, UK: Edward Elgar, 225–229.

Jennings, Ann and Dell Champlin (1994), 'Cultural Contours of Race, Gender, and Class Distinctions', in Janice Peterson and Doug Brown, eds, *The Economic Status of Women Under Capitalism*, Cheltenham, UK: Edward Elgar, 95–110.

MacDonald, Martha (1995), 'The Empirical Challenges of Feminist Economics: The Example of Economic Restructuring', in Edith Kuiper and Jolande Sap, eds, *Out of the Margin*, London: Routledge, 175–197.

Miller, Edythe (1972), 'Veblen and Women's Lib: A Parallel', *Journal of Economic Issues*, **6**, September, 75–86.

Mutari, Ellen and Deborah Figart (1997), 'Comparable Worth in a Restructuring Economy', in Ellen Mutari, Heather Boushey and William Fraher IV, eds., *Gender and Political Economy*, Armonk, NY: M.E. Sharpe, 115–130.

Nelson, Julie (1993), 'The Study of Choice or the Study of Provisioning? Gender and the Definition of Economics', in Marianne Ferber and Julie Nelson, eds, *Beyond Economic Man*, Chicago: University of Chicago Press, 23–36.

Newland, Kathleen (1980), 'Women, Men and the Division of Labor', *Worldwatch Paper*, **37**, Washington, DC: Worldwatch Institute.

Peterson, Janice (1993), 'What's in a Number? Gender Bias in Economic Statistics', *The Social Science Journal*, **30**, July, 285–290.

Seiz, Janet (1997), Review of *Beyond Economic Man*, Marianne Ferber and Julie Nelson, eds., and *Out of the Margin*, Edith Kuiper and Jolande Sap, eds, in *Feminist Economics*, **3**, Spring, 179–188.

Veblen, Thorstein (1953[1899]), *The Theory of the Leisure Class*, New York: Macmillan.

Waddoups, Jeffrey and Rick Tilman (1992), 'Thorstein Veblen and the Feminism of Institutional Economics', *International Review of Sociology*, **3**, 182–204.

Waller, William and Ann Jennings (1990), 'On the Possibility of a Feminist Economics', *Journal of Economic Issues*, **24**, June, 613–622.

Ward, Kathryn, ed. (1990), *Women Workers and Global Restructuring*, Ithaca, New York: ILR Press.

Williams, Rhonda (1993), 'Race, Deconstruction, and the Emergent Agenda of Feminist Economics', in Marianne Ferber and Julie Nelson, eds, *Beyond Economic Man*, Chicago: University of Chicago Press, 144–153.

8. Veblen and the 'Woman Question' in the Twenty-First Century

Gladys Parker Foster

1 INTRODUCTION

As we stand poised to enter the second century since the publication of Thorstein Veblen's brilliant treatise on manners and morals, the women's movement could be characterized as 'on its way' but far short of realizing its goals. 'On its way' because it seems unlikely at this time that it will be squelched, in spite of ups and downs during the past century and a backlash at the present time. For one thing, there are too many women in the labor force for it to be ignored. But it is having a mighty struggle, which is perhaps inevitable given its revolutionary nature. For what is happening is much more wrenching than purging the language of sexist words or offering flex-time in the workplace. What is happening is that our most fundamental institution, the family, is undergoing basic change.

Will Veblen's *The Theory of the Leisure Class* be relevant to the women's movement in the twenty-first century? This chapter says yes. This is so because it provides arguably the best basic framework available on the nature of institutions and the nature of societal change. Institutions are not 'given,' as they are assumed to be in neoclassical economic theory. Nor is the market 'natural.' More specifically, Veblen's theory about the two ways of behaving, the ceremonial and the instrumental — the so-called dichotomy — not only captures the essence of the position of women in American society, it describes it so clearly and in such a way that the need for change seems simple and obvious. Ideological, or 'ismatic,' approaches, such as capitalism or socialism, are hopelessly inadequate to the task of providing understanding of women's issues. Equally inadequate are the traditional economic theories based on factors of production and supply and demand. Veblen, on the other hand, who is frequently regarded as if from another planet, arrives on the American scene with an original theory of human behavior, one that is universally applicable and sufficiently novel to offer fresh insight into the question at hand.

It is not that a great deal of space in *The Theory of the Leisure Class* is devoted explicitly to women. In fact, I suppose one could read the book without thinking that it has much of anything of importance to say about women. But in those areas where it does discuss women and the relationships between women and men, the argument is so compelling that once one has noticed it, it is impossible to ignore it. And when one sees how these passages about women fit into the basic thesis of the book, the dichotomy, the argument indeed becomes powerful. In fact, the fit is so good that I noticed at times as the book progressed I was reading sections as if the book were specifically about the behavior of men and women rather than about the behavior of the leisure class and the working class. For example, the discussion about the leisure class being sheltered from the 'real world' and thus being less responsive to the need for change sounds like a description of the men in the United States Congress resisting changes that are being pushed by the female members, because the latter confront problems every day that the men are shielded from — the need for day care, problems in nursing homes, care of the elderly, abortion, sexual assault, and so on (Veblen 1953[1899], p. 137).

Veblen's occasional denial that he is making any judgement about the relative worth of the two ways of behaving deserves comment because this question is critical to what follows. He says, for example, that 'the exigencies of the language make it impossible to avoid an apparent expression of disapproval,' but 'it is not intended to imply anything in the way of depreciation or commendation' (Veblen 1953[1899], p.176; see also Tilman 1996, and Bush 1996). This propensity of his to deny making judgements has been variously interpreted. Perhaps he felt that to express an opinion about relative worth would be considered unscientific. In any case, the fact that he devotes the entire book to a detailed, carefully reasoned, and very meticulously expressed discussion of these two ways of behaving (not to mention that the same theme provides the framework for all of his subsequent works) indicates that he thinks it worthy of serious consideration — although he does seem to have fun doing it, and maybe that is enough. Perhaps his only goal, or at least his major one, is satire.

My own interpretation, however, is that he is in fact doing exactly what he disavows, in other words he is in reality saying that ceremonial behavior is to be condemned and instrumental behavior is to be valued. The latter kind of behavior forms the core of the criterion of judgement, or theory of value, that subsequent scholars have gleaned from his work. His denials about making judgements are the more remarkable in light of the fact that he chooses words that are so expressive of strong approval or disapproval, such as 'worthy, honorable, noble' employment (of men) and 'unworthy, debasing, ignoble' employment (of women) (Veblen 1953[1899], p. 29). One might well ask what all of this has to do with economic theory. Veblen goes on in the passage mentioned above to observe that:

> These phenomena are here apprehended from the economic point of view and are valued with respect to their direct action in furtherance or hindrance of a more perfect adjustment . . . to the environment and to the institutional structure required by the economic situation . . . (Veblen 1953[1899], p. 176).

What is the significance of 'the economic point of view' to what appears to be his central thesis, the dichotomy? His occasional references to economic theory suggest that his purpose is to set forth a theory that is essentially economic but that it is necessary to place it in a broader cultural context (Veblen 1953[1899], p. xx). Also, in such references he seems to be suggesting that he deems economics to be of fundamental importance.

Pertinent here is the question of how he defines economics; the answer is that he sees economics as 'provisioning.' From the above, he seems to think this important, and again, he notes that this is what women do — a value judgement about women's work.

Whatever his intent, his work suggests a way of evaluating human behavior and institutions and policies, if one takes it seriously. That is the way I take it.

2   OWNERSHIP OF WOMEN

Veblen begins by describing the institution of the leisure class, consisting of non-industrial occupations roughly comprised under government, fighting, hunting, religious observances, and sports activities pursued by men. The 'productive work' is done by the rest of society, the 'inferior class' — slaves and other dependents, and ordinarily also all of the women. This work consists of manual labor, industry, whatever has to do directly with the everyday work of getting a livelihood. His choice of words is telling as he describes the division between men's work and women's work, exploit versus drudgery, prowess versus diligence, predation versus the 'assiduous and uneventful shaping of materials' (Veblen 1953[1899], pp. 22–30).

The notion of ownership developed early, says Veblen, and the earliest form of ownership was the ownership of women by men, seemingly begun because of their usefulness as trophies. This gave rise to a form of ownership-marriage. From the ownership of women the concept of ownership comes to include the product of their industry, and so there arises the ownership of things as well as of persons. The motive that lies at the root of ownership is emulation. The possession of wealth confers honor; it is an invidious distinction (Veblen 1953[1899], pp. 34–35). The incentives for acquiring women as property have apparently been: (1) a propensity for dominance and coercion; (2) the utility of these persons as evidence of the prowess of their owner; and (3) the utility of their services. The women are commonly slaves; the great, pervading relation in such a system is that of master and servant (Veblen 1953[1899], p. 52). The wife, or the chief wife, will gradually, however, come to be exempted from production.

Thus we see the development of the role of women as indicators of the conspicuous consumption and conspicuous leisure of their masters. It is a fine thing to be wealthy enough to abstain from work oneself. It is finer still to be able to afford women who also abstain from production. And, what is perhaps finest of all, these women can themselves engage in conspicuous consumption, which of course amounts to vicarious consumption for their masters.

3   BODY MUTILATION AND DRESS

When valued for their services, Veblen points out, women should be robust and large-limbed. But to show evidence of abstention from work, a woman should be delicate and slim, especially slim-waisted, even to the point of debility (Veblen 1953[1899], p. 106). There have been changes since then, of course. Women now compete in athletics, for example, for which they develop their bodies, and they are even honored for it. Surely, however, women who work now as fashion models are as severely mutilated by diet as anyone in Veblen's time, and adolescent girls suffer from bulimia and other eating disorders as a result of the portrayal of the desired female form as defined by the media (Pipher 1991). The corset — which is 'in economic theory, substantially a mutilation, undergone for the purpose of lowering the subject's vitality and rendering her permanently and obviously unfit for work' (Veblen 1953[1899], p. 121) — has largely passed out of favor. But it survives to some degree at least, under the name of 'body shaper,' as I noted recently at a department store.

It requires no stretch of the imagination to see echoes of these phenomena in our own culture. The feeling of propriety in the relationship between men and women is clearly present today. Given this, it becomes easy to see how the women's movement would appear to many as a threat.

If the wife goes into the job market her role of conspicuous consumption and conspicuous leisure will probably be compromised. In addition, the husband may come to be perceived as economically unable to support her, at least as the embodiment of wealth and leisure. The notion of the man-of-the-house as provider for the family remains a significant component of his masculinity. Veblen's analysis could be very helpful in bringing into the open the reasons for this possibly largely subconscious but still nagging anger, sometimes out-and-out fury, at women entering the labor market.

The phenomenon of heads of corporations marrying pretty young women as trophies has also been observed and remarked upon in the current media (Collins 1989). This is perhaps an illustration of the all-too-prevalent perception of sex as sport, as conquest, as predation, as described in *The Theory of the Leisure Class*. As the twentieth century ends, the struggles over sex in the military, adultery by persons in public life, rape, sexual harassment, and so on, are matters of varying but considerable concern in American society, providing evidence of our inability to handle the changing relations between the sexes. While Veblen makes no suggestions for policy in *The Theory of the Leisure Class*, his exposure of the attitudes and the motivations behind such problems should help us to think more clearly about them. This would indeed be a valuable service.

It should come as no surprise that the canons of conspicuous waste, conspicuous consumption, and conspicuous leisure are manifested in other areas as well, particularly in dress, and more particularly in female dress. Some items are undeniably beautiful, Veblen notes, as, for example, the feather mantles of Hawaii, but others are not. Therefore,

> The result is quite as often a virtually complete suppression of all elements that would bear scrutiny as expressions of beauty, or of serviceability, and the substitution of evidences of misspent ingenuity and labor, backed by a conspicuous ineptitude; until many of the objects with which we surround ourselves in everyday life, and even many articles of everyday dress and ornament, are such as would not be tolerated except under the stress of prescriptive tradition. Illustrations of this substitution of ingenuity and expense are to be seen, for instance, in domestic architecture, in domestic art or fancy work, and in various articles of apparel, especially of feminine or priestly apparel (Veblen 1953[1899], p. 110).

Expenditure on dress has the advantage of being always in evidence. Veblen goes on:

> and affording an evidence of pecuniary standing at first glance, and probably at no other point is evidence of shabbiness so keenly felt as it is if we fall short of the standard set by social usage in the matter of dress. An inexpensive article of

apparel is held to be inferior; while an expensively hand-wrought article is much to be preferred even if the difference defies all scrutiny. Additionally, a garment should make plain to all observers that the wearer is not engaged in any kind of productive labor. The more elegant styles of feminine bonnets go even further towards making work impossible than does the man's high hat. The woman's shoe adds the so-called French heel to the evidence of enforced leisure afforded by its polish; because this high heel obviously makes any, even the simplest and most necessary manual work extremely difficult. The same is true even in a higher degree of the skirt and the rest of the drapery which characterizes woman's dress. The substantial reason for our tenacious attachment to the skirt is just this, it is expensive and it hampers the wearer at every turn and incapacitates her for all useful exertion. The like is true of the feminine custom of wearing the hair excessively long (Veblen 1953[1899], p. 120).

So here we see in evidence, Veblen notes, the broad principle of conspicuous waste, and secondarily the principle of conspicuous leisure. Not only this, dress must be up to date, which of course is another corollary of the principle of conspicuous waste. The dress of schoolchildren, of both sexes, is particularly prescriptive. This is reported to be a worldwide phenomenon, even in developing nations. How do you sell $75 designer jeans or $150 wireless phones in a country where per-capita gross domestic product is only a couple thousand dollars a year? One answer is that extended families are showering their money on the kids — a common form of conspicuous consumption in the developing world (Wysocki 1997).

The phenomenon of changing fashions every season is sufficiently familiar to everyone, 'but the theory of this flux and change has not been worked out' (Veblen 1953[1899], p. 122). Veblen asserts there is an antagonism between expensiveness and artistry, that the norm of conspicuous waste is incompatible with the requirement the dress must be beautiful or becoming. Wastefulness is offensive to native taste: it requires an obviously futile expenditure, and the resulting conspicuous expensiveness of dress is intrinsically ugly. Thus each innovation must show some ostensible purpose, which is always so transparent that it soon becomes unbearable and we must take refuge in a new style. Hence the essential ugliness and the ceaseless change of fashionable attire. None of the shifting fashions, of course, will bear the test of time; in a few years the best of our earlier fashions strikes us as grotesque, if not unsightly. The presumption, therefore, must be that the wealthier the community, the more grotesque and intolerable will be the styles that successively come into vogue (Veblen 1953[1899], pp. 124–125).

And what of the relevance of Veblen's analysis of dress to the century about to begin? Prescriptions regarding dress, fortunately, have relaxed considerably in recent decades in some respects, notably in the requirement that one's attire must attest to the wearer's wealth. For most everyday activities it has become more difficult to determine one's affluence by one's dress, except possibly for the very poor. Also, most dress nowadays is not seriously constricting; one is expected to dress in such a way as to be able to pursue athletic activities and the like. Additionally, some places of business even permit casual wear on Fridays! It would seem likely that such changes would remain and perhaps be further extended. Thus Veblen's descriptions of fashion as evidence of affluence may become less relevant in some respects in the twenty-first century.

Constant changes in fashion, however, are quite another story; there is nothing to suggest any abatement of this folly. Well, perhaps in at least one area there has been an improvement. Even though manufacturers keep changing skirt lengths, women now wear almost any length of skirt they fancy, without arousing opprobrium or even raising eyebrows. The fashion industry has, one might hope, lost the battle to prescribe skirt lengths.

But the frequency of change regarding almost everything else seems more bewildering than ever, what with instant communication and the increasingly widespread dissemination of television and computers and videophones and so on. And it is not only the frequency of style change. It is also that nothing is too outrageous — hair color and style, body-piercing, tattooing, and so on — so much so that people-watching has become a spectator sport. Often it appears that a major decision in the morning is what kind of statement one wishes to make that day by one's choice of attire. This is not always or necessarily bad. There is often a bit of whimsy here, and sometimes of artistry. Is it perhaps a reflection of post-modernism? Or have the garments been assembled by someone with impaired vision, or a warped sense of humor? Most fashion today is quite ugly.

Whatever else may be the case, however, the expenditure on dress is both huge and extremely wasteful, inasmuch as the bulk of it is for ostentation rather than protection from the elements. If the expenditure were known for clothing hidden in closets, especially women's, much of it never to be worn, the sum would no doubt boggle the mind. Not only that, as wealth increases, so too will the waste, and this may continue as long as humankind remains human. In all of this Veblen's analysis is uncannily astute and applicable, both now and, one would expect, for the indefinite future, almost certainly well into the coming century. Although this is a women's issue, perhaps it is just as much, if not more, a comment on capitalism as well.

4   WORK AND INCOME

Perhaps the most consequential women's issue raised in *The Theory of the Leisure Class* has to do with work. Veblen was making a point about upper class men comprising the leisure class, while the rest of society did the work. There have, we should note, been significant changes in work patterns since Veblen wrote. The upper classes today contribute substantially more to 'provisioning,' it seems safe to say, than in the earlier eras Veblen describes, when they engaged only in fighting, hunting, sports, government, and religious activities — although hunting at one time was a major contribution, which it is not now. Veblen himself points out that a curious inversion has appeared; the head of the household comes to perform useful work, while the wife carries on the burden of vicarious leisure (Veblen 1953[1899], p. 68). How much leisure time the modern wife has might be questioned (usually precious little), but it also seems that few men today, even upper class men, could be described as members of the leisure class. Many if not most might more accurately be classified as members of the 'business' community (which is still largely unproductive, according to Veblen), as contrasted with other workers, both men and women, who work in 'industry.' In other words, the dichotomy has made a shift from 'leisure class' to 'business,' but the basic analysis about the dichotomy remains.

Another major difference, of course, is that women now constitute an increasingly significant portion of the US paid labor force: 46 percent in 1995, and projections are that they will make up 48 percent by 2005 ('Trends' 1997). As a result they perform many of the same kinds of tasks that men perform, although many of the occupations filled by women continue to be similar to those performed in the home: child care, care of the elderly, nursing, cooking in schools and hospitals, and the like. Thus the line separating men's work from women's work has been blurred but not erased. One might expect a continued blurring in the twenty-first century.

The focus here, however, is on the unpaid work that women do in the home, which is still very substantial — the 'breeder-feeder' role that Elise Boulding talks about (Boulding 1977). A great deal of it is encompassed by the word 'provisioning.' It is informative to realize that women do a very large share of this as housewives and that it is not counted in Gross Domestic Product in the US, or scarcely anywhere else either. Nor is it so considered in most economic theory. Veblen, almost alone, seemed to be aware of the importance of the provisioning done by housewives.

Daphne Greenwood, in an explicit elaboration on Veblen's thesis, considers childbearing and nurturing to be part of the productive process (Greenwood 1984). The work of housewives and mothers in the home constitutes production. It is economic in nature. The experiences of US society in confronting the problems in this area as women go into the workplace suggest that this question will continue to be extremely relevant in the coming century. Stories about the two-earner household have helped to enlighten the community somewhat. It is beginning to become apparent that the work of housewives actually needs to be done in order for society to function. For example this includes stopping at the cleaners, getting the children off to school, waiting for the repairman, driving the children to piano lessons, preparing meals, shopping for groceries, doing the laundry, and so on. Probably the care of infants is the biggest service provided by housewives. It is pretty much a twenty-four-hour-a-day job, with no days off. Caring for the elderly, the sick, and the disabled is also a major task, done almost entirely by women. Thus while the household *is* a consuming unit, more importantly it is a unit of production; and it produces not only consumption goods but invests as well. It makes an investment in the human race by turning infants into adults, both physically and socially.

If the enormous contribution of housewives were recognized by society generally and reflected in public policy it would make a great deal of difference. Not only might women cease to be considered as second-class citizens, which would help their morale and probably their productivity, it might become apparent that society ought to find ways to get the income to them that is required to do their job well. It also might become a part of public policy to make adjustments to them rather than the other way around. Women have always been expected to do the adjusting to permit society to run smoothly, to go into the labor force if needed, and to get out if society says so. Also they have been expected to organize the household in such a way that the husband can do his job in the work force, in short to adjust their behavior in almost every way to cater to the 'real' world of work. It is not here argued that women should not help out as needed; it is simply that *everyone* should. And at the present time more of the helping out should be *for* mothers and children, not *by* them. Parents are overworked and children are hurting, lacking supervision and lacking sufficient income for them to grow into productive adults.

All of this remains to be faced in the twenty-first century. *The Theory of the Leisure Class* provides the outline of a theory that can help society to face it. Serious institutional adjustment will be required. Society might even discover that the 'real' world is to be found in the bearing and nurturing of children rather than in business.

Closely related to the question of women's work is the question of income distribution. The fact that housework is unpaid is a major factor in the disparity of income between men and women. Also of course is the fact that women in the labor force are paid less. This latter fact is being addressed — although gains have been small — and it could be expected to be largely remedied at some point. But the problem of the lack of remuneration for housework and childbearing and child care gives no indication of any possibility of resolution; the fact is that society simply does not see that anything much can, or should, be done about it. We do, indeed, apply bandaids, in the form of 'welfare' programs that go largely to women and children, pension plans that include the spouse, tax exemptions for dependents, school lunch programs, and so forth. The federal budget affords many additional opportunities for special programs that could help, but their philosophical underpinning is not well articulated, and they are always under attack. The fact remains that these nods in the direction of income for women in the 'breeder-feeder' role are so meager that a large income gap promises to remain. Elderly women are likely to live in poverty. And children are disproportionately represented among the poor.

It is of course true that some other countries provide better than we do for children and mothers, but nowhere is this sufficient to provide adequate income for them. Capitalism is particularly deficient in this area: mothers and children simply do not fit. Veblen makes no suggestions, but an effort to apply his theory of institutional adjustment based on an instrumental rather than a market-based criterion of judgement would constitute a huge step forward.

5   WOMEN AND 'PERSONHOOD'

There is yet another important aspect to woman's role in society and what Veblen says about it. The community wonders, he observes, why woman is not content. She is petted, and is permitted, even required, to consume conspicuously for her husband; she is exempted, or debarred, from 'vulgarly useful employment' in order to consume leisure vicariously for him. What then is the problem? Veblen's response:

> These offices are the conventional marks of the un-free, at the same time that they are incompatible with the human impulse to purposeful activity. But the woman is endowed with her share — which there is reason to believe is more than an even share — of the instinct of workmanship, to which futility of life or of expenditure is obnoxious. She must unfold her life activity in response to the

direct, unmediated stimuli of the economic environment with which she is in contact. The impulse is perhaps stronger upon the woman than upon the man to live her own life in her own way and to enter the industrial process of the community at something nearer than the second remove (Veblen 1953[1899], p. 232).

Obviously there is a reference here to the important matter of women joining the labor force. But there is also something more. Veblen observes earlier that traditionally a woman is assigned a 'sphere' ancillary to that of a man, and it is felt that any departure from this is unwomanly. A woman should be represented in the body politic or before the law through the mediation of the head of the household to which she belongs. It is unfeminine of her to aspire to a self-directed, self-centered life, and her direct participation in the affairs of the community is a menace to that social order which expresses our habits of thought. The woman's life must be an expression of the man's life at the second remove (Veblen 1953[1899], p. 230; see also Matthaei 1982).

In other words, a woman is not quite a person in her own right. A great deal of the women's movement has been about this, that is, about a woman gaining a measure of control over her own life, about achieving independence similar to that which a man enjoys, about more opportunity to develop her own potential as she sees it. This is fundamental. My own observation of women I know is that this is what many of them have very earnestly been seeking, however hesitantly, however indirectly, however cautiously. And when they achieve some measure of this 'personhood,' they blossom. Although substantial progress has been made — after all, women now vote and even run for office — the idea of independence is slow to change and will surely be a part of the women's movement in the twenty-first century.

6 THE THEORY OF VALUE

The criterion of judgement implicit in *The Theory of the Leisure Class* as well as in Veblen's subsequent work is not something mysterious and arcane but rather something most of us should find both comfortable and familiar from everyday life — although not from academic literature. The locus of value in Veblen's work is in the kind of behavior referred to as instrumental or technological or industrial. It simply says that value lies in serving or enhancing human life or human well-being on the whole, in furthering the life process taken impersonally (Veblen 1953[1899], pp. 78–79). Goods are produced and consumed 'as a means to the fuller unfolding of human life, and their utility consists, in their efficiency as means to this end' (Veblen 1953[1899], p. 111).

> The collective interests of any modern community center in industrial efficiency. The individual is serviceable for the ends of the community somewhat in proportion to his efficiency in the productive employment vulgarly so called. This collective interest is best served by honesty, diligence, peacefulness, good-will, an absence of self-seeking, and an habitual recognition and apprehension of causal sequence, without admixture of animistic belief and without a sense of dependence on any preternatural intervention in the course of events. The successful working of a modern industrial community is best secured where these traits concur, and it is attained in the degree in which the human material is characterized by their possession. These traits are present in a markedly less degree in the man of the predatory type than is useful for the purposes of the modern collective life (Veblen 1953[1899], p. 154).

Further on Veblen has this to say:

> The aristocratic and the bourgeois virtues — that is to say the destructive and pecuniary traits — should be found chiefly among the upper classes, and the industrial virtues — that is to say the peaceable traits — chiefly among the classes given to mechanical industry. The 'economic man', whose only interest is the self-regarding one and whose only human trait is prudence, is useless for the purposes of modern industry. The modern industry requires an impersonal, non-invidious interest in the work in hand. This interest in work differentiates the workman from the criminal on the one hand, and from the captain of industry on the other (Veblen 1953[1899], p. 162).

And still more:

> The progress which has been made and is being made in human institutions and in human character may be set down, broadly, to a natural selection of the fittest habits of thought and to a process of enforced adaptation of individuals to an environment which has progressively changed with the growth of the community and with the changing institutions under which men have lived (Veblen 1953[1899], p. 131).

These statements about value can be augmented by reference to the three so-called 'instincts' (whether this is the right word cannot be pursued here) suggested in *The Theory of the Leisure Class* and pursued in subsequent works: (1) the instinct of workmanship, or industrial efficiency; (2) the parental bent, or altruism; and (3) idle curiosity, or the development and exercise of critical intelligence (Veblen 1953[1899], pp. 29, 75, 79, 154,

247–252; Tilman 1996, p. 9). These proclivities can provide transcultural standards against which institutions can be evaluated (Tilman 1996, p. 101).

As institutions are being reevaluated, adjustments should be made in the direction of a 'partnership' society where the sexes share in decision-making, rather than continuing with the 'dominator' society we have always known (Eisler 1991).

Veblen was aware that the institution of a leisure class has an effect not only upon social structure but also upon individuals, and this effect tends to be conservative (Veblen 1953[1899], p. 145). The message of the book suggests, on the other hand, that the community should expect institutional adjustment, including innovation, and that social welfare will be better served if this change occurs in response not to ideological criteria but to the application of an instrumental criterion of judgement.

REFERENCES

Boulding, Elise (1977), *Women in the Twentieth Century World,* New York: John Wiley & Sons.

Bush, Paul D. (1996), 'Veblen's "Olympian Detachment" Reconsidered', Paper presented at the meetings of the *Association for Institutional Thought,* Reno, Nevada, April, Revised September.

Collins, Thomas (1989) 'Powerful Men Begin to Demand Trophy Wives', *Denver Post,* August 20.

Eisler, Riane (1991), *The Chalice and the Blade,* San Francisco: Harper and Row.

Greenwood, Daphne (1984), 'The Institutional Inadequacy of the Market in Determining Comparable Worth: Implications for Value Theory', *Journal of Economic Issues,* **18**, June, 457–64.

Matthaei, Julie (1982), *An Economic History of Women in America: Women's Work, the Sexual Division of Labor, and the Development of Capitalism,* New York: Schocken Books.

Pipher, Mary (1991), *Reviving Ophelia: Saving the Selves of Adolescent Girls,* New York: Putnam.

Tilman, Rick (1996), *The Intellectual Legacy of Thorstein Veblen: Unresolved Issues,* Westport, CT: Greenwood Press.

'Trends: Better Conditions for US Working Women', (1997), *Denver Post,* April 27.

Veblen, Thorstein (1953[1899]), *The Theory of the Leisure Class,* New York: Macmillan: Mentor Edition, The New American Library.

Wysocki, Bernard, Jr. (1997), 'In Developing Nations, Many Youths Splurge, Mainly on US Goods', *Wall Street Journal,* June 26.

9. *The Theory of the Leisure Class* in Relation to Feminist Thought

James Ronald Stanfield, Jacqueline B. Stanfield and Kimberly Wheatley-Mann

1 INTRODUCTION

This chapter argues that the analysis of *The Theory of the Leisure Class* is very relevant to an examination of gender inequality in contemporary American society. The argument is that the Marxian view supplied primarily by Engels lacks the all important cultural context of gender inequality that is suggested by *The Theory of the Leisure Class* and that Veblen's analysis remains very relevant to *fin de siecle* feminist analysis. In this regard, it is important to note that, although the once dominant influence of Engels is waning, feminist analysis still tends to neglect the importance of *The Theory of the Leisure Class* and the subsequent Original Institutionalist Economics (OIE). Nelson uses the looming choice between provisioning and economizing in her title but does not mention the OIE scholarship that develops the provisioning view. Her conclusion that a provisioning definition of economy is necessary for feminist thought is sound but a reader is left with little to take away in terms of the nature of such a definition. Indeed the conclusion is weakened by the inclusion of a brief discussion of the material bias in classical economics which leaves the impression that this problem continues to confound the development of the provisioning approach. In Jaggar's influential discussion of the varieties and history of feminist thought, there are numerous mentions of Marx, Engels, and Marxism but none of Veblen or OIE. This suggests that the continuing relevance of *The Theory of the Leisure Class* to feminist analysis is a case that still needs to be made.

Feminist thought has been framed by Engels's historical materialist analysis (Hartmann 1981; Hartsock 1983) and his conclusion that gender inequality is rooted in men's and women's relationship to the paid labor force. 'The emancipation of women will only be possible when women can take part in production on a large scale, social scale, and domestic work no longer claims anything but an insignificant amount of her time' (Engels 1972, p. 221). The presumption is that a more balanced distribution of gender participation in the paid labor force would spontaneously generate more equitable sharing of domestic or caring labor outside the paid labor force. As the capitalist organization of industrialism pulled women from working class family homes into the factories and shops, Engels expected the elimination of the material basis for male superiority. But, to the contrary, it appears that patriarchy was instead carried into the work place where women have faced lower pay, occupational segregation, and sexual harassment, and that no fundamental shift in domestic labor roles unfolded. Feminists have also come to doubt that socialism is a panacea for the inequality of men and women.

It should also be noted that occupational segregation in industrial societies does not seem to vary significantly with the extent of women's employment in the paid labor force (Jacobsen 1994, p. 158). This suggests that something other than labor market participation is at work. This could culturally be given attitudes with regard to appropriate work for men and women in the paid labor force. These attitudes likely interact with attitudes about gender roles in non-market labor and the employment attributes of particular occupations. Given that women bear the principal burden of nurturing labor, occupations which are less amenable to part time and serial employment may be difficult for women to fulfill.

In sum, it would appear that Engels either incompletely specified the material basis of gender inequality or that this material basis was not determinant, at least within the time frame. That is, it may be that the material base of gender inequality must include the social structuring of caring or domestic labor or that the capitalist material basis of gender coexists with the traditions of patriarchal culture which limit the working out of the laws of motion or tendencies of capitalism (Hartmann 1976; Brown 1987). In either case, this appears to be an instance in which Classical Marxism overestimated the defining power of the capital and wage labor relationship.

2 CULTURE AND HUMAN NATURE

Thorstein Veblen's theory of women's secondary status parallels Engels's theory in many respects. Veblen provided an evolutionary perspective which focuses on his notion of human instincts and their role in a comprehensive theory of social change. Veblen's cultural theory of the irksomeness of labor is potentially significant to feminist thought. In particular, so-called socialist feminist theory partially captures the Marxist theory and partially integrates other analyses. Many of their revisions correlate closely with institutional perspectives, though Veblen is largely neglected.

In *The Theory of the Leisure Class*, Veblen made use of the instinct of workmanship, which is foremost among a set of instinctive human tendencies or proclivities that play an important role in his view of the general scope of human behavior. Although Veblen was later to shift the terminology somewhat, all the major instinctive proclivities except perhaps idle curiosity appear to have been present in *The Theory of the Leisure Class* (Veblen 1953[1899], pp. 39–40 and ch. 13; Gruchy 1967, pp. 61–70). Veblen's instincts were not mechanically physiological and indeed he seems to have had in mind inveterate cultural tendencies rather than instincts in the modern sense. Moreover, it seems clear that he considered these instincts to be modified or shaped by culture, that is, by the socially constructed patterns of interaction within which individuals transact in the conduct of everyday life. Institutions, the 'prevalent habits of thought,' are the 'persistent element in the culture of an organized group'; institutions channel the inveterate tendencies of the individual (Veblen 1953[1899], p. 132; Gruchy 1967, p. 68). Instinctive predispositions are a formative influence on institutions, yet in turn, institutions influence the operation of the instincts in a given culture (Veblen 1953[1899], pp. 131–134). Nonetheless, there does seem to have been a genetic element to Veblen's views and his notion of instincts remains controversial among the scholars who look to his work as a paradigmatic point of departure. It can also be said that in *The Theory of the Leisure Class* and later works, Veblen appears to have seen the need to integrate the psychoanalysis and socio-analysis of human life. It is worthy of note that this intellectual project remains undone even now (Heilbroner 1981). Today's promising research into the structure and function of the human brain and its relation to knowing may eventually shed some light on Veblen's speculations and enable an advance in this integrative project. This advance may eventually prove *The Theory of the Leisure Class* to have been very prophetic.

Of the many instincts Veblen noted, four were most prominent in his theory of social behavior and are of particular interest for a theoretical examination of the status of women. These are the parental bent, the self-regarding bent, the instinct of workmanship and the instinct of idle curiosity. The parental bent influences individuals to have concern for the welfare of their families, tribes, communities, nations and the human race. The polar opposite of the other-regarding parental bent is the self-regarding or acquisitive instinct which implies that the individual considers self before others. Every individual is faced with an unending dynamic conflict between the other-regarding, parental bent and the self-regarding, acquisitive bent. Of course, the specification of the substance of one's own interest versus the collective interest is cultural, although, as Marx insisted, there are powerful regularities established by the evolving process of getting a living. The instinct of workmanship is the human proclivity toward efficiency and serviceability and the hatred of futility and wasted effort (Veblen 1953[1899], p. 29). The instinct of workmanship must also be given cultural expression and its relation to the parental and self-regarding bents is also an important cultural consideration (Veblen 1953[1899], p. 39–40). The fourth important instinct, the instinct of idle curiosity, refers to an epistemological urge to comprehend or understand the phenomenological world. Idle curiosity seems to play about the same role in relation to the instinct of workmanship as basic research plays in relation to applied efforts in the vernacular of those who study the contemporary scientific and technological process.

The pervasive bents play an important role in Veblen's social evolutionary theory and he asserted that the need to examine how the instinctive proclivities cross, blend, overlap, neutralize or reinforce one another is of the utmost importance in the exploration of human nature. In conjunction with instincts Veblen argues that humans 'strive, work, think, and act' with regard to the effect their behavior will have upon the thinking of others. The human creature is a social creature and necessarily mindful of the approval or disapproval of others (Veblen 1953[1899], p. 38). There is a powerful imprinting process by which humans learn through observation of others. Veblen labeled this the 'emulative process' and emphasized the cultural context of human behavior throughout *The Theory of the Leisure Class* and his later work (Veblen 1953[1899], p. 41).

Veblen uses the notion of instincts as the basis for his explanation of the transition from early primitive society of 'peaceable savagery' to the rise of predatory barbarianism. A combination of idle curiosity, the instinct of workmanship, and the parental bent led to the technological development of primitive societies. Accomplishments that are attributed to this development include the domestication of both plants and animals as well as the development of tools and weapons for efficient hunting.

With the advent of predation, women became secondary citizens. Initially slight differences in physical structure and 'perhaps even more decisive' differences in temperament become more marked as cultural selection proceeds (Veblen 1953[1899], p. 28). Veblen cited women's role in agriculture and men's role in animal husbandry and hunting as responsible for both a widening gap in the sexual division of labor and a widening gap in character traits between women and men. Men were responsible for hunting and herding because they were physically larger, able to react quickly with a violent strain, more apt to be self assertive and exercise aggression. Also, men were more mobile since it was women who gave birth to and nursed children. The predacious work of hunting required 'more of the manly qualities of massiveness, agility, and ferocity' and herding required traveling long distances from the household as rangeland expanded (Veblen 1953[1899], p. 28 and 1964, pp. 156–157). This left women to do the more routinely productive everyday work of 'assiduous and uneventful shaping of materials' (Veblen 1953[1899], p. 28). As hunting and war-like competition among tribes increasingly became habit, men became more involved in predacious behavior and the gap in the division of labor widened.

The increased dependence on hunting for subsistence brought about a change in the organization of society's productivity and eventually led to predation for several reasons. First, hunting became the primary employment for some individuals of the tribe. Second, higher productivity led to larger and denser populations. Close proximity of tribes meant the rise of competition for subsistence and likelihood of increased hostility and aggression. Third, tribes were able to produce a surplus beyond the culturally specified immediate needs of its members. This allowed some members of the tribe to be engaged in non-subsistence activities and sustained the social stratification of individuals and groups into ranks of privilege, responsibility, and prestige (Veblen 1953[1899], pp. 25 and 32; see also Stanfield 1992).

The domestication of animals had a similar effect to that of hunting. This form of production had the peculiar trait of reproducing itself, and since cattle were relatively easy to care for, they were tempting to acquire by predation. As rangelands became scarcer and populations became denser, there was increased incentive for aggression. These circumstances required tribes to be prepared for defense. Veblen argued that 'pastoral pursuits will somewhat readily take to a predatory life' (Veblen 1945, pp. 50–51).

Both hunting and herding initiate the habit of war. According to Veblen 'with the advent of warfare comes the war chief, into whose hands authority and pecuniary employment gather somewhat in proportion as warlike exploits and ideals become habitual in the community' (Veblen 1964, p. 157). These changed conditions for primitive tribes initiated the passage from a peaceable culture to a predatory culture. The gap between men's and women's work as well as the habits associated with their roles widened. The predatory culture respected the 'honorific employment' of severe and war-like behavior. Emulation was displayed through prowess. Those who were engaged in the nonaggressive, productive, socially necessary labor, that is, women, were looked down upon. Practices such as avoiding involvement with women before war-like activity were common. Men would not eat the same food as a women nor engage in sexual intercourse before raids. Fighting became the major aspect of men's lives while non-fighting activities were regarded as secondary employment and left to the women or subordinate men.

> Therefore the able-bodied barbarian of the predatory culture, who is at all mindful of his good name, severely leaves all uneventful drudgery to the women and minors of the group. He puts in his time in the manly arts of war and devotes his talents to devising ways and means of disturbing the peace. That way lies honor (Veblen 1945, p. 48).

Veblen saw this transition of society from the 'poverty stricken peace' to the 'predatory culture' as a result of the increased incentive for aggression and the custom of men engaging in aggressive activity to demonstrate their success. 'Exploit becomes the conventional ground of invidious comparison between individuals and repute comes to rest on prowess' (Veblen 1945, p. 93). He referred to the degradation of domestic or socially necessary work as the 'irksomeness of labor,' maintaining that there is nothing inherently unpleasant about 'women's work.' Instead, labor is degraded through predatory habits of thought (Veblen 1953[1899], p. 25); 'labor acquires a character of irksomeness by virtue of the irksomeness imputed to it' (Veblen 1953[1899], p. 30). Veblen states, 'Physical irksomeness and distastefulness can be borne, if only the spiritual incentive is present' (Veblen 1953[1899], p. 95). It is certainly not a lack of social and reproductive importance which made women's work unpleasant.

> Instead of a valuation of serviceability, there is a gauging of capability on the ground of visible success. And what comes to be compared in an invidious comparison of this kind between agents is the force which the agent is able to put forth, rather than the serviceability of the agent's conduct (Veblen 1945, p. 90).

This advent of predatory culture meant, according to Veblen, the beginning of ownership, and women were the first 'objects' owned. The institutions of coercive marriage and ownership 'are not distinguishable in the initial phases of their development' (Veblen 1953[1899], p. 34). Ownership initially meant 'the habit of coercion and service' in early times (Veblen 1945, p. 48). One tribe would raid another tribe, seizing objects for their own use. The objects being seized more and more often became women who became the property of the seizing male. Women were easily captured and they served as 'trophies' for the men. Eventually practice became custom and the captor held exclusive right to 'use and abuse' over the captured women (Veblen 1945, p. 47).

Veblen called this relationship between captor and captive ownership — marriage. This form of relationship between man and woman became the predominant habit of thought. Veblen saw ownership — marriage — as the first form of private property, the beginning of the patriarchal family and a means of status distinction for men. 'The ownership and control of women is a gratifying evidence of prowess and high standing' (Veblen 1945, p. 59).

Veblen's image of social change in *The Theory of the Leisure Class* includes speculation that predatory society someday might be eclipsed by an institutional configuration that is more pragmatic and less invidious than the commodity production stage of barbarism, that is, capitalism. He clearly introduces in *The Theory of the Leisure Class* (Veblen 1953[1899], pp. 157–164) what he later was to refer to as the 'cultural incidence of the machine process' (Veblen 1904). The industrial employment tends to inculcate a matter of fact, non-animistic habit of thought that might someday come to the fore in place of the invidious reckoning of predatory culture. If so, labor would then be evaluated by its degree of contribution to furtherance of the life process in a non-invidious manner. This would eliminate the basis for the spiritual irksomeness of labor. Veblen, however, recognized that institutional change is an extremely slow process and that archaic habits of thought would not easily yield to the new context of technologically generated abundance. But since he asserted that technology is the 'prime mover' of society he did place some reliance on technology to loosen the psychological bonds of the past (Diggins 1978, p. 167). Such change would of course have enormous repercussions on the relations between the genders. Technology without the repressive ceremonial aspects or archaic habits of thought could free men and women from 'animism, from a subservience to supernatural forces, invisible economic laws, sanctified institutions and all irrational forces that perpetuate the mystification of feminine subordination' (Diggins 1978, p. 167).

In *The Theory of the Leisure Class*, Veblen concurred with Engels's recognition that the technological changes that enabled production of an economic surplus were correlated with the beginnings of stratification and the degradation of women's status. However, Veblen implies that individuals, especially men, possess a predatory instinct which may be left dormant until sufficient conditions such as the ability to accumulate wealth draw predatory behavior out. If it is possible for tribes to seize wealth without apparent repercussions it will become custom (Veblen 1964, p. 156). Custom provides values to a culture and in this case predatory behavior and invidious comparison became the expressions of emulation. Women, who were not involved in predatory behaviors became victims of exploitation. Their work was devalued due to the nonaggressive nature of it, not its lack of importance to continuation and reproduction of the life process. The 'irksomeness of labor' was established in which men were designated honorific employment and women the humiliating employment. We can generalize Veblen's notion of the irksomeness of labor. It states that culture specifies that which is regarded as demeaning or subordinate activity and that which is regarded as honorable and prestigious activity. Veblen saw nothing in the work itself that would account for this invidious distinction; it is solely the result of the habitual emotional conditioning that relates industrially serviceable activities to the predatory habits of mind.

3 SOCIALIST FEMINIST THEORY AND VEBLEN

The origin and maintenance of the sexual division of labor is of utmost importance to both feminist theorists (Hartmann 1981; Jaggar 1983) and Veblen. It is the sexual division of labor which assigns women the drudgery chores and men the more powerful and prestigious positions. Socialist feminists do not have a well-defined explanation as to why certain tasks are more prestigious than others, and Veblen's theory of the irksomeness of labor fills this gap in socialist feminist theory.

To see the importance of the cultural approach set out in *The Theory of the Leisure Class*, consider the seminal article in which Hartmann (1981, p. 3) addresses the sexual division of labor issue, noting that Marxist categories are sex blind and tend to focus on the relationship between women and economies rather than women and men. Consequently, the system of patriarchy, which she holds responsible for determining who fills the various categories, is not thoroughly examined. Hartmann argues that the material base of patriarchy is men's control over women's labor power. For example, in Western societies men have control over the jobs that pay a 'living wage.' Women are economically dependent on men. By men excluding women from necessary economic productive resources and restricting women's sexuality they are able to receive sexual services and avoid unpleasant tasks. They are also able to maintain their power by avoiding participation in household tasks and child rearing (Hartmann 1981, p. 18).

But Hartmann's argument makes sense only with the assumption that household tasks and child rearing are demeaning and repressive work. Yet she offers no explanation as to why or whether this was always so. She assumes a bias common to much of Marxist feminist literature, but without clarification as to how patriarchy evolved, it is difficult to determine the underlying forces which maintain a system involving the oppression of women. She argues that the sexual division of labor is the base of male power. But why did men exclude women from the means of production as she suggests? Surely the division in itself does not create oppression of a particular group.

The basis for this neglect among Marxist feminists perhaps stems from Engels's view of domestic work as 'dull and undignified' (Diggins 1978). Diggins argues that Veblen's distinction in *The Theory of the Leisure Class* 'between those who create value through socially useful labor and those who thrive and command status on the basis of non-productive exploit plays no role in Engels' analysis of the oppression of women' (Diggins 1978, p. 149).

Veblen's *The Theory of the Leisure Class* does explain that domestic work is less worthy because of its non-exploitative nature. It is the culturally specified 'irksomeness of labor' that defines domestic work as dull and undignified.

Hartmann's article discusses the idea of male and female characteristics as portrayed by society. Her example and conclusions are analogous to Veblen's theory of the sexual division of labor. Hartmann refers to a study of attitudes toward gender work roles and finds that presuppositions about gender roles and personalities is more important than the concrete nature of the work activity.

> So, for example, the authors of *Crestwood Heights* found that while the men, who were professionals, spent their days manipulating subordinates (often using techniques that appeal to fundamentally irrational motives to elicit the preferred behavior), men and women characterized men as rational and pragmatic. And while the women devoted great energies to studying scientific methods of child rearing and child development, men and women in *Crestwood Heights* characterized women as 'irrational and emotional' (Hartmann 1981, p. 28)

Hartmann concluded by noting that this cultural rendering of women's and men's work and personalities is permeated with capitalist culture even as it perpetuates patriarchal culture because the honor accorded to rationality in capitalism leads to its use in identifying men rather than women.

It is also important to note the presence of the ideology of patriarchy in the outlook of women. The oppressed are very often oppressed by their own habitual outlooks and acceptances of the enabling ideologies of inequality.

Hartmann's discussion provides a clear demonstration of the usefulness of Veblen's *The Theory of the Leisure Class* for analysing why certain tasks are seen by society as prestigious and others demeaning. Men in her example were involved in honorific and worthy employment in which force or fraud are used to exploit those in submissive and humiliating employment (Veblen 1953[1899], p. 29). This explanation is essential for understanding why domestic work performed in the private household is demeaning and why the participation of women in the paid labor force will not be a complete solution. Women are subjugated in the culture of patriarchy and their roles and personalities will be reinterpreted by patriarchy as they change with social evolution.

The analysis of *The Theory of the Leisure Class* seamlessly integrates the analysis of socially structured inequality, not only of sexism and classism but also of nationalism and ethnicism. These four modes of socially constructed inequality must be addressed simultaneously in a manner that is cognizant of their differences and their interactions. This can only be accomplished by the sort of concrete cultural criticism that is evident in *The Theory of the Leisure Class*. The enabling ideologies of these modes of inequality are very important, not least in the minds of the oppressed and exploited themselves.

In a manner that is very similar to the analysis of *The Theory of the Leisure Class*, socialist feminists encourage the broad interdisciplinary study of other social sciences and in particular psychology, sociology and anthropology in order to understand a social economy. Specifically they utilize some version of psychoanalysis for researching questions as to how the individual psyche is structured by gender. From this perspective they conclude, in a similar vein to *The Theory of the Leisure Class*, that gender structuring is mostly not innate but is socially imposed by historically prevailing systems of organizing production. This gender structuring reinforces the dominant ideologies.

These predacious habits of thought are so ingrained that still today predacious or exploitative behavior is seen as becoming to men but not to women. Such behavior in the case of women is often characterized as overly aggressive and insensitive to others. Hence, despite much commentary in current business literature about the necessity of women learning traditional 'male characteristics' in order to participate successfully in business, women who do so are often characterized as ruthless 'ball-busting bitches.'

Socialist feminists view human nature as partially constructed through biology and partially through historically specific ways in which society is organized. Consequently, human nature is subject to change in an evolutionary process. Jaggar states that 'our form of social organization is determined not by our biology alone, but rather by a complex interplay between our biological constitution, the physical environment we inhabit and our current type of technological and social development' (Jaggar 1983, p. 109). Veblen's theory of instincts is certainly consistent with this definition of human nature. He argued that instincts are fixed tendencies which are shaped by culture and take on an 'institutional character.' Human nature is a result of the evolutionary interaction of instincts and institutions. Both Veblen and socialist feminists reject biological determinism.

There are apparent gaps in Engels's and Marx's theories that are filled by the cultural nature of the analysis in *The Theory of the Leisure Class*, which provides a historical evolutionary approach for the examination of social change. The analysis of *The Theory of the Leisure Class* is particularly important in clarifying why women will not so easily regain status upon entering the paid labor force. The cultural roots of gender inequality run deep and will only gradually change.

The cultural analysis of *The Theory of the Leisure Class* adds a dimension to this change for which Engels's model has no place at all. As Greenwood points out, the liberation of women was of utmost importance to Veblen, not only for the sake of women, but for the change in cultural values he expected to occur as a result (Greenwood 1984, pp. 676–677). As society becomes less male-dominated, Veblen expected a decline of emphasis on male virtues such as competitiveness and an increased emphasis on female virtues such as nurturance and cooperation. In *The Theory of the Leisure Class*, he often refers to women being more imbued with the instinct of workmanship in its genetic sense of industrial serviceability, to their 'larger share of this instinct that approves peace and disapproves futility,' to their relatively greater 'sense of human solidarity and sympathy,' and to their 'more pronounced, non-invidious temperament' (see Veblen 1953[1899], pp. 30, 217, 220, 229). In the vernacular he adopted later, Veblen thought that women were more imbued with the parental bent which included a concern for the genetic or solidaristic interest of the human species. In the discussion in *The Theory of the Leisure Class* of the 'new woman movement' as well as in the analysis of the cultural incidence of the machine process, there is then a perhaps uncharacteristic note of optimism (Veblen 1953[1899], pp. 157–164 and 231–234).

A feminist theory should provide a sound historical interpretation of the origins of oppression and therefore offer sound guidance for proposals for the liberation not only of women but of human beings universally. But this universal liberation cannot be pursued by a theory that sweeps patriarchal (or ethnicist and nationalist) culture under the rug of classist culture.

Concrete cultural analysis of the type Veblen championed in *The Theory of the Leisure Class* is essential. Socially structured inequality is based on unequal power and access to life chances and much of this inequality resides in the acculturated imaginations of the oppressed as well as their oppressors.

4   SOCIAL CONSTRUCTION OF GENDER

Gender is socially constructed, and the idea of separate male and female cultures and knowledge is well documented (Belenky et al., 1986; Hekman 1990; Schaef 1981; Gilligan 1982; Harding 1986; Tannen, 1990). Dual culture and gendered knowledge imply that females and males, even though they live side by side in the same society, experience different cultural spheres and have different social realities beginning in childhood.   De Beauvoir (1952, p. 161) argued that the world is the work of men who describe it from their point of view.   The dominant cultural sphere in this society is male, and during childhood male socialization is oriented to the world outside of the home while female socialization is oriented to the world inside of the home (De Beauvoir 1952, p. 161).

In *The Theory of the Leisure Class*, Veblen recognized the role of socialization of men in sports, games, and warfare. This conditioning is important preparation for men who must undertake the exploits of business and politics. It is also important to the development of male camaraderie and networking to the exclusion of women, and this cultural duality is a significant source of gender differences and inequity that has been widely noted in contemporary gender studies (Bem 1974; Hartsock 1983; Lipman-Blumen 1984).

Recent evidence suggests that although gender segregation is pervasive in industrial and pre-industrial societies, there are important differences across cultures.   The occupational segregation in industrial societies is similar in that particular occupations tend to be segregated in respect to gender in different industrial societies. However, gender is relevant in very few instances.   Nonindustrial societies display a consistent pattern of occupational segregation but not of similar occupations being segregated in the same direction with regard to gender (Jacobsen 1994, p. 158). Hence it is not the activity in question so much as the cultural ordering of the activity that is significant.

This seems to be consistent with Veblen's emphasis on culture but inconsistent with his instinctual tendencies between the genders. But it is important to recall that he employed the term instinct to refer to culturally prevalent propensities not physiological tendencies. But still if women and men have these pervasive tendencies across cultures, would we not expect a persistent pattern of occupational segregation for given occupations? Not necessarily. As noted above, the analysis of *The Theory of the Leisure Class* refers to the aggressive, exploitative tendencies of men versus the more cooperative, nurturing tendencies of women. Moreover, also as emphasized above, the analysis of *The Theory of the Leisure Class* insists that not the character of work activity but its cultural positioning accounts for its 'irksomeness.' Hence, if in a given culture a particular activity is assigned a lower status, we should expect it to be performed by individuals who are accorded a lower status. If patriarchy generally assigns a lower social status to women, then we should expect a given patriarchal culture to assign its lower status activities to women. Given the many variables that go into assignment of social status, we should be surprised if particular activities are consistently segregated unless we have some cross cultural influence — such as similarities in industrial societies in the employment attributes of particular occupations or of a persistent tendency for women to fill the nurturing activities which are instituted within the household. Some paid labor force occupations may be more nurture oriented and a persistent gender segregation pattern might be found therein. However, the experience with physicians in Western industrial nations versus the Former Soviet Union leads us to be very reluctant to press the case. Physicians in the West tend to be high status, high paid, male occupations but in the Former Soviet Union they were relatively low paid and predominantly filled by women.

At any rate, the interaction between low status individuals and low status assignments for productive activities is a two way street. People may be accorded low status because they perform low status tasks and tasks may be assigned low status because they are performed by low status people. Precise social formulation in these regards will be socially defined and culturally relative, notwithstanding some cross-cultural tendencies.

This conclusion has been reached in the gender studies field. England observes that the feminist discussion of gender inequality has emphasized two themes, one emphasizing 'the exclusion of women from traditionally male activities and institutions' and the other emphasizing 'the devaluation of and low material rewards accorded to activities and traits that traditionally have been deemed appropriate for women.' The crucial role of cultural tradition could hardly be more emphatic (England 1993, pp. 38–39).

England also notes the strategic importance of this finding by noting that efforts to break down activity segregation by gender are thoroughly consistent with efforts to enhance the cultural evaluation of women's activities. A very concrete example of this strategy can be found in the Swedish effort to effect a solidaristic wage policy alongside policies intended to reduce occupational segregation and gender discrimination. Solidaristic wage policy seeks to institute higher percentage pay increases for workers whose wages fall below the median income in order to compress wage differentiation and, hopefully, increase solidarity among workers. From a cultural perspective such policies should work together. Efforts to reduce segregation and allow the success of women in traditionally male activities should serve to provide role models of women who succeed in pattern-breaking activities. This would not only encourage other women who seek to break through such pattern models but raise the social estimation of the capabilities and value of women in non-traditional roles. Solidaristic wage policies reduce the significance of occupational segregation which should undermine the cultural pattern model which segregated activities by gender. Efforts aimed at enhancing the social estimation of the importance of activities traditionally performed by women should also negatively sanction the attitude that it is beneath men to perform such roles. Inclusion of domestic labor in social policy formulation and income and product accounting should empower women and undermine the cultural pattern model of gender roles. Such policies are also needed to foster social change to re-institute nurturing activities outside the structure of the patriarchal family (Stanfield and Stanfield 1997).

5   CONCLUSION

Strategies to combat socially structured gender inequality must be far more complex than the simple entry of women into the paid labor force. The analysis of *The Theory of the Leisure Class* suggests that the institutional analysis of the socially structured transactions by which integration of the division of labor is achieved must be comprehensive and not obsessed with market transactions. The analysis of *The Theory of the Leisure Class* suggests that the institutional analysis of the socially structured transactions by which integration of the division of labor is achieved must be comprehensive and not obsessed with market transactions. Hence a feminist emphasis solely upon the promotion of women's participation in the paid labor force is problematic in another way. As noted above, this strategy may entail disastrous neglect of the nurturing activities traditionally performed by women in the domestic economy (Stanfield and Stanfield 1997). Not that entry into the paid labor force should be neglected. Strategies to reduce market discrimination, reduce occupational wage differentials, secure comparable worth, and accommodate flextime employment are important. Affirmative action or positive discrimination policies are also important because the presence of role models is necessary to break down occupational segregation. But improved accounting for the significance of domestic labor and the extension of entitlements to non-paid nurturing labor are also important. In general redistributive policies should be reformed to empower women and children.

In light of these wider concerns, it is evident that the struggle against gender, and other, inequalities must also be cultural. The enabling myths of socially structured inequality must be debunked. As the cultural analysis of *The Theory of the Leisure Class* emphasizes, the habitual propensity to invidiously rank individuals by pecuniary success must itself come under attack and the fetishism of commodities demystified. Only then can the focus shift to the quality and reform of human relationships that Marx and Engels, as well as Veblen, seek. But *The Theory of the Leisure Class* provides a significant contribution to this task of re-viewing the past and the present so to imagine an alternative future.

REFERENCES

Belenky, M.F., B.M. Clinchy, N.R. Goldberger, and J.M. Tarule (1986), *Women's Ways of Knowing,* New York: Basic Books.

Bem, S. (1974), 'The Measurement of Psychological Androgyny,' *Journal of Consulting and Clinical Psychology,* **42**,155–162.

Brown, D. M. (1987), 'A Hungarian Connection: Karl Polanyi's Influence on the Budapest School,' *Journal of Economic Issues,* **21**, March, 339–347.

De Beauvoir, S. (1952), *The Second Sex,* New York: Basic Books.

Diggins, J. (1978), *The Bard of Savagery,* New York: Seabury.

England, P. (1993), 'The Separative Self: Androcentric Bias in Neoclassical Assumptions', in M.A. Ferber and J.A. Nelson, eds, *Beyond Economic Man: Feminist Theory and Economics,* Chicago: University of Chicago Press, 37–53.

Engels, F. (1972), *The Origin of the Family, Private Property, and the State,* New York: International Publishers.

Gilligan, C. (1982), *In a Different Voice,* Cambridge, MA: Harvard University Press.

Greenwood, D. (1984), 'The Economic Significance of "Women's Place" in Society: A New-Institutionalist View,' *Journal of Economic Issues,* **18**, 663–680.

Gruchy, A. (1967), *Modern Economic Thought,* New York: Augustus M. Kelley Publishers.

Harding, S. (1986), *The Science Question in Feminism,* Ithaca, NY: Cornell University Press.

Hartmann, H. (1976), 'Capitalism, Patriarchy, and Job Segregation by Sex', *Signs: Journal of Women in Culture and Society,* 1, Spring, 137–169.

Hartmann, H. (1981), 'The Unhappy Marriage of Marxism and Feminism: Towards a More Progressive Union,' in L. Sargent, ed., *Women and Revolution: A Discussion of The Unhappy Marriage of Marxism and Feminism,* Boston: South End Press, 1–41.

Hartsock, N. (1983), *Money, Sex, and Power: Toward a Feminist Historical Materialism,* New York: Longman.

Heilbroner, R.L. (1981), *Marxism: For and Against,* New York: Norton.

Hekman, S.J. (1990), *Gender and Knowledge: Elements of a Postmodern Feminism,* Boston: Northeastern University Press.

Jacobsen, J.P. (1994), 'Sex Segregation at Work: Trends and Predictions,' *Social Science Journal,* 31, 2, 153–169.

Jaggar, A. (1983), *Feminist Politics and Human Nature,* Totowa, NJ: Rowman & Allanheld.

Lipman-Blumen, J. (1984), *Gender Roles and Power,* Englewood Cliffs, NJ: Prentice Hall.

Miller, E. (1972), 'Veblen and Women's Lib: A Parallel', *Journal of Economic Issues,* 6, 75–86

Schaef, A.W. (1981), *Women's Reality,* Minneapolis, MN: Winston Press.

Stanfield, J.R. (1992), 'The Fund for Social Change', in J. Davis, ed., *The Economic Surplus in Advanced Economies,* Brookfield, VT: Edward Elgar, 130–148.

Stanfield, J.R. and J.B. Stanfield (1997), 'Where Has Love Gone? Reciprocity, Redistribution, and the Nurturance Gap', *Journal of Socio-Economics,* 26, April, 111–127.

Tannen, D. (1990), *You Just Don't Understand: Women and Men in Conversation,* New York: Ballantine.

Veblen, T.B. (1904), *The Theory of Business Enterprise,* New York: New American Library.

Veblen, T.B. (1945), *Essays in Our Changing Order,* New York: Viking.

Veblen, T.B. (1953[1899]), *Theory of the Leisure Class,* New York: Mentor.

Veblen, T.B. (1964), *The Instinct of Workmanship,* New York: Augustus M. Kelley Publishers.

10. Women and the Higher Learning in America: Veblenian Insights on the Leisure of the Theory Class

Ann Mari May

1 INTRODUCTION

Virginia Woolf, writing about women and fiction, once observed that when a woman writes,

> She will find that she is perpetually wishing to alter the established values — to make serious what appears insignificant to a man, and trivial what is to him important. And for that, of course, she will be criticized; for the critic of the opposite sex will be genuinely puzzled and surprised by an attempt to alter the current scale of values, and will see in it not merely a difference of view but a view that is weak, or trivial, or sentimental because it differs from his own (Woolf 1972[1929], p. 146).

Of course the observation applies equally well to the writing of economics as it does to the writing of fiction — a narrow distinction to be sure.

It is, of course, this reality that has made academe so profoundly exasperating for many women academics. Because in reality, academe, which at its best is presumed to be a fertile breeding ground for the idle curiosity of the devout scholar, and at its worst is alleged to be fully infiltrated with radicals and other suspicious 'change agents,' is in fact, neither. The higher learning in America mimics neither an unfettered forum for disinterested inquiry nor a conspiracy of the left to overthrow the institutions of Western culture. Instead, the higher learning often reflects the status seeking priorities of the theory class as much as the pecuniary values of the larger culture — both of which have had significant implications for women in higher education. As a result, women have been effectively excluded from participating in the higher learning in the nineteenth and twentieth centuries.

Now, most of our colleagues in the discipline of economics and on the faculties in general, will object to the use of the term 'exclude' and would prefer to 'argue' instead, that women have simply not *chosen* to enter economics or academe for that matter, and that if they had, women would have been welcomed, judged, and allowed to progress just like any of their male colleagues. According to this view, the profession is like one big free market wherein the talented in this meritocracy prosper, and the weak, well, they wither away.

But who are the weak and just what is considered 'weak' or, in Woolf's words, 'trivial and sentimental?' What are the institutions that have framed, not only the discipline of economics, but higher education for women? In what specific way does the internal structure of academe interact with societal imperatives to shape women's experiences in the enterprise as well as the outcome of academic discourse? And finally, how does the 'text' — not only the 'text' which describes the outcome of theorizing, but also the 'text' which describes our internal structures and rationalizes these academic institutions — reveal a rich subtext concerning gender, authority, and higher education in American culture?

Of course it was Thorstein Veblen who, in his *The Theory of the Leisure Class* and *The Higher Learning in America*, provided important and critical insights on human behavior in general and the institution of higher learning in particular. Moreover, in contrast to most of his contemporaries, Veblen offered important observations on 'the woman problem' in its many forms. His many insights, made almost 100 years ago, offer a useful framework for examining the experiences of women in the higher learning in America.

Stories about the development of economic thought — histories about the development of economic thought — have tended to emphasize individual efforts to rationalize and formulate 'value free' judgements amid a few references to historical circumstances (Blaug 1978). This approach, not confined to the history of the development of economic thought, gains its authority from the progressive view of science — a view which holds that each addition to the body of accepted knowledge represents an improvement over past notions. Therefore, what should be emphasized in the course of time is not the temporal (historical) but the outcome (theoretical) (Feyerabend 1988, p. 109).

In reality, this approach draws its authority through patriarchy of a particularly academic sort in which men's views gain authority through the sheer 'forcefulness' of their personalities while women's views must surely be constructed on something more firm. However, a more complete story of the development of our accepted knowledge recognizes that 'knowledge' is influenced by the external environment in which academe locates itself, as well as the internal organization and rituals practiced in institutions of higher learning.

Moreover, the internal institutions in academe often mediate conflicting social values to provide a framework where, for example, exclusion can be rationalized and justified when that exclusion might possibly be at odds with our fundamental precepts, for example, equal opportunity. These factors together shape the boundaries of a discipline, help to determine the outcome of theorizing, and ultimately help to determine who will and who will not participate in the activity of knowledge creation.

In the US, the development of higher education was most certainly influenced in some subtle and not so subtle ways, by the business enterprise and the development of capitalism. The needs of the state, not of course unrelated to the needs of the business enterprise, have also shaped the academic enterprise from the Morrill Act to the GI Bill to grant activity and defense spending. And of course, existing notions of women's sphere have influenced the ways in which these factors impacted women. Veblen's insights into the business enterprise and its influence on the higher learning reveal much about not only the evolution of higher education in American in the late nineteenth and twentieth centuries, but about higher education today.

2   VEBLEN AND THE HIGHER LEARNING

Veblen's most extended discussion of academe comes in his book *The Higher Learning in America*. In this work he examines the evolution of the higher learning and the institutions impacting the character of the higher learning in the US in the last half of the nineteenth century. He directs his attention to the 'captains of erudition' commonly known as administrators, their leader — so affectionately known in a generic sense as 'president strong man,' and — 'the adepts' — the many faculty who provide the 'standardized erudition' for the 'corporation of learning.' Veblen examines the higher learning as a cultural artifact emanating from two impulsive traits of human nature — the instinct of workmanship and idle curiosity; and that is, in a variety of ways and at various developmental stages, influenced by ceremonial behavior (Veblen 1993[1918]).

According to Veblen, every civilization cultivates esoteric knowledge that is considered to have intrinsic value apart from material considerations. Such knowledge comes to be considered as 'eternal truth,' although as Veblen said, 'it is evident to any outsider that it will take its character and its scope and method from the habits of life of the group' (Veblen

1993[1918], p. 1). Although the adepts pursuit of knowledge is taken by many, most vociferously by the adepts themselves, to be an unadulterated search for 'truth,' it is itself a reflection of the habits of thought of the adepts themselves. These 'habits of thought' are given expression through what Veblen called the 'paraphernalia of learning,' that is the precedent, gradations of rank, ritual and ceremonial vestments of the theory class (Veblen 1981[1899], p. 367). They are rightly thought of as a residual of the primitive community that maintains it as 'some sort of scholarly apostolic succession' and it is the status maintenance of the theory class that occupies much of the activities of the adepts (Veblen 1981[1899], pp. 368–369). Veblen considers the relationship between the growth of the barbarian temperament, with its insistence of status and clannishness, and the predatory habits of thought. Veblen links the growth of the predatory business habits in academe in the late nineteenth century to the 'psychologically disintegrating effects of the Civil War' and to the habituation to war that necessarily follows (Veblen 1981[1899], p. 373).

For Veblen, the character of the higher learning is influenced by the business culture in a variety of ways. Veblen speaks of the influence that emanates from the imperatives of a pecuniary culture that seeks, for example, to fit youths for careers in commerce. This motive drives the curriculum to prepare students or 'inmates' for engaging in the mechanics of commerce as well as to shape their values so that they appreciate rather than question existing arrangements. More to the point, the purpose of the higher learning is increasingly to fit youths of the leisure class for the 'consumption of goods, material and immaterial, according to a conventionally accepted, reputable scope and method' (Veblen 1981[1899], p. 370).

It is this pressure to accommodate the inmates so as to avoid the drop in enrollment and loss of goodwill in genteel circles that leads to the growth of a variety of 'student activities' which of course Veblen sees as 'sideshows to the main tent' in the higher learning (Veblen 1993[1918], p. 74). Hence the growth in 'scholastic accessories' — collegiate sports, fraternities, clubs, and exhibitions, all reflect the pandering of the corporation of learning to the business culture.

The pernicious influence that the pecuniary culture wages upon the curriculum of the higher learning and other student activities is not unrelated to the changing nature of the governing boards. According to Veblen, the 'substitution of businessmen in the place of ecclesiastics' resulted in the seating of regents and others whose only claim to ascendancy lay in their pecuniary prowess (Veblen 1993[1918], p. 48). Such prowess, he believed, was of only limited usefulness in addressing the fiscal affairs of the university and held more danger than benefit in determining the values and direction of the university through control over appointments of academic personnel.

It is for the captains of erudition and 'president strong man' that Veblen holds forth his most vitriolic prose, for it is the growing cadre of administrators that brings the business culture in all its glory into academe. Veblen describes how delicate the procedure is through which the academic executive and his loyal minions secure acceptance for the most arbitrary of acts and how important is the role of oversight that the witting faculty provides in securing acceptance of these acts (Veblen 1993[1918], pp. 68–69). For Veblen, these trusted aids and advisors must surely 'be selected on the same grounds of fitness as their chief, — administrative facility, plausibility, proficiency as public speakers and parliamentarians, ready versatility of convictions, and a staunch loyalty to their bread' (Veblen 1993[1918], p. 69).

It is the businesslike mentality of the corporation of learning and the resulting expansion of undergraduate education for that purpose that Veblen argues has led to the degradation of the higher learning. The large edifice to erudition requires 'such a system of authoritative control, standardization, gradation, accountancy, classification, credits and penalties, (and) will necessarily be drawn on stricter lines the more the school takes on the character of a house of correction or a penal settlement' (Veblen 1993[1918], pp. 162–163). For Veblen, the businesslike administration of the scholastic routine is to be decried because of its deleterious effect on the pursuit of knowledge.

While most of the discussion of the higher learning in both *The Higher Learning in America* and *The Theory of the Leisure Class* is without reference to women, Veblen does note the unusual location that women have occupied in the corporation of learning. And although the framework that he develops throughout is also useful in examining the experience of women in the higher learning, it is especially noteworthy to examine Veblen's specific references to women.

In *The Theory of the Leisure Class* Veblen notes the inferior status of women and refers to them as the 'original subservient class.' Veblen indicates that among many there has prevailed a strong sense that the inclusion of women in the hallowed halls of academe might serve to lower the status of those already occupying such a station (Veblen 1981[1899], pp. 375–376). Veblen notes the reluctance of the most reputable universities in moving toward inclusion and argues that the 'sense of class worthiness, that is to say of status, of a honorific differentiation of the sexes according to a distinction between superior and inferior intellectual dignity, survives in a vigorous form in these corporations of the aristocracy of learning' (Veblen 1981[1899], p. 376).

When speaking directly about women and the higher learning, Veblen points out that even when women are accepted within these institutions, they are often properly afforded only 'such knowledge as conduces immediately to a better performance of domestic service — the domestic sphere' and 'such accomplishments and dexterity, quasi-scholarly and quasi-artistic, as plainly come in under the head of a performance of vicarious leisure' (Veblen 1981[1899], pp. 376). Even more revealing, Veblen points out that:

> Knowledge is felt to be unfeminine if it is knowledge which expresses the unfolding of the learner's own life, the acquisition of which proceeds on the learner's own cognitive interest, without prompting from the canons of propriety, and without reference back to a master whose comfort or good repute is to be enhanced by the employment or the exhibition of it (Veblen 1981[1899], pp. 376–377).

The analysis that Veblen provides of the higher learning in general and his observations on women in particular present us with a useful framework for examining the evolution of women's experiences in the higher learning in the nineteenth century in the US. Veblen's notice of a separate sphere for women in the higher learning was born out in the development of separate women's colleges, in curriculum matters, and also through legislation. Moreover, the general reluctance to accept women in the higher learning, especially among well established universities, was painfully evident.

However, what is most interesting is the way in which institutions of higher learning responded to the growing participation of women through the development of new schemes of status maintenance and arguments against diversification in the higher learning. These schemes and arguments used prevailing notions of femininity and masculinity to coerce and discipline. Moreover, the mechanisms and arguments for preserving the status of men, both in their role as 'inmates' and as the 'adepts,' have served as the foundation for the continued dominance of men in the higher learning throughout much of the twentieth century.

3   STRONG MINDED WOMEN AND UNMANLY MEN

The colonial college in America was borrowed from Europe and founded to supply a learned clergy for the moral betterment of society. Higher education was, like its European counterpart, an elitist institution not open to women.   Yet after the Revolution, the ideals of 'Republican Motherhood,' which increasingly emphasized the role of women in educating future citizens of the new republic, led to a greater recognition of the importance of education for women (Rudolph 1968, pp. 308–309). From the early 1800s, however, it was well recognized that a particular type of education would be appropriate for women, even in their role as Republican mothers — an education that emphasized domestic studies.

To make educational opportunities available for the peculiar 'needs' of women, women's colleges were formed in the 1830s (Rudolph 1968, p. 311). The rise of these women's colleges were not met with unquestioning enthusiasm, as a satire in the Springfield, Massachusetts Republican Journal (March 14, 1835) demonstrates.   Upon the granting of a charter for Van Doren's Institute for Young Ladies by the Kentucky legislature, a satire appeared calling for the additional degrees for women of M.P.M. (Mistress of Pudding Making), M.D.N. (Mistress of the Darning Needle), and M.S.B. (Mistress of the Scrubbing Brush).   So as not to neglect any women who might be hired to teach at the Institute, they added, 'to fit the girls for those degrees, it will be necessary to organize a new department.   We further recommend them to procure some well qualified Professors, from among the farmers' wives, and especially from some of the best regulated kitchens' (Cohen 1974, p. 1573).

Along with women's colleges, state supported universities began to expand in the 1850s and opened their doors to women as well.   The University of Utah in 1850, Iowa in 1855, Wisconsin in 1863, Kansas in 1866, Minnesota in 1868 and Nebraska in 1871 were all coeducational from the beginning (Rudolph 1968, p. 314).   As these new coeducational universities in the middle and western states expanded, other established universities were pressured to turn coeducational.   Just as women in the west won suffrage earlier than women in the east, universities in the west admitted women earlier than more prestigious eastern schools.   However, the inclusion of women was not achieved without controversy.   The most well known of the state universities, the University of Michigan, founded in 1817, first enrolled women in 1870, against the will of the faculty (Thomas 1969, p. 325).   At Cornell, founded in 1865, where it was said that 'anyone could study anything,' women were finally allowed to enroll in 1872, when a large endowment for a woman's dormitory was forthcoming (Rudolph 1968, p. 316).

The expansion of higher education in the second half of the nineteenth century was, of course, greatly aided by the passage of the Morrill Act of 1862 (Ross 1942).   The Morrill Act was proposed and intentionally sold as a democratic piece of legislation aimed at creating a system of 'people's colleges' useful for expanding education in agriculture and the 'mechanic arts.' However, like many other 'democratic' or 'universal' programs, expectations varied greatly and what was 'useful' for men was different from what was 'useful' for women, at the same time that both terrains were contested. Given nineteenth century notions of the 'domestic code,' women were expected, when they did attend university classes, to avail themselves by studying domestic economy or the household arts as Veblen pointed out. Men were more appropriately suited for the more rigorous studies of political economy, history, agriculture, and the mechanical arts.

Although the Morrill Act was aimed primarily at expanding study in areas not thought to be useful to women, the Act did, by virtue of its timing, lay the foundation for increasing access to higher education for women. By subsidizing higher education at a time when new universities in the middle and western states were expanding, the movement to expand coeducational opportunities for women accelerated. Universities in these states were modeled after the so-called 'American system of free elementary and primary schools' which were, more from lack of population than any egalitarian impulse, necessarily co-educational (Thomas 1969, p. 322). Moreover, the teaching of secondary schools had become largely feminized by the mid to late 1800s (Thomas 1969, p. 324). Allowing women to attend institutions of higher learning was important, if only to guarantee that boys in their secondary school training would not be deprived of qualified women secondary school teachers.

As educational opportunities for women expanded, male privilege in education diminished, threatening to undermine the status of men in society. This threat was particularly significant in a society that was increasingly complex and where education was increasingly an avenue to commercial success. It was in this environment of conflict that discussions of the relationship between sexuality and education became more salient. Arguments that women would become 'desexed' as a result of too much education emerged and drew upon a notion that too much education, meaning as much or more than a man, was somehow unnatural. In 1895, for example, faculty at the University of Virginia pronounced that women students were indeed often 'unsexed' by academic strains (Rudolph 1968, p. 326–327).

Interestingly enough, as the experience of women in higher education began to demonstrate that 'a woman could do everything that a man could do,' the focus began to subtly shift to focus on the impact of coeducation on men. Coeducation raised suspicion and heightened self-consciousness of appropriate gender roles not only of women, but of men. Andrew D. White, president of Cornell, raised the issue of gender and coeducation by asking whether 'coeducation nurtured "strong-minded" women and "unmanly" men' (Rudolph 1968, p. 317). As Frederick Rudolph points out, suspicions would long linger that coeducation 'deprived women of some of their infinite charm and gentleness and robbed men of some of the sternness and ruggedness on which society depended for its protection' (Rudolph 1968, p. 327).

Given the blurring of traditional gender divisions in higher education, it is perhaps not surprising that collegiate football gained enormous popularity in the last third of the nineteenth century. Although in the early 1870s Andrew D. White of Cornell could still safely state that he would 'not permit thirty men to travel four hundred miles merely to agitate a bag of wind.' By the 1890s such a statement would have come close to heresy (Rudolph 1968, p. 376). By then football, rather than being viewed as a misguided waste of human energy, was touted as an antidote to the 'physical softness' that had been created by material plenty (Rudolph 1968, p. 377).

Contemporary observers as well have identified the rise of collegiate football in the nineteenth century with broader cultural changes in society. Noted men's historian E. Anthony Rotundo, for example, identifies the increased popularity of collegiate football with the valorization of the Civil War and the rise of competitive capitalism (Rotundo 1993, pp. 240–246). Although Rotundo acknowledges that women were 'entering many public worlds,' he nonetheless does not specifically argue that the rise of collegiate football is directly related to the growth in coeducational institutions of higher learning or the increasing participation of women in higher education.

Yet the growing numbers of women students represented a real and immediate threat to existing gender relations and a growing number of universities reflected the acceptance of co-education. While the number of men receiving bachelor's degrees increased 177 percent from 1870 to 1900, the number of women receiving bachelor's degrees increased 280 percent (*Historical Abstracts of the United States*). Moreover, whereas in 1880 over 30 percent of American colleges admitted women, by 1900 that figure was 71 percent (Rudolph 1968, p. 322).

While the Morrill Act greatly encouraged the expansion of largely coeducational universities and the founding of private women's colleges opened up educational possibilities for women, changes in the notion of what constituted scholarship emerged to create a gendered division of study within the university. The same impetus that moved the university of the nineteenth century to the 'practical' fields of agriculture, political economy, and history eventually led to the development of 'applied research' in the 1880s. Curriculums were changed from the 'classical curriculum' to include political economy, history and other more 'relevant' areas of study

(Ross 1991, p. 36). Interestingly enough, the liberal arts, which had been considered beyond the comprehension of women only decades earlier, were now considered to be essentially 'feminine.' As Frederick Rudolph stated 'Coeducation helped to divide the subjects of the curriculum and the courses of study into those which were useful, full-blooded, and manly, and those which were ornamental, dilettantish, and feminine' (Rudolph 1968, p. 325).

CONCLUSION

Veblen's *The Higher Learning in America* and *The Theory of the Leisure Class* provide useful insights in the workings of the higher learning and the ways in which the progressive movement of women into academe was resisted in an effort to maintain the status of men. For Veblen, much of what would appear to others to be mere fancy, represents instead, remnants of barbarian culture replicating and recreating invidious distinctions made long ago.

Even a brief examination of the history of women in the higher learning shows quite clearly how the institutions of higher learning can be utilized to retard progressive change and rationalize inequality despite a strong cultural allegiance to notions such as equality of opportunity and its corollary — equal access to education. Arguments against women's equal participation in the higher learning often turned on what were asserted to be natural differences between men and women and lamented the loss of femininity and masculinity that an equal co-education might produce.

All this might properly be viewed as a punitive effort to protect that which is really at stake in the democratization of the higher learning. That is, the specter of an educated female population raises the possibility that the division of labor might just change in the home and at work. As a student from Vanderbuilt argued 'No man wants to come home at night and find his wife testing some new process for manufacturing oleomargarine, or in the observatory sweeping the heavens for a comet' (Rudolph 1968, p. 327). Probably more to the point, no man wants to come home at night and find that he has to make dinner for himself or anyone else.

Of course anyone who has ever attended a faculty meeting will no doubt have immense appreciation for what Veblen called 'imbecile institutions.' Yet what is most valuable, but perhaps less entertaining, in Veblen is not his notoriously perceptive observations on the adepts, the captains of erudition, or the inmates that make up the penal settlement we call a university. It is the perspective that he brings on the institution of the higher learning — that of the Outsider. This is, of course, the same perspective that women continue to bring today. A perspective that, as Virginia Woolf observed long ago, threatens to alter the established values.

REFERENCES

Blaug, Mark (1978), *Economic Theory in Retrospect,* Cambridge: Cambridge University Press.

Cohen, Sol (ed.) (1974), *Education in the United States: A Documentary History,* Volume 3, New York: Random House.

Feyerabend, Paul K. (1988), 'Knowledge and the Role of Theories', *Philosophy of the Social Sciences,* **18**, 157–178.

Ross, Dorothy (1991), *The Origins of American Social Science,* Cambridge: Cambridge University Press.

Ross, Earle D. (1942), *Democracy's College: The Land-Grant Movement in its Formative Stage,* Ames, Iowa: Iowa State College Press.

Rotundo, E. Anthony (1993), *American Manhood: Transformation in Masculinity from the Revolution to the Modern Era,* New York: Basic Books.

Rudolph, Frederick (1968), *The American College and University: A History,* New York: Alfred A. Knopf.

Thomas, M. Carey (1969), 'Education of Women', in *Education in the United States,* Nicholas Murray Butler, ed., New York: Arno Press and the New York Times.

Veblen, Thorstein (1981[1899]), *The Theory of the Leisure Class,* New York: Book-of-the-Month-Club edition.

Veblen, Thorstein (1993[1918]), *The Higher Learning in America,* New Brunswick, NJ: Transaction Publishers.

Woolf, Virginia (1972[1929]), 'Women and Fiction', reprinted in Leonard Woolf, ed., *Collected Essays: Virginia Woolf,* Vol. II, London: Chatto and Windus.

PART IV

Veblen and the Global Economy

11. Capital and Inequality in Today's World

Phillip Anthony O'Hara

1 INTRODUCTION

The purpose of this chapter is to examine capital accumulation and inequality starting from an analysis of collective wealth generation originally enunciated in *The Theory of the Leisure Class* (Veblen 1970 [1899]). Then I modernize Veblen's ideas through an analysis of wealth in its various forms, such as ecological, human, social and private business capital; and specific forms of inequality based on species, gender, class, race and nation.

Veblen's work on wealth was innovative because he examined capital which is collectively-generated wealth. He paid special attention to the collective generation of wealth through the industrial arts, knowledge and institutional relationships. In many ways he foreshadowed later work on the contribution of technology, social capital, human capital, and ecological capital to the reproduction of material life.

In order to comprehend the nature of inequality it is necessary to examine the major forms of wealth or capital that generate unequal shares. Inequality depends on the nature of the forces propelling wealth production and distribution. These various forms of wealth — ecological, social, human and private business capital — are heterogeneous and not easily reduced to a common measure of value. It is important to have a broad view of wealth, as Veblen recognized, because a narrow view leads to the 'destruction' of critical forms of wealth as they are abstracted from the analysis. Many forms of capital compete with each other, as an increase in one often leads to a decrease in another. Indeed, in this paper we explore the hypothesis that what passes for 'economic growth' in the modern world is to some degree a transfer of resources from ecological (and sometimes social capital) to private business capital.

2   VEBLEN'S THEORY OF COLLECTIVE WEALTH

Few secondary sources emphasize Veblen's analysis of collective wealth. Harris (1934), Gruchy (1958), Stanfield (1989), and Tilman (1992), however, are scholars who do recognize the importance of collective wealth in Veblen's political economy. As Tilman said:

> Veblen's emphasis on the *social* nature of the stock of industrial knowledge and tools, his stress on the *organic* character of all economies, and his focus on the *collective* process by which goods and services are produced led him to *egalitarian* conclusions regarding the distribution of wealth and income. He did not believe it was possible to trace the origin of the value of a commodity to a particular input of land, labor, or capital (Tilman 1992, p. 22; emphases added).

The collective process of wealth creation is fundamental to Veblen's analysis, and he modified the context of the process according to the subject matter. At times his scope was narrow, centering on technology and the industrial arts. And at others times it was broad, including technology and the industrial arts, but also incorporating language, community bonding, and cooperation between people.

For instance, when he delimited the scope of the analysis to matters directly relevant to the instinct of workmanship, in *The Instinct of Workmanship and The State of the Industrial Arts* (1914), the nature of collective wealth is usually more narrowly conceived. As he said of this more narrow formulation of collective wealth:

> Technological knowledge is of the nature of a common stock, held and carried forward collectively by the community, which is in this relation to be conceived as a going concern. The state of the industrial arts is an affair of the collectivity, not a creative achievement of individuals working self-sufficiently in severalty or in isolation (Veblen 1914, p. 103).

Knowledge is embedded in the culture, technical colleges and universities, technological structures, and corporations. New knowledge and industrial arts are always modifications and extensions of the previous body of knowledge and science (O'Hara 1993; 1997). As Veblen said:

> In the main, the state of the industrial arts is always a heritage out of the past; it is always in process of change, perhaps, but the substantial body of it is knowledge that has come down from earlier generations. New elements of insight and proficiency are continually being added and worked into this common stock by the experience and initiative of the current generation, but such novel elements are always and everywhere slight and inconsequential in comparison with the

body of technology that has been carried over from the past (Veblen 1964[1914], p. 103).

Veblen's theory is not reductionist in the sense of leaving 'real people' out of the process. He recognized that every new invention and innovation is to some degree made by individuals. However we are 'social individuals' since every change 'so made is necessarily made by individuals immersed in the community and exposed to the discipline of group life as it runs in the community, since all life is necessarily group life' (Veblen 1964[1914], pp. 103–104). He believed that the productivity or contribution of individuals can rarely be assessed, because of the group nature of work in modern corporations; but, more importantly, because 'productivity is but a function of the immaterial technological equipment (which is a) slow spiritual distillate of the community's time-long experience and initiative' (Veblen 1908, p. 339).

Veblen's theory is not just related to technology and workmanship, important though this is. In some of Veblen's works on collective wealth, most notable *The Theory of the Leisure Class* and to some degree the *Instinct of Workmanship*, the contributing elements to collective wealth are defined very broadly. Veblen examines the traits which promote group livelihood, trust and bonding; in a phrase, 'social capital.' As he said:

> Along with these traits go certain others which have some value for the collective life process, in the sense that they further the facility of life in the group. These traits are said to include truthfulness, peaceableness, good-will, and a non-emulative, non-invidious interest in men and things (Veblen 1970[1899], p. 152).

Veblen's analysis of wealth generation was, for its time, pathbreaking. He recognized the collective contribution of technology, knowledge, and skill capital to the general welfare. And he was the first economist to emphasize the importance of social capital for the institutions underlying long-term economic performance. He found that economies which neglect their technological, educational, and social capital develop competitive tendencies which predicate extremes of inequality and conspicuous consumption thus negating the common good. This is probably Veblen's greatest achievement in political economy.

Capital or wealth, generally speaking, is the dynamic stock of durable structures, whatever those structures may be. Investment, therefore, as a flow, is the process whereby these durable structures are created and maintained. Capital in its many forms provides the foundation for a flow of services over time.

Capital is heterogeneous and therefore takes many forms. The forms it takes are finite because the world is asymmetrical, complex, imperfect and subject to irregularities. In this chapter, we delineate four main forms of capital: ecological capital; social capital; human capital; and private business capital. Conceptually, the linkages between these forms of capital are complex and multifarious. But, in general, two links stand out as being critical. First, some forms of capital are increased at the expense of others; often this takes the form of private business capital being increased at the expense of ecological capital and/or social capital. And second, some forms of capital are increased in tandem with increases in other forms of capital; for instance, increases in social capital may provide the foundations for increases in private business capital in the long term. Special emphasis will be placed on these interactions in the process of generating inequality.

3 ECOLOGICAL CAPITAL

Veblen, of course, dealt with aspects of ecological capital. He was the first great evolutionary economist, and attempted to link the economy with aspects of the gene pool, racial and ethnic factors, instincts, and plant and animal life. However, Veblen did not develop the notion in such a general form as is needed today.   Ecological capital is the stock of all environmental and ecological resources. It is a dynamic stock involving the biosphere, the gene pool, plant and animal species, the weather, the cycles of nature, and the physical environment. Here the concern is with the long-term regeneration of the biosphere, or the long-term survival of all plants and animals plus certain environmental conditions. This view of ecological capital, based on 'deep ecology,' seeks to promote ecological harmony and balance, biospecies equality and simple material needs (Bartelmus 1994). In the wake of the worldwide devastation of ecological capital we must transcend the concerns of one species (human beings) and take an ecological view of the matter.

There are various ways of looking at the question of the sustainability of natural capital and the relationship between ecological and other forms of capital.   For instance, it could be argued that ecological capital is sustainable if certain forms of ecological capital are destroyed but other forms expand so that the net ecological capital stock has risen or at least remains constant.   When examining the total capital stock (ecological, social, human, and business capital), it could be argued that sustainability holds if a decrease in, say, ecological capital occurs through an expansion of private business capital, while the total capital stock remains constant.

However, there are two problems with this latter perspective. The first is that ecological capital relates to the very survival of life on earth, while business capital relates only to the growth of one element of human needs. Ecological capital is thus primary. And second, questions of valuation are notoriously difficult when dealing with heterogeneous forms of capital, and again depend on the population whose benefits are valued. The history of humanity, and particularly of capitalism, has seen a rapid destruction of ecological capital as the stock of fixed business capital expands inexorably.

The most obvious case of a trade-off between capitals relates to the switch from ecological capital to private business capital. For instance, the human population on earth increased from an estimated 1 billion in 1800 to 1.8 billion in 1900 to 5 billion in 1990. Projections show that with a low population growth rate this will increase to 8 billion in 2100, while with a high growth rate the figure could be 11.5 billion by 2100 (Ekins 1992, pp. 108–109). The fivefold increase in the stock of the human population between 1800 and 1990 has occurred in tandem with a far greater expansion of the stock of private business capital in advanced economies. For example, UK non-residential capital stock per capita increased over twenty times between 1820 and 1991, while the US capital stock per capita increased forty times over the same period (Maddison 1995, p. 143).

This expansion of the stock of human population and private capital has been at the expense of ecological capital. Inequalities between the species have grown larger, the stock of old natural forests has declined markedly, and the rate of species extinction and hence loss of biological diversity has been increasing in broad proportion to the total consumption of energy by human beings. Ekins (1992, p. 16) documents some dimensions of this loss of ecological capital. For instance, forests once covered over 70 percent of total land area, but now the figure is less than 30 percent; and for tropical forests the figure has halved to under 7 percent. He points out that these tropical forests have contained the vast majority of earth's species, and are under threat worldwide. Between 50–100 animal species are estimated to be extinguished every day.

The growth of automobiles, for instance, is especially problematical. The stock of automobiles increased from zero in 1900 to an estimated 470 million in 1994. Western Europe has 161 million automobiles, followed by the USA with 146 million, Japan with 41 million, Central and South America 31 million, and Eastern Europe and Asia (excluding Japan) each with 28 million. Density levels are especially high in the USA (1.7 persons per automobile), Western Europe (2.5 persons per automobile), and Japan (3.1 persons per automobile) (see Freund and Martin 1996).

The stock of automobiles, as Fruend and Martin (1996) argue, requires an enormous amount of nonrenewable energy; consuming about one-fifth of all industrial energy and one-half of all petroleum used in the USA. For instance, they point out that a single occupant automobile uses 1860 calories per mile, compared with 35 calories for a bicycle and 885 for a train. The chief problem is the pollution produced by automobiles, including 60 percent of the carbon monoxide, 33 percent of the nitrous oxide, and 25 percent of the hydrocarbon emissions in the USA. Automobiles have been implicated as an important player in the creation of acid rain, depletion of the ozone layer, and reducing the self-cleansing capacity of the atmosphere.

In short, the recent history of humanity, and in particular the expansion of capitalism, has seen the wholesale slaughter and destruction of most of the animal kingdom and a great percentage of the plant kingdom. Inequality between the species has risen to extreme proportions. We can generalize the trade-off between capitals explained above. The switch from ecological to human types of capital means that, in large measure, the growth of capital is derivative. One form of capital tends to grow at the expense of another. At the greatest level of generality, the history of humanity has seen the destruction of ecological capital in favor of human-centered forms of capital (especially business capital).

Figure 11.1: Hysteresis and the Trade-Off Between Capitals

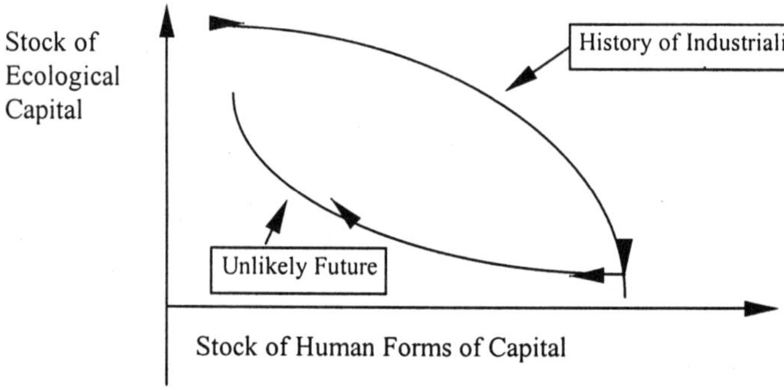

This illustration shows, in a stylized fashion, how industrialization has been possible through the exploitation and destruction of ecological capital. The downward sloping curve is indicative of the process whereby the marginal rate of industrial expansion declines as the marginal rate of ecological capital destruction increases. In other words, in the latter phase of industrialism, a given increase in human forms of capital results in an accelerated destruction of ecological capital. As the extent of genetic diversity diminishes, the destruction of ecological capital is propelled in a circular and cumulative fashion. In large measure, reversing the process is not possible, and therefore history (hysteresis) is important. Species extinction cannot be reversed and less genetic diversity is extremely difficult to reverse. Hence the 'unlikely future' scenario illustrates that building ecological capital by reducing the stock of human forms of capital is unlikely to be very successful, even with a substantial effort. However, if the destruction of ecological capital was reversed before the process became too extreme, some degree of success is likely. As Setterfield recognizes (1997, p. 14), the emphasis on long-run outcomes draws attention to the permanence of hysteresis effects. Human dominance via hysteresis is endemic to a process of perpetual, self-propelling motion.

4   SOCIAL CAPITAL

In *The Theory of the Leisure Class*, in particular, Veblen was the theorist of social capital par excellence. Much of his analysis of collective wealth examined the process whereby institutions are developed for the benefit of the collectivity. Social (or institutional) capital comprises those norms, mores, relationships and organizational arrangements which help to bond people together. Some minimal degree of trust, respect, dignity and communication between people is necessary with this form of capital. Durable relationships and behaviors are created within, for instance, specific sites or spheres such as families, corporations, governments, markets and nations (Tomer 1998).

The dynamic stock of social capital has been demonstrated to be critical to both human relationships and the long-term economic performance of nations and the world. Political economy has for many decades recognized that the basic substance of the economy is its institutions. More recently it has been recognized that stability and flexibility in the institutions is a necessary condition for sustained economic growth and performance. When the institutions are suitable, growth and accumulation of private business capital is encouraged; and when the institutions are in disarray, such growth and accumulation tend to falter.

For instance, during the post WW II period, the stock of suitable social capital is said to have increased during the 1940s–60s. Especially important in this context is the stock of durable relationships within the family, durable agreements between capital and labor, stabilizing processes initiated by the state, the provision of credit by the financial system, organizational and informational relations within corporations, and international leadership and coordination. These institutions were especially favorable in the long term to the expansion of private business capital in advanced capitalist economies, especially in the 1950s and 1960s (O'Hara 1994).

However, over time the institutions became less durable and eventually failed to propel the required level of confidence and trust for sustained growth and accumulation. This helped to initiate the deep recessions of the mid-1970s, early 1980s and early 1990s when lower levels of confidence and stability led to a lowering of the floor of the business cycle. Families began to break down at a high rate, which adversely affected the quality of labor power. The agreements between capital and labor dissolved as productivity declined. The state became implicated in the process of stagflation during the 1970s, precipitating a more laissez-faire form of government and a structural decline in aggregate demand. And leadership provided by the USA declined as the system of fixed exchange rates (Bretton Woods System) dissolved; they lost the war in Vietnam; and other nations such as Japan, Europe and other parts of Asia gained in international competitiveness. Despite some re-establishment of social capital through the 'flexible mode of accumulation,' various regional trading blocks, and new forms of the state and financial system, sustained stability and economic performance has yet to be achieved in the West. It may be that the distribution of social capital appropriate to growth and accumulation is changing to favor certain areas such as East and South East Asia (despite recent instabilities there).

This is an instance when institutional and private business capital are positively related. However, especially in the past three decades, critical forms of social capital have been destroyed as individuals spend less time in the process of bonding with family and friends and more time at work helping to sustain corporate hegemony over the other institutions. This has also led to the transfer of production from the home to the marketplace. Hence, certain dimensions of social capital and fixed commodity capital may be inversely related. For instance, Jefferson (1997, p. 110), dealing with flow aspects of these stocks, provides an indication of the possible switches between social and private business capital. She calculates the value of household production in Australia to have declined from 54 percent of GDP (as an addition to GDP) in 1976/77 to 43 percent in 1994/95, as commodity production took over a certain percentage of household tasks.

Cloud and Garrett (1997) support this 'shift in capital between sectors' argument with data for the US. Normal GDP growth, investment and capital stock figures may thus be misleading because they do, in part, represent the extent to which production (and therefore capital) is transferring from the home to capitalist market activities, rather than necessarily increasing total production (and capital). In advanced capitalist economies, especially over the last couple of decades, people on average are investing less in family, relationship and community capital and more in human, corporate and market forms of capital (Dollahite and Rommel 1993). This is an important instance of a shift from social to private forms of capital, which is similar in some ways conceptually to the shift from ecological to business capital previously discussed. This trend is troublesome because it reduces the social safety nets that people can depend upon during stressful socioeconomic times, and reduces the quality of life for the most vulnerable.

Heller (1996) examines the relationship between social and business capital in a fascinating case study of the state of Kerala in India (population: 29 million). He shows that data for per capita GDP (and private business capital stock) gives a misleading indication of the standard of living of the people in Karela. For instance, while GDP per capita is lower in Kerala (US$260 per capita) than for India as a whole (US$310), other indicators of the standard of living in Kerala suggest that it is much higher than for India (and within reach of much more developed nations). For instance, average life expectancy in Kerala is 70 years compared with 59 for India, 76 for the US and 70 for South Korea; infant mortality in Kerala is 17 per 1000, compared with 91 for India, 9 in the US and 13 in South Korea; and adult literacy is 91 percent in Kerala, compared with 52 percent in India, 99 percent in the US and 97 percent in South Korea. Hence, the human development index (HDI), which includes composite indicators of income, schooling and life expectancy, is high at 0.65 for Kerala, compared with 0.38 for India, 0.96 for the US and 0.76 for South Korea. Kerala seems to be at a medium to moderately high level of social development, compared with a relatively low level for India, a moderately high level for South Korea and a very high level for the USA (1991 data from Heller 1996).

Heller isolates the large dynamic stock of social capital as the main reason for Kerala's relatively high standard of living. Important components of the social capital which were developed, especially since the 1940s, are said to include the 'high density of civic organizations,' the 'vigor of associational life,' an 'extensive network of cooperative societies,' 'numerous non-government organizations,' vigorous 'communal and caste organizations,' and the 'size and activism of the state.' Expansion of social capital was made possible by the extensive system of land reform which created a new class of small proprietors; the government-run primary health care units which reduced infant mortality; active state regulations in the workplace which improved work conditions and enhanced employment;

and an extensive system of social security and elementary schools which raised the standard of living for poor people. The social relationships which stimulated these developments are closely linked with the high level of participation and association of people in a system of community (civil society).

This successful expansion of civil society is said to have been due to the policies of the Communist Party of India (CPI), which became the dominant party at the state level; and the high level of grassroots mobilization which created pressure from below for institutional reform and basic goods. The first decades of this program in the 1950s and 1960s were periodically characterized by industrial chaos and conflict, in order to direct resources from business capital to social capital. In this phase of the program there was clearly a shift of economic surplus from privileged landowners and big capitalists to investment in capitals which support the social development of the community. In more recent years, there has been an extension of social capital in the form of institutionalized long-term labor — management agreements and industrial harmony. The emergence of 'class compromise,' initiated by the CPI, was seen as a way of expanding the economic surplus, productivity, private investment as well as wages (through productivity bonuses, for instance). This latest program of conciliation has reduced the level of uncertainty, increased cooperation, and possibly in the long run enabled some degree of dual expansion of social and business capital. As Heller stated:

> The 'synergy' of state and class mobilization in Kerala has produced two forms of social capital. The first underwrote the provision of redistributive goods, the second facilitated class coordination. What is certain is that the synergy has directly contributed to building the political and institutional foundations most likely to effectively 'manage' the contradictions of democratic capitalist development (Heller 1996, p. 1067).

Overall, then, social capital is a critical dimension of wealth, which provides a foundation for increasing the standard of living of whole societies. In some respects it can help to sustain business capital, and in other contexts social and business capital are in competition with each other. There is, however, every justification for including social capital in an assessment of the wealth of nations, and as an important determinant of inequality.

5 HUMAN CAPITAL

Veblen was concerned with human capital through his analysis of workmanship, idle curiosity, and knowledge. He believed that these forms of human capital were in large measure a product of the community, being handed down from the past. Rather than seeing it as being embodied in individuals *per se*, Vebien recognized a critical dimension of socially-generated knowledge and skills.

Human capital is usually related to those skills and knowledge that are capable of general application, although 'firm specific' human capital and 'learning by doing' are of considerable importance, perhaps being part of 'organizational capital' (Tomer 1998). A large proportion of the knowledge and skills that are incorporated in individuals emanate from collective sources, such as schools, universities, libraries, organizational structures, and the like. Regardless of the source, though, such human capital provides the bearers of such knowledge with potential flows of effort and productive labor which can be exchanged for flows of income over time.

Since the 1950s, studies have been done on the contribution of human capital to economic growth, and on the role of education in the distribution of income. Economists have attributed between 20–50 percent of productivity growth in advanced nations to the growth of human capital (see Griliches 1997 and Cloud and Garrett 1997, p. 159). In general, human capital is now recognized to be critical, especially to endogenous growth theory; and some economists think obtaining credentials performs a screening device for employers, by indicating those people who are likely to perform well.

The importance of education and skills in explaining inequality can be seen from the pattern of unemployment. Nickell and Bell (1996) examined the pattern of unemployment for those with high and low levels of education in many OECD nations. The results are clear. Those people with low levels of education have, in all nations studied except Italy, a much higher rate of unemployment relative to those with a high level of education.

Their results show that, in general, people with low levels of 'education' are likely to have from two to five times the rate of unemployment of those with a high level of education. This is important because unemployment adversely affects one's material and psychological well being. During the 1970s and 1980s, for instance, earnings differentials between people with high and low levels of education were consistently wide for the vast majority of OECD nations studied. The ratio of income for the highly educated divided by income for the low educated in the 'late 1980s' was 1.65 for the UK, 1.61 for Italy, 1.42 for Germany and Canada, 1.22 for Holland and 1.19 for Sweden. Therefore, the differential level of acquisition of human capital is a critical factor in the inequality of nations; although in advanced social democracies such as Sweden these inequities are much less.

Radical economists have taken traditional human capital theory to task for not adequately incorporating questions of class, gender and race — and more generally socioeconomic reproduction — into the analysis. As Bowles and Gintis state, 'schooling, occupational training, child rearing, and health care perform dual economic functions: they play an essential, if indirect, role in production; and they are also essential to the perpetuation of the entire economic and social order.' They go on to say that 'these processes can not be understood without reference to the social requirements for the reproduction from period to period of the capitalist class structure, the individuals who compose it, and the economic institutions that regulate it' (Bowles and Gintis 1975, p. 75). In other words, human capital comprises not only technical capital, but also social capital, and it is the latter which orthodox economics has problems with.

As Veblen recognized, there are considerable externalities associated with human capital, such as it being embodied in new physical capital, advances in knowledge, new organizational structures, better social modes of communication, and planning for future life experiences. Many of the advantages of human capital concern flows of experience associated with non-monetary rewards, including dealing with an uncertain future. All this, of course, relates to 'capital invested in institutions such as families, friends, and firms, and in the creation of our own identities and reputations' (Griliches 1997, p. S338).

Many scholars believe that some of the major forms of racial, gender and class inequality can to some degree be resolved by the expansion of human capital for less privileged groups. However, the structure of the education system is by no means consistent with the resolution of these problems. Indeed, as Bowles (1975) and others argue, an important function of the education system in modern capitalism is to prepare people for their class role in segmented labor markets. Rather than helping to spread human capital evenly in the community, the education system is said to help to reproduce inequality to the extent that it does not challenge the basic property relations of capitalism. Schools and universities do not just teach 'knowledge' and 'skills,' but also function to help students fit into the roles they are supposed to play in the wider society and the workplace. Also, schools are not uniform, since their quality depends on funds available and the class interests certain schools entertain.

For instance, Egerton (1997) found that certain occupations are in large measure inherited. Her study of British occupational inheritance found class background to be the main factor influencing the acquisition of human capital; although gender played an important role as well. Specifically she found that sons of professionals and managers were more likely than others to enter professional and managerial occupations, respectively. Also, daughters of professionals were more likely to become professionals, while daughters of managers, however, were not more likely to become managers.

Egerton's conclusion is that upper classes are better able to provide their offspring with the 'cultural capital' of cognitive, personal, educational, property and social network assets which bring material success. This is consistent with the findings of Gottschalk (1997), who studied the nature of inequality of income in the US. He found that the greater income inequality that occurred during the 1970s–90s, from a Gini Coefficient of 0.353 (1970) to 0.365 (1980) to 0.396 (1990) to 0.426 (1994), 'reflects an absolute as well as a relative decline in the earnings of less skilled workers' in an era of greater wage flexibility (Gottschalk 1997, p. 39). He concluded that the occupational mobility of workers — their ability to shift from low to higher wage jobs — is relatively low and during the 1970s–90s has either declined or experienced no change. This reflects to some degree class differences in family cultural capital, which in turn is a major determinant of individual human capital formation.

The situation is more problematical from the view of race or ethnicity. The net worth asset ownership of households is heavily skewed in favor of whites in the US. For instance, in 1993 31.5 percent of whites and 8.1 percent of blacks had a net worth of $100,000 or over; while 9.8 percent of whites and 25.6 percent of blacks have negative or zero net worth (USCB 1997). Jianakoplos and Menschik demonstrate that blacks are more likely to move down to the bottom quintile; less likely to move up to the top decile; and the 'chances that a black in the poorest group will reach the richest group in fifteen years is approximately zero' (Jianakoplos and Menschik 1997, p. 28). An important reason for this is differential levels of human and cultural capital. In 1993 for instance, 0.9 percent of individuals with less than 12 years of schooling (a high proportion of blacks) and 8.6 percent of those with 4 or more years of college (a low proportion of blacks) had a net worth of $500,000 or more (USCB 1997). In relation to wealth and education, blacks are 'significantly worse off' in segregated communities (ghettos) than in those which are integrated with whites, presumably because of a lack of suitable cultural capital (Cutler and

Glaeser 1997). Darity (1994) attributes some of the inequality to discrimination.

A significant proportion of this cultural capital (for all 'racial' categories) is provided by household workers. Household workers still contribute a substantial amount to the reproduction of human capital. Cloud and Garrett sought to estimate the extent to which this household formation of human capital contributed to GDP in 1990 (where revised GDP estimates include such household labor). On average for the 132 countries they examined, it was found (given certain assumptions) that household labor expanded the stock of human capital by approximately US$8 trillion, which was about 24 percent of the revised GDP figure of just over US$30 trillion. The smallest gains in GDP were for Finland (21 percent), and the largest Bangladesh (90 percent) (Cloud and Garrett 1997).

Thus, household labor contributes a flow of services to enhance the human capital stock of nations. But, ironically, in undertaking such household labor women reduce their lifetime earnings as employers assume that their lack of involvement in the formal labor market reduces their 'human capital.' This probably explains much of the income inequality that exists between women and men, including the much lower 'work experience wage premium' that women have compared to that of men (Gottschalk 1997, p. 32).

6 PRIVATE BUSINESS CAPITAL

The last form of capital examined is private business capital. This category includes the creation of durable structures within corporations, such as machinery, factories, tools, warehouses, buildings, and inventories. Private business physical capital, historically speaking, has been the dominant form of capital in the economists' language; physical investment is the accumulation of such structures. Fixed capital has had such a dominant hold over economists, historically speaking, that few recognize the existence of any other forms of capital, besides perhaps human capital.

Recent debates about human and social capital have downplayed the relative importance of private business capital in the total wealth stakes. The World Bank, for instance, has produced world-wide figures for natural capital, human resources and produced assets (World Bank 1995, 1997; Serageldin 1996).

Natural capital is not the same as ecological capital, but is mainly the stock of ecological capital that is available for potential use by human beings in one form or another. This includes agricultural land, minerals/fossil fuels and forests and protected areas. Human resources include mainly human capital (the dollar value of 'years in education'), plus 'raw labor' and to some degree social capital. Their estimates of human resources are calculated by using a residual method; the 'residual of the (discounted) future income stream for today's population after deducting estimates for produced assets and natural capital' (World Bank 1995, p. 61). Produced assets are figures for fixed capital, including inventories. Hence, their figures examine the major forms of wealth from the point of view of human beings.

These figures clearly show the dominance of mostly western economies in the wealth stakes. Much of the wealth is a product of firstly British (1820s–70s) and later United States (1940s–60s) hegemony, both of which are related to the mostly western nations which have been interlocked into the hegemonic and post-hegemonic structures. Most non-western nations have historically been left out of these structures of productive, commercial and financial dominance and leadership. This has great significance for race/ethnicity, since the dominant nations have historically been mostly white and the lesser states non-white. The relative lack of accumulation of wealth, especially human resources, in Latin America, North Africa, South Asia and Sub-Saharan Africa has led to an increase in the head count index (percent) of poverty for these areas between 1985 and 1990 (World Bank 1995, p. 67). The flows of income, therefore, tend to emanate from the dynamic stock of capital or wealth. Some challenge to western dominance was achieved through the OPEC oil price rises of the 1970s and 1980s; and more recently with the rising nations of Asia (especially Japan); but this has not challenged western power, and hence global inequality, sufficiently at this point in history.

CONCLUSION

The objective of this chapter has been to examine and extend Veblen's notion of collective wealth to the contemporary world. In doing so we have recognized the primary importance of ecological wealth to human well-being. However, in large measure there is an inverse relationship between the stock of ecological wealth and human forms of wealth. The history of humanity, especially in the past 100 years, has seen the massive destruction of ecological wealth, through the extinction of species and a reduction in genetic diversity. In the long term, the expansion of human forms of wealth may diminish due to severe damage to the biosphere.

Of the human sources of wealth, the most important forms are social and human capital. Social capital is a critical form of collective wealth because it provides benefits to the whole community. In some respects, social wealth and business capital are positively related, since stable and suitable institutions provide the foundations for long-term business capital accumulation. However, they are also to some extent in competition with each other, since business capital is more easily measured and brought to the attention of economists; and also because business attempts to exploit the wealth of the community in the private interests of industrial profit, interest and rent. Increases in social capital, more than any other, are positively related to equality and the quality of social life.

Human capital is in large measure dependent upon social, cultural and organizational capital. The way in which many economists associate human capital with individual benefits ignores the social generation of knowledge, communication, and skills which is the reproductive basis of labor power. The ability of parents to instill in their children the desire and ability to acquire knowledge and skills is one critical factor in the development of human capital; the other factor is the accumulation of broader social capital which cannot be privatized. A policy conclusion which can be drawn from this is that inequality can be reduced if the dynamic stock of social capital is expanded.

Western economies (and Japan) have a disproportionate share of world wealth, especially human resources. This international inequality acts as a form of conspicuous consumption, whereby the lower developed nations tend to try and emulate the more wealthy nations. The wealthy nations acquired their wealth from imperialism and later through hegemonic dominance of world resources via market economics. However, as more nations join the race for greater private business capital and social capital, the stocks of ecological capital will most likely deteriorate to new lows. More emphasis needs to be placed on the collective stock of ecological capital for reducing inequality between species and, ultimately, ensuring survival of the planet. Much of the growth of human forms of capital is at a considerable expense to the ecological environment; and this trend must be reversed.

This broadened approach to wealth and its social creation is in many respects attributable to Veblen's insights in *The Theory of the Leisure Class*. To better understand the growing inequality in today's world, and how it is socially constructed, we can continue to draw on Veblen's cultural approach to wealth as it was first revealed in *The Theory of the Leisure Class*.

REFERENCES

Bartelmus, Peter (1994), *Environment, Growth and Development: The Concepts and Strategies of Sustainability*, London and New York: Routledge.

Bowles, Samuel (1975), 'Unequal Education and the Reproduction of the Social Division of Labor', in Martin Carnoy, ed., *Schooling in a Corporate Society: The Political Economy of Education in America*, New York: David McKay Company, 38–66.

Bowles, Samuel and Herbert Gintis (1975), 'The Problem with Human Capital Theory — A Marxian Critique', *American Economic Review: Papers and Proceedings*, **65**, 2, May, 74–82.

Cloud, Kathleen and Nancy Garrett (1997), 'A Modest Proposal for Inclusion of Women's Household Human Capital Production in Analysis of Structural Transformation', in *Feminist Economics*, **3**, 151–177.

Cutler, David and Edward L. Glaeser (1997), 'Are Ghettos Good or Bad?', *Quarterly Journal of Economics*, **CXII**, 3, August, 827–872.

Darity, William A. Jr. (1994), 'Loaded Dice in the Labor Market: Racial Discrimination and Inequality', in Susan Feiner, ed., *Race and Gender in the American Economy: Views from Across the Spectrum*, Englewood Cliffs, New Jersey: Prentice Hall, 18–21.

Dollahite, D. C. and J. I. Rommel (1993), 'Individual and Relationship Capital: Implications for Theory and Research on Families', *Journal of Family and Economic Issues*, **14**, 1, Spring, 27–48.

Egerton, Muriel (1997), 'Occupational Inheritance: The Role of Cultural Capital and Gender', *Work, Employment and Society*, **11**, 2, 263–282.

Ekins, Paul; with M. Hillman and R. Hutchinson (1992), *Wealth Beyond Measure: An Atlas of New Economics*, London: Gaia Books.

Freund, Peter and George Martin (1996), 'The Commodity that is Eating the World: The Automobile, the Environment, and Capitalism', *Capitalism, Nature and Socialism*, **7**, 4, December, 3–29.

Gottschalk, Peter (1997), 'Inequality, Income Growth, and Mobility: The Basic Facts', *Journal of Economic Perspectives*, **11**, 2, 21–40.

Griliches, Zvi (1997), 'Education, Human Capital, and Growth: A Personal Perspective', *Journal of Labor Economics*, **15**, 1, part 2, S330–S344.

Gruchy, Allan (1958), 'Veblen's Theory of Economic Growth', in Douglas Dowd, ed., *Thorstein Veblen: A Critical Appraisal*. Westport, Connecticut: Greenwood Press.

Harris, Abram L. (1934), 'Economic Evolution: Dialectical and Darwinian', *Journal of Political Economy*, **42**, 1, February, 34–79.

Heller, Patrick (1996), 'Social Capital as a Product of Class Mobilization and State Intervention: Industrial Workers in Kerala, India', *World Development*, **24**, 6, 1055–1071.

Jefferson, Therese (1997), *Some Implications of the Commodification of Activities Previously Carried Out Within Households*, Bundoora, Australia: Master of Economics Thesis, School of Business, Faculty of Social Sciences, La Trobe University.

Jianakoplos, Nancy A. and Paul L. Menschik (1997) 'Wealth Mobility', *Review of Economics and Statistics*, **LXXIX**, 1, February, 18–31.

Maddison, Angus (1995) *Explaining the Economic Performance of Nations: Essays in Time and Space*, Aldershot: Edward Elgar Publishing.

Nickell, Stephen and Brian Bell (1996), 'Changes in the Distribution of Wages and Unemployment in OECD Countries', *American Economic Review: Papers and Preceedings*, **86**, 2, 302–308.

O'Hara, Phillip Anthony (1993), 'Veblen's Analysis of Business, Industry and the Limits of Capital: An Interpretation and Sympathetic Critique', *History of Economics Review*, **20**, 95–119.

O'Hara, Phillip Anthony (1994), 'An Institutionalist Review of Long Wave Theories: Schumpeterian Innovation, Modes of Regulation, and Social Structures of Accumulation', *Journal of Economic Issues*, **28**, 2, June, 489–500.

O'Hara, Phillip Anthony (1997), 'Veblen's Critique of Marx's Philosophical Preconceptions of Political Economy', *European Journal of the History of Economic Thought*, **4**, 1, Spring, 65–91.

Serageldin, Ismail (1996), *Sustainability and the Wealth of Nations: First Steps in an Ongoing Journey*, Washington DC: World Bank.

Setterfield, M.A. (1997), *Rapid Growth and Relative Decline: Modeling Macroeconomic Dynamics with Hysteresis*, London: Macmillan.

Stanfield, Ronald James (1989), 'Veblenian and Neo-Marxian Perspectives on the Cultural Crisis of Late Capitalism', *Journal of Economic Issues*, **23**, 3, September, 717–734.

Tilman, Rick (1992), *Thorstein Veblen and His Critics, 1891–1963: Conservative, Liberal, and Radical Perspectives*, Princeton, New Jersey: Princeton University Press.

Tomer, John F. (1998), 'Capital: Social and Organizational', in Phillip Anthony O'Hara (editor), *Encyclopedia of Political Economy*, London and New York: Routledge.

USCB (US Census Bureau) (1997), *The Official Statistics: Asset Ownership of Households: 1993*, Http://www.census.gov/hhes/www/wealth/wlth93t4/html.

Veblen, Thorstein (1908), 'On the Nature of Capital: I. The Productivity of Capital Goods', *Quarterly Journal of Economics*, **22**, 3, August, 517–542.

Veblen, Thorstein (1964[1914]), *The Instinct of Workmanship and the State of the Industrial Arts*, New York: Kelley.

Veblen, Thorstein (1970[1899]), *The Theory of the Leisure Class: An Economic Study of Institutions*, London: Unwin Books.

World Bank (1995), *Monitoring Environmental Progress: A Report on Work in Progress*, Washington DC: World Bank.

World Bank (1997), *Expanding the Measure of Wealth: Indicators of Environmentally Sustainable Development*, Washington DC: World Bank.

12. My Dam is Bigger than Yours: Emulation in Global Capitalism

Paulette Olson

1 INTRODUCTION

As with the work of any great scholar, Thorstein Veblen's nineteenth century classic *The Theory of the Leisure Class* continues to provide many valuable insights as we enter the twenty-first century. Veblen's key insight that consumption is driven by the desire for social status and esteem remains valid. Veblen also identified conspicuous consumption and conspicuous leisure as the two main methods for demonstrating social standing in the community. One hundred years later, conspicuous consumption continues to provide an important mechanism for demonstrating social status. However, the form that conspicuous consumption takes has evolved to reflect a new set of hierarchical relationships under global capitalism. It will be argued that the industrialized countries of the West have replaced Veblen's nineteenth century leisure class in setting the standards of decency and pecuniary canons of good taste for the rest of the world.

The purpose of this chapter is to reconceptualize Veblen's nineteenth century analysis of consumption in the historical context of global capitalism. This chapter expands Veblen's analysis of consumption in three basic ways. First, whereas Veblen analysed consumer behavior within American culture, I will explore consumption patterns across cultures. Second, whereas Veblen focused on the advantages of using high fashion and other 'private' methods for demonstrating pecuniary prowess, I will show how countries display their pecuniary prowess using public assets. Third, whereas Veblen analysed the instrumental and ceremonial features of consumption goods, I will explore this tension focusing on producer goods. I will begin by summarizing Veblen's theory of consumption, highlighting concepts which are particularly relevant to my analysis of consumer behavior under global capitalism.

2   A SUMMARY OF VEBLEN'S THEORY OF CONSUMPTION

For Veblen, much of consumption behavior is driven by emulation, 'the stimulus of an invidious comparison which prompts us to outdo those with whom we are in the habit of classing ourselves' (Veblen 1987[1899], p. 103). Emulation leads to 'discrimination in favor of visible consumption' and a concentration of consumption 'upon the lines which are most patent to the observers whose good opinion is sought' (Veblen 1987[1899], p. 112). That is, the goods we purchase to impress others must be visible to those with whom we compare ourselves. But visibility, according to Veblen, is a necessary not sufficient characteristic of emulation. Consumption also requires a conspicuous waste of goods. That is, consumption must convey economic extravagance in excess of what is required for physical comfort. The more wasteful the expenditure, the more meritorious it is because it allows for invidious comparisons and thereby reinforces one's pecuniary superiority.

Throughout *The Theory of the Leisure Class*, Veblen emphasizes the tension between predatory instincts and the instinct of workmanship as expressed in the goods we produce and consume. Like other social theorists of his era, Veblen argues that human activity is essentially purposive and that people possess 'a taste for effective work, and a distaste for futile effort' (Veblen 1987[1899], p. 15). In pecuniary society, however, this instinct is perverted by predatory behavior and is dominated by the canon of conspicuous waste. That is, emulation can perform a positive or negative function depending on social conditions. According to Veblen, in peaceful societies emulation played a positive role. Esteem was gained by putting one's efficiency in evidence, fostering the well-being of the community. In pecuniary society, emulation jeopardizes the future of humanity because status is gained by demonstrating wastefulness in consumption and predatory behavior; the use of force and fraud for individual gain. But the tension between wastefulness and usefulness in consumption persists because 'all wastefulness is offensive to native taste' (Veblen 1987[1899], p. 176). Hence, goods tend to provide some combination of status and serviceability. That is, goods can serve both a ceremonial and instrumental purpose.

For Veblen, conspicuously wasteful consumption expresses a desire to live up to the conventional standard of decency as defined by the wealthy leisure class. During the nineteenth century, this reference group determined what constituted a decent and honorific standard of living for the rest of society. But as Veblen pointed out, this standard is 'indefinitely extensible.' As the 'pecuniary ability' of the lower classes increases, the 'scale of decent consumption' expands. Cellular phones, computers and other important sources of social status become indispensable. What passes as status goods in one time period become basic needs in the next. To maintain their relative position within the social hierarchy, the leisure class is forced to increase their level of consumption. In the process, the pecuniary canons of good taste and standards of reputable living are redefined for those below. From a global perspective, the implications are obvious.

3 THE CONSTRUCTION OF EMULATION UNDER GLOBAL CAPITALISM

As we approach the twenty-first century, emulation continues to govern consumer behavior. However, emulation has evolved to reflect a new global order in which the industrialized countries of the West define the standards of decency and pecuniary canons of good taste for the rest of the world. As a result the process of emulation can no longer be understood as a cultural phenomenon defined within the boundaries of nation states. Instead, emulation is a global process in which countries compete for economic status and esteem.

Writing at the turn of the twentieth century, Veblen analysed invidious distinctions within American culture. A century later, global capitalism promotes cross-cultural emulation. In the quest for global status and esteem, invidious comparisons are not only made between people of the same culture, but between people of very different cultures. However, because of the dominance and supremacy of western culture and pecuniary values, many people around the world attempt to emulate the consumption patterns of the West. That is, the cultural hegemony of the West now substitutes for the cultural dominance of Veblen's nineteenth century leisure class. Status in the global community is increasingly linked to the ability to successfully emulate the West.

Western cultural hegemony can be traced to colonial rule when 85 percent of the world had been colonized by the West (Goldsmith 1996, p. 257). Economic globalization has exacerbated rather than alleviated the hierarchical relationships of the colonial era. As a result of the 1980s debt crisis, many 'underdeveloped' countries have been re-subordinated by western banks via structural adjustment programs. Loans from the International Monetary Fund are granted to debtor countries which have agreed to dismantle their social and economic structures, and redesign them according to an imposed free market or free trade ideology. Likewise, as a result of the GATT Uruguay Round Agreement, 'underdeveloped' countries will lose further control over their economies to western interests. Control over manufacturing and agriculture has already been lost to transnational corporations, either through investments or dependence upon global product markets. Under GATT, they are positioned to lose control over their service industries such as banking, insurance, information, communication, the media, law, medicine, tourism, accounting, and advertising. Under GATT, transnationals are not only given the freedom to trade and invest in 'underdeveloped' countries, they also benefit from what is called 'national treatment'; that is, they must be treated the same as national or local companies. Moreover, host governments must allow equal treatment of foreign and domestic companies in the provisioning of public goods and services (Khor 1996, pp. 55–56). The implications for 'underdeveloped' countries are obvious. Transnationals have the power to gain full control over local banks and other businesses. This suggests that the balance of world power is firmly held by western political elites and the corporate interests they represent (Clarke 1996).

This imposed hierarchical relationship is exemplified in the classification system used in development theory to characterize the various economies of the world. Countries are typically classified as either developed, developing, or underdeveloped. Each term represents a different level of status in the global hierarchy. The highest status is accorded to 'developed' nations such as the United States, Canada and western Europe, among others. These countries are considered superior and dominant in every way — technologically, economically, culturally and militarily. Consequently, they set the standards and norms by which all other countries are judged backward, inferior, different, deviant or subordinate. Development theory, like Social Darwinism in the nineteenth century, serves as a convenient cultural myth legitimating the hierarchical global order and subservience to western interests.

Because of the global reach of capitalism, even those unfamiliar with development theory are acutely aware of western superiority. For instance, more than 75 percent of the world's population now have access to daily television reception via satellite (Mander 1996a, p. 350), and 99 percent of the 4000 films shown on Brazilian television are produced in the West (Barnet and Cavanagh 1996, p. 77). People in remote parts of the world are watching old television shows like Mr Ed, Dallas, or L.A. Law, and movies like Rambo or Pretty Woman. The youth of the world are watching MTV, Nickelodeon, and other cable networks, and listening to commercially produced popular music, all of which peddle western goods and vicarious experiences. Indeed, the American music industry, Hollywood film studios and global advertising agencies have become the most powerful and influential teachers of the next generation. In this way, the superiority of western culture and pecuniary values is reinforced through the gospel of consumerism and western imagery produced by western corporate interests. Emulation of the West is most advanced in the newly industrializing countries (NICs) of Asia. These nations are able to demonstrate their pecuniary prowess in the most conspicuous and wasteful ways. The process of emulation in 'underdeveloped' countries, however, is restricted by the inability to pay for western goods. This is consistent with Veblen's observation that each layer in the social hierarchy is governed by different norms of consumption depending on the 'ability to pay.' It also reflects the varying degrees of ease with which different habits of thought are formed or given up. Countries which are more socially removed from the West are slower at adopting western values and attitudes. In the following sections, I discuss the various forms that emulation has taken in 'developing' and 'underdeveloped' countries. First, I focus on 'micro-emulation'; emulation at the individual level. Then, I discuss 'macro-emulation'; emulation between countries.

4 MICRO-EMULATION UNDER GLOBAL CAPITALISM: THE CASE OF PRIVATE GOODS

Emulation by the 'new rich' in Asia takes the form of increasingly wasteful expenditures on western-style luxury and leisure goods. In Indonesia, residential estates complete with security guards and swimming pools are mushrooming around the capital, Jakarta (Robison 1996, p. 80). In Singapore, the proportion of spending on food has dropped while expenditures on leisure have increased. In 1991, for instance, Singaporeans took 1.6 million vacations abroad (Rodan 1996, p. 24). In Thailand, private motor vehicles have become increasingly common even in rural villages. By 1993, Thailand became the seventeenth largest automobile market in the world (Hewison 1996, p. 151). Expenditures on expensive consumer goods such as computers, air conditioners, refrigerators and mobile phones have also increased among Bangkok's population. Young people dress in the latest western fashions, eat at fast-food outlets, and listen to western music as a mark of social status. In Taiwan, the desire to have a European-made car and European-designed clothes reflects a cultural preference for western standards of taste (Chu 1996, p. 214). As one author explains, 'the prime difference that distinguishes [the new rich in Taiwan] from their predecessors is that their aim is not so much to accumulate wealth for investing in business but to purchase goods associated with western middle-class lifestyles' (Chu 1996, p. 215). Emulation of the West is no less pronounced lower down on the Asian social ladder. In fact, a class composed of the 'not quite there's' (NQTs) has been identified by market researchers in Malaysia. 'The NQTs have a lower average income than the Upper Echelons. They appear to be halfway up the ladder of success but, as the name suggests, they are not quite there. This group is particularly introverted, spending-oriented, neurotic, unadventurous, traditional and lacking in confidence, (Kahn 1996, p. 67).

Throughout Asia, the popular insistence on conformity to western standards and consumer culture is evident in the proliferation of department stores, shopping malls, fast-food outlets and convenience stores such as 7–Eleven, all of which replace local markets and street-stalls. As Asian analysts have observed:

> The vibrant economic growth has brought this (region) to a new level of affluence and with it a degree of westernization. Now it looks good and feels good to live and consume with style — the western style. The era of mass consumerism is upon us. The globalization of consumerism transcends cultural differences and leaves the value of restraint as expounded by Buddhism a relic of the past. Consumerism puts the whole show on stage (Hewison 1996, p. 149).

In poorer countries, what the West exports is the taste for western lifestyles, not the lifestyle itself. The case of the Ladakhis people serves as one example. For over 2000 years they have survived and prospered on the wild and inhospitable Tibetan Plateau without the assistance of the West. However, as a result of tourism, media images, western-style education, and other 'development' projects promoting progress and modernity, their ancient culture is rapidly disintegrating. In the pressure to conform to the idealized images of the American dream, they have redefined their needs. In the desire to appear modern, they have rejected their own culture. Even their traditional foods are no longer a source of pride. Their self-respect and self-worth has been shaken, generating a greater demand for material status symbols. People wear wristwatches they cannot read or use. Women are more concerned with appearances than with their traditionally valued capabilities. A mutual intolerance between the young and old has emerged. In general, the Ladakhis feel ashamed about their traditional practices and increasingly depend on the West for food and other basic necessities (Norberg-Hodge 1996).

The story of the Ladakhis is repeated throughout the world wherever satellite communication technology is combined with a technical infrastructure to speed up the pace of 'development.' Most of this activity is funded by the World Bank and the International Monetary Fund together with agencies such as US AID, the Inter-American Bank, and the Asian-American Bank, all of which serve the interests of multinational corporations. Creating a global economy means transforming the vast majority of largely self-sufficient people living in 'underdeveloped' countries into consumers of western goods provided by transnational corporations. As the president of Nabisco Corporation explains, 'I am looking forward to the day when Arabs and Americans, Latins and Scandinavians will be munching Ritz crackers as enthusiastically as they already drink Coke or brush their teeth with Colgate (Mander 1996b, p. 321).

5 MICRO-EMULATION UNDER GLOBAL CAPITALISM: THE CASE OF GOVERNMENT-PROVIDED GOODS

Emulation not only takes place at an individual level, but at the level of the nation-state. At this level, the mark of pecuniary strength and superior status is the ability to put government-provided or publically-owned assets in evidence rather than private goods. Indeed, expenditures on skyscrapers, hydroelectric projects, militaries and other public assets serve an invidious purpose not unlike the fancy bred dogs, racehorses and high fashion, of which Veblen wrote. Government expenditures are obviously for display. They are incurred for the sake of a respectable appearance more so than for their serviceability. They bear the mark of reputability which follows from their expensiveness, adding an expression of invidious distinction. This explains why hydroelectric dams have replaced cultural artifacts such as cathedrals as major tour destinations in non-western countries, and why national parades celebrate military rather than cultural prowess. These practices reflect economic globalization and the primacy of pecuniary values under global capitalism.

The advantages of public assets as evidence of superior pecuniary status can be understood by turning our gaze once again towards Asia. The Petronas Twin Towers in Kuala Lumpur, Malaysia, set a new world height record for skyscrapers at 1,482 feet. This is significant because until recently skyscrapers have been considered a particularly American genre, sprouting up in major cities like New York and Chicago. Today, most of the tallest buildings in the world are being proposed and built in locations such as Taiwan, Hong Kong, Shanghai and in other Asian cities, where government image-building and the desire to showcase surging economic growth are propelling the boom in 'ego towers.' This reflects the increased ability of the NICs to pay for architectural extravagance and to engage in conspicuously wasteful consumption — the mark of superior status in the global community. At $800 million, the Petronas Towers have become the symbol of Malaysian national prestige and status attainment. As Prime Minister Dr Mahathir bin Mohammed stated in 1992, 'this uniquely Malaysian project is consistent with the government's objective to transform Malaysia into a developed nation by the year 2020, and it will definitely put Kuala Lumpur on the map' (Bergsman 1996).

Other efforts to put Kuala Lumpur on the map include the Kuala Lumpur City Center (KLCC), which is described as the largest single urban construction project in the world. When completed, KLCC will include a 50-acre landscaped park and lake, 1.5 million square feet of shops, an 850-seat concert hall, a 13-screen movie theater, a mosque that will hold 6,000 people, a hotel, office buildings, a convention center, a civic center, and a plant for cooling the entire complex (Bergsman 1996; Petroski 1996, p. 323).

Another mega project is the $2 billion, 8.08 million square foot Kuala Lumpur Linear City (KLLC), which at 7.4 miles will be the longest, multi-use complex in the world. The centerpiece of KLLC is Giga World, a 1.5 mile, 14-story tube-like structure that will follow the Klang River. It will house retail malls, four 30-story office towers, four 30-story residential/hotel towers, a landscaped park on the roof, and a man-made indoor river that extends along the entire length of the building. Visitors will cruise in electric-powered flat-bottomed boats past landscaped terraces, shops and restaurants housed in historical structures that recall the riverside cities of Paris, London, Venice, and Amsterdam (Kai-sun Chia 1997; Pura 1996). As one Malaysian executive explains, 'this will be the happiest place in Asia. Someday, someone may beat the Kuala Lumpur City Center, but no one will beat the longest building in the world' (Pura 1996).

By building the tallest and the longest, Malaysia has begun to assert itself as a foremost pecuniary society in the image of the West. State officials have been more interested in transforming Kuala Lumpur into an international financial center than in developing a manufacturing base. While the state has tried to make Malaysia a desirable place for foreign investment, transnationals have been allowed to determine the nature and progress of industrialization (Jomo 1994). The objective is to attract information technology firms to the new high-tech center of Cyberjaya, freight traffic to the new port near Malacca, and tourists to their new airport, sports complex, race track, concert halls, shopping malls and high-rise hotels. All of these mega projects serve a higher need to live up to the standards of taste and reputability of the West, while simultaneously demonstrating to the world the 'ability to pay' for the best, including American architects, engineers and technocrats.

Of course, Malaysia faces fierce competition from other NICs in the pursuit of global esteem. In the case of skyscrapers, each new record set by the 'erection index' is short-lived (*The Economist* 1996). When the Shanghai World Financial Center is completed, it will surpass the 88-story Petronas Twin Towers at 1,509 feet (Pacelle 1996, p. 1). In Bangkok, the Baiyoke Tower II with 89 stories is now the highest hotel in the world (Reina 1996, 14). As an American architect explains, 'many Asian countries see the tall building as a device to move them quickly into the twenty-first century, to catch up quickly. These guys really want cutting-edge modern design, things that people have not seen before. They want to be in the top echelon of global players (Pacelle 1996, p. 2).

Like skyscrapers, hydroelectric projects are symbolic of western technology and progress, and thereby serve an invidious global purpose. With dam building virtually over in the United States and other industrialized countries, transnationals with the aid of western governments, the World Bank and other multilateral finance institutions are targeting industrializing countries for new business opportunities. Hydroelectric projects can generate huge profits for transnationals who win contract bids to build them. And although they often leave the host country indebted, hydroelectric projects serve as evidence of superior pecuniary status. As many as 843 large dams are under construction around the world — 430 of them in Asia (Lachica 1996).

China, for instance, has joined the race to the top of the global status heap with its proposal to build the world's largest dam on the world's third largest river, the Yangtze. At an estimated cost of $100 billion the Three Gorges Dam is the most expensive project ever undertaken. When completed it will stand at 607 feet high and 1.2 miles wide with a generation capacity of over 18,000 megawatts. The reservoir behind the dam will equal the length of Lake Superior and cover over 621 square miles (Sullivan 1995, p. 266). As one author observed, 'the dam represents yet another attempt by China to rapidly catch up with developed nations through a single grand project — as occurred during the Great Leap Forward of the late 1950s and early 60s — instead of long-range sustainable planning' (Edmonds 1992).

China's prime minister, Li Peng, put it this way, 'The Three Gorges will show the rest of the world that the Chinese people have high aspirations and the capabilities to successfully build the world's largest water conservancy and hydroelectric power project' (Sullivan 1995, p. 269).

In India, pecuniary prowess is equally evident. The $1.6 billion Sardar Sarovar hydroelectric project in Gujarat will reach a height of 470 feet and flood nearly 150 square miles of land, and the 281-mile main canal connected to the dam will rank among the world's largest water supply. The entire project along the Narmada River will eventually include another superdam in the neighboring state of Madhya Pradesh, 30 additional large dams, 150 medium-sized dams, and 3000 smaller dams, dikes, and irrigation schemes, making it one of the most ambitious power projects and irrigation systems in the world (Fineman 1990, pp. 118–119, 122, 126).

Not to be outdone by its Chinese and Indian neighbors, Malaysia is building the largest hydroelectric dam in Southeast Asia on the Bakun River. The $6.2 billion Bakun Dam will reach 60 stories and its reservoir will flood 170,000 acres in the center of Borneo's tropical rain forest (Lachica 1996; Schulz 1997, p. 8). Prime Minister Mahathir Mohamad confronting critics of the dam has claimed that 'Malaysia wants to develop, and I say to the so-called environmentalists, "mind your own business"' (Schulz 1997, p. 9).

There are numerous types of public assets which are symbolic of pecuniary status in the global community. Military aircraft, nuclear bombs and other items of warfare quickly come to mind. I will explore the tension between the instrumental and ceremonial aspects of skyscrapers and hydroelectric projects. Not surprisingly, I find that ceremonial values tend to dominate under global capitalism.

6   THE INSTRUMENTAL AND CEREMONIAL
FEATURES OF GOVERNMENT-PROVIDED GOODS

As Veblen observed, consumer goods, even the highly honorific ones, have both instrumental and ceremonial features. He argued that although ceremonial or wasteful elements tend to predominate in consumer goods, traces of conspicuous waste are equally evident in producer goods (Veblen 1987[1899], p. 100). However, it is beyond the scope of this chapter to discuss them all. Again, Kuala Lumpur provides a fine example. The construction boom has the potential to serve the useful and productive purpose of improving infrastructure and attracting investment to Malaysia. However, the ceremonial aspects of downtown development often overshadow its serviceability. Clearly, building the tallest flagpole in the world is ceremonial (Jayasankaran 1995a, p. 36). Certainly lengthening the spires at the top of the Petronas Twin Towers to 20 feet, to surpass the height of the Sears Tower in Chicago, also serves a ceremonial purpose (Pacelle 1996, p. 1). Likewise, as one of the world's tallest structures, the $110 million Kuala Lumpur Tower suggests the dominance of ceremonial values. As one executive admits, 'a smaller tower on one of the hills outside Kuala Lumpur would have done just as well. It would have certainly cost much less' (Jayasankaran 1995a, p. 36). Indeed, Christopher Boyd, a local developer, points directly to the ceremonial features of Kuala Lumpur's skyline when he observes that, 'it's wonderfully diverse, but I'd suspect that many of our buildings are constructed more for outward appearances than any efficiency of design' (Jayasankaran 1995a, p. 36). In other words, these towers are coveted because they demonstrate the ability to engage in superfluous, wasteful spending. As symbols of worth, they allow Kuala Lumpur to strut its new wealth. Their architectural beauty derives from their expensiveness and uniqueness, not from their serviceability and efficiency. In addition, Kuala Lumpur's construction boom has raised efficiency concerns. Because of heavy government subsidies, real estate investment offers high rates of return to investors. As a result, some predict a massive office glut (Jayasankaran 1995b). This prediction was supported when Petronas, the national oil company, announced it would move into the Twin Towers to assure it has tenants (*The Economist* 1995). Compounding the potential overproduction of office space is the plan to move all the state agencies to the new M$20 billion administrative capital of Putrajaya (Jayasankaran 1995a, p. 37). In the meantime, working-class neighborhoods in the Peel-Cochran area of downtown are being 'redeveloped' to make room for a $3.3 billion Super-Vision City which will double the city's 5.5 million square feet of office space. To deal with the problem of displaced civil servants and workers, private developers have proposed building houses or apartments in return for government land (Jayasankaran 1997).

Overproduction not only serves the purpose of invidious distinction, it also supports a predatory class of politicians, private developers, engineers, and other foreign and domestic elites who benefit financially from wasteful public expenditures at the expense of working people and the environment. In the effort to make Kuala Lumpur a world-class tourist destination and financial capital, working-class neighborhoods are being destroyed and the ecosystem of the Klang River is severely threatened. But in a country where political elites and developers are one and the same, the voices of workers and environmentalists are often ignored. Profits and image are more important than protecting natural and human resources. Indeed, the main goal of political elites is to make Kuala Lumpur 'an urban icon of the twenty-first century' (Kai-sun Chia 1997).

Likewise, hydroelectric projects can demonstrate the instrumental and ceremonial features of 'development.' From an environmental perspective, they represent a positive alternative to coal-fired power, allowing the government to reduce its emissions of carbon dioxide and other greenhouse gases. Clearly, this contributes to the furtherance of human life. Indeed, advocates of hydroelectric power can point to many instrumental features. The Chinese, for instance, argue that the Three Gorges Dam will improve navigation, increase regional development, generate electric power for the surrounding communities and protect the middle and lower reaches of the Yangtze River from devastating floods (Sullivan 1995, p. 266). Similar claims have been made by the proponents of the proposed Usumacinta River Dam on the border between Mexico and Guatemala. For the first time, both industrial and private users in surrounding areas and distant cities will benefit from electric light and water for irrigation (Fagan 1992, p. 76).

The instrumental value of hydroelectric projects around the world is their capacity to generate huge amounts of energy required by modern industrial plants and infrastructure. It is also difficult to argue against irrigation and flood control. Successful societies must find ways of producing energy and improving agriculture, or perish. Unfortunately, mega projects rarely accomplish either goal as efficiently as a series of smaller, less costly dams could, and they often create more problems than they solve. Reservoir siltation, loss of silt and fertility downstream, destruction of wildlife, flooding of agricultural land and forests, soil erosion, massive landslides, deforestation and mass population displacement are a few of the well publicized drawbacks. Less well known are the potential threats to the structure itself. In 1975, for instance, 200,000 Chinese died in Henan province when the dam collapsed due to lack of quality control in the construction industry (Sullivan 1995, p. 267). The Three Gorges Dam is even more precarious. The dam site is riddled with fault lines and located near the huge, unstable, Huangla rock formation capable of triggering massive landslides. But the scientific and environmental communities that propose alternative, more efficient projects are often silenced or ignored by political elites who are focused on catching up with the West irrespective of the economic or human costs of the project (Sullivan 1995, pp. 267–268; Gwynne and Li 1992). As Jan Veltrop, a dam builder for 37 years with Chicago's Harza Engineering Company, explains, 'water is essential, power is needed, flood control is beneficial, and therefore, dams are indispensable. Nature can't be preserved in an altered state' (Lachica 1996).

Apparently, people and their traditional livelihoods cannot be preserved either. One of the most extravagant displays of conspicuous waste is the massive population displacements that accompany dam construction. For instance, the reservoir behind China's Three Gorges Dam will raise water levels to 574 feet above its current level, submerging 13 cities, 140 towns, 1352 villages, 1600 factories and 8000 sites of historical, archeological, paleontological and biological interest. Nearly 1.5 million people will be relocated, making it the largest resettlement program ever for a civil-engineering project (Sullivan 1995, pp. 266–267; Childs-Johnson, *et al.* 1996, p. 39). Likewise, in India, the Narmada River project will flood out 245 villages and displace 1.2 million people (Fineman 1990, p. 130; Chatterjee 1994, p. 20).

Approximately 10 million people have been displaced by hydroelectric dams constructed under the direction of the World Bank, but massive dislocations are rarely a concern for World Bank employees (Jeffrey 1996). An American engineer with the World Bank put it best when he praised the Sardar Sarovar Project in India, 'here they are, flooding 150 square miles, and you only have to remove some 40,000 people. We're lucky it's not 400,000 people. From this perspective, it's a pretty darn good reservoir site' (Fineman 1990, p. 123). Of course, from another perspective, 40,000 people are forced to make major life changes because they have lost their homeland. In another report, the World Bank again cheerfully claims that 'China has had a remarkable satisfactory resettlement performance during the 1980s and 1990s' (Becker 1997, p. 8). The term 'resettlement' implies compensation and government assistance. Since most people end up fending for themselves, this claim ignores the reality of people's daily lives. For instance, the dam on the Xinfeng River in China forced 100,000 peasants from their homelands. Forty years later the displaced population has doubled and many still live in poverty (Becker 1997, p. 7). Likewise, the Bakun Dam forced indigenous groups in east Malaysia to resettle in Belaga where they were housed in apartments, and forced to work on plantations as coolies for subsistence wages (Schulz 1997, p. 9). The list goes on and on. Government compensation remains a paper fiction, and resettlement land when it is awarded is not always of the best quality or suitable for farming. As an Indian farmer displaced by the Sardar Sarovar Project observes, 'it is the land that makes us so sad. We live, after all, not for luxury. We live for the land. And half the land the government gave us is full of rocks' (Fineman 1990, p. 127).

Displacement not only changes people's location, but their traditional way of life. Dams may offer protection from floods, but they often rob millions of down streamers of their traditional livelihoods. The Kainji Dam on the Niger River reduced rice production downstream by 18 percent and the fish catch by 70 percent. Likewise, the downstream villagers of the Bakolori Dam on a tributary of the Niger experienced serious crop, fish and livestock reductions (*World Press Review* 1997, p. 7). In Java, the Kedung Ombo project forced rice farmers to live in the forest without compensation. In Sarawak, indigenous cultures based on farming, fishing, rain forest hunting and gathering are being destroyed by the Bakun River Dam (Schulz 1997, p. 9). Likewise, the Great Whale project in Canada threatens the traditional fishing, hunting, and trapping culture of the Cree on James Bay and the fishing culture of the Belcher Island Inuit (Jenish 1990, p. 81; Fenge 1992, p. 48). In Thailand, the recently completed $231 million Pak Mun Dam has devastated the fish population in the large tributary of the Mekong River. Downstream villagers who depended on fishing have consequently migrated to Bangkok to find work, leaving the village half empty and families broken up (Sherer 1996). Rather than raising the standard of living of indigenous groups and rural farmers as promised, hydroelectric projects have had the opposite effect. As a Witness for Peace report claims, 'bank loans have not reduced poverty, but they rather have impoverished the very men and women that this development institution should benefit' (Jeffrey 1996).

Conspicuous waste is also evident in the ecological destruction in countries attempting to 'catch up' with the West. In China, for instance, the Three Gorges Project Development Corporation has authority over the construction of the dam as well as the environmental protection work. This does not bode well for the Yangtze sturgeon and alligator, the freshwater finless dolphin, the cloud leopard and the Siberian white crane, all on the endangered species list (Sullivan 1995, p. 267). Forty-seven species of rare plants and trees are also endangered, including the lotus leaf maidenhair fern used in Chinese herbal medicine to treat kidney stones (Hoh 1996, p. 33). In Guatemala, the Chixoy River basin is almost entirely deforested and silted up. Sedimentation has shortened the dam's effective life to 20 years from the projected 200 (Jeffrey 1996). In Malaysia, the Bakun Dam will raise dammed rivers to new heights, allowing loggers to access Sarawak's previously inaccessible tropical rain forests (Schulz 1997, p. 9). In Canada, the creation of reservoirs by the Great Whale project has released mercury into the water, killing fish and endangering the survival of migratory birds (Schulze 1989). In Mexico, the proposed Usumacinta Dam will flood what remains of Guatemala's Maya Biosphere Reserve and Mexico's Lacondon tropical rain forest, and destroy the river's fish and crocodile populations (Perera 1992, p. 509). The list of ecological disasters associated with large dams is endless.

Conspicuous waste is also evident in the destruction of historical sites of cultural value. In Central America, the Usumacinta project will submerge two unexcavated Mayan civilizations, Piedras Negras and Yaxchilan, together with dozens of towns and unexplored Maya villages (Fagan 1992, p. 22). In India, the eighteenth century temple of Ahilya Bai will be submerged with the completion of the Narmada River valley project (Fineman 1990, p. 133). In China, the three scenic gorges which have inspired Chinese poets and painters for over two millennia will soon disappear, destroying evidence of human habitation in the valley dating as early as the Paleolithic period. The money for rescuing archaeological sites has not materialized and excavations have grounded to a halt. But the Chinese government found the money to set up giant illuminated billboards in Xiling Gorge to advertise China's growing alcoholic beverage industry (Sullivan 1995, p. 266).

Like the building boom in Southeast Asia, hydroelectric projects in non-western countries are rarely justified on efficiency grounds. Observed or predicted inefficiencies are well-documented. For instance, Guatemala's $2.5 billion Chixoy project is a notorious disaster. Today only 30 percent of Guatemalans have electrical service and hook up rates are the most expensive in the region. And because of its shabby construction, its tunnel has to be reinforced every two years to keep it from collapsing. This has forced the World Bank to admit that 'The Chixoy project has proved to be an unwise and uneconomic investment' (Jeffrey 1996; Perera 1992, p. 509). But while some projects are not able to supply enough electricity, other projects are guilty of overproduction. For example, the final plan for the Usumacinta River project predicts production of electricity 'greatly exceeding Guatemala's current and future needs' (Fagan 1992, p. 21). Clearly, efficiency considerations are not at the top of the agenda of hydroelectric planning schemes. So what is?

Veblen's insights about the predatory leisure class are again instructive. The benefits accrue largely to a set of corrupt bureaucrats, business interests and members of the professional classes in both western and non-western countries. US companies, for instance, won $2.7 billion in World Bank contracts in 1993, and this is considered a low estimate. Consultants hired by the World Bank to discredit independent studies which condemn projects for lack of environmental assessments and resettlement plans pocketed more than $35 million (Chatterjee 1994, p. 20). On the local level, developers and government officials make millions from the logging spoils, dam construction, kickbacks and bribes, among other things (Schulz 1997; Jeffrey 1996).

Meanwhile, opposition movements are crushed and civilians are silenced and sometimes massacred. In China, a book criticizing the Three Gorges project has been banned and opponents have been charged with contributing to 'creating the atmosphere of public opinion that led to the turmoil and riots of 1989!' (Qing 1993, p. 277). As Dai Qing, a Chinese activist, argues:

If the dam is such a fantastic idea, a unique feat of engineering, as is claimed, then why in Heaven's name is the government unwilling to allow a public debate on the subject in China? If not a public debate, then why can't scientists and specialists discuss the pros and cons of the project? (Qing 1993, p. 277).

In Guatemala, hundreds were killed with the complicity of the World
Bank because the 400 year-old settlements on the Chixoy River blocked
'progress.' Corrupt generals and politicians wanted to eliminate the people
of Rio Negro, in order to quiet vocal opposition to the dam, and to avoid
paying communities' resettlement costs. World Bank personnel supervised
the site between 1979 and 1991 when the killings occurred, but there is no
mention of the massacres in its reports on the dam (Jeffrey 1996). From
these accounts and others, it is evident that global capitalism is a breeding
ground for exploitative and predatory instincts that result in economic
waste and inequality, environmental devastation and sometimes genocide.
As Baba Amte, a 77 year old Indian anti-dam activist argues, 'in this
country, they're using dams to store the water to power skyscrapers, the
five-star hotels, and the factories that are polluting our fields, and they
don't even see that, under their noses, the common people continue to
starve and to thirst' (Fineman 1990, p. 132).

CONCLUSION

Veblen's observation that, 'it is much more difficult to recede from a scale
of expenditure once adopted than it is to extend the accustomed scale in
response to an accession of wealth' (Veblen 1987[1899], p. 102) contains a
powerful message for our generation and beyond. Status attainment in the
global community will require ever greater levels of conspicuously
wasteful expenditures. In an effort to 'catch up' with the West, Asian
countries are prepared to spend what it takes. The Asian construction
market alone will approach $900 billion annually within the next 10 years
(Reina 1995, p. 10). In addition, high economic growth rates have raised
the expectations of government elites about 'surpassing' the West. For
instance, in his Vision 1999 statement, the Deputy Prime Minister of
Singapore, Goh Chok Tong, set the goal of surpassing the 1984 Swiss
standard of living before 2000, and more recently, the Strategic Economic
Plan sets a goal of 'catching up on a moving target basis with American
standards by the year 2030' (Rodan 1996, pp. 22–23). If Veblen was
correct, western countries will be forced to increase their consumption
levels to maintain status differentials, which in turn will raise the
consumption standards for 'developing' and 'underdeveloped' countries.

   This global path of pecuniary emulation is clearly unsustainable. The
implications of expanding conspicuous consumption in the form of private
status goods such as infant formula, automobiles and televisions is one
thing. The implications of expanding conspicuously wasteful consumption

in the form of government-sponsored mega projects is quite another. Will instrumental values, as Veblen suggested, be reasserted to ensure the survival of the human species? Will the instinct of workmanship, parental bent and idle curiosity triumph over pecuniary values predicated on ceremony, superstition and blind faith? If Veblen was correct in his predictions, men and women will ultimately reject the present global order in favor of an alternative order that maximizes the collective well-being of the global community. As we enter the twenty-first century, there is some support for Veblen's prediction, but it is not overwhelming (Mander and Goldsmith 1996).

REFERENCES

Barnet R. and J. Cavanagh (1996), 'Homogenization of Global Culture', in *The Case Against the Global Economy and For a Turn Toward the Local,* edited by J. Mander and E. Goldsmith, San Francisco: Sierra Club Books.
Becker, J. (1997), 'The Human Debris of China's Mega-Dams: Relocation's Lingering Effects', *World Press Review,* **44**, 8, August, 7.
Bergsman, S. (1996), 'Thriving Malaysia Propels an Office-Tower Boom In Its Biggest City, and You Know What Follows a Boom', *Barron's,* **76**, 33, August 12, 32.
Chatterjee, Pratap (1994), 'Slush Funds, Corrupt Consultants and Bidding for Bank Business', *Multinational Monitor,* **15**, 7–8, July/August, 17–20.
Childs-Johnson, E., J.L. Cohen, and L.R. Sullivan (1996), 'Race Against Time', *Archaeology,* **49**, 6, November/December, 39–43.
Chu, J.J. (1996), 'Taiwan: A Fragmented "Middle" Class in the Making', in *The New Rich in Asia: Mobile Phones, McDonald's and Middle-Class Revolution,* edited by R. Robison and D.S.G. Goodman, London: Routledge.
Clarke, Tony (1996), 'Mechanisms of Corporate Rule', in *The Case Against the Global Economy and For a Turn Toward the Local,* edited by J. Mander and E. Goldsmith, San Francisco: Sierra Club Books, 1996.
Edmonds, R.L. (1992), 'Against the Flow', *Far Eastern Economic Review,* **155**, 20, May 21, 24.
Fagan, B. (1992), 'Flooding the Maya Heartland', *Archaeology,* **45**, 5, September, 20–22, 76.
Fenge, T. (1992), 'Damning a People? The Great Whale Project and Inuit of the Belcher Islands', *Alternatives,* **19**, 1, September, 48–49.
Fineman, M. (1990), 'A Scheme to Harness India's Sacred Waters Brings Tempers to a Boil', *Smithsonian,* **21**, 8, November, 118–133.
Goldsmith, E. (1996), 'Development as Colonialism', in *The Case Against the Global Economy and For a Turn Toward the Local,* edited by J. Mander and E. Goldsmith, San Francisco: Sierra Club Books.

Gwynne, P. and Y.Q. Li (1992), 'Yangtze Project Dammed With Faint Praise', *Nature,* **356**, 6372, April 30, 736.

Hewison, K. (1996), 'Emerging Social Forces in Thailand: New Political and Economic Roles', in *The New Rich in Asia: Mobile Phones, McDonald's and Middle-Class Revolution,* edited by R. Robison and D.S.G. Goodman, London: Routledge .

Hoh, Erling (1996), 'The Long River's Journey Ends: China's Three Gorges Dam Will Soon Transform the Yangtze', *Natural History,* **105**, 7, July, 28–39.

Jayasankaran, S. (1995a), 'Towers of Pride: The Sky's No Limit in Affluent Kuala Lumpur', *Far Eastern Economic Review,* **158**, 31, August 3, 36–37.

Jayasankaran, S. (1995b), 'Heat Stroke?' *Far Eastern Economic Review,* **158**, 33, August 17, 69.

Jayasankaran, S. (1997), 'Big Fish, Big Pond: Malaysian Land Deal Boasts Some Powerful Partners', *Far Eastern Economic Review,* **160**, 13, March 27, 62.

Jeffrey, P. (1996), 'The World Bank, a Giant Dam and a Massacre', *National Catholic Reporter,* **32**, 26, April, 8.

Jenish, D. (1990), 'Disputed Impacts: A New Controversy over James Bay II', *Maclean's,* **103**, 49, December 3, 81–82.

Jomo, K.S. (1994), *U-Turn? Malaysian Economic Development Policy After 1990,* Australia: James Cook University of North Queensland.

Kahn, Joel S. (1996), 'Growth, Economic Transformation, Culture and the Middle Classes in Malaysia', in *The New Rich in Asia: Mobile Phones, McDonald's and Middle-Class Revolution,* edited by R. Robison and D.S.G. Goodman. London: Routledge.

Kai-sun Chia, K. (1997), 'A New Record for Kuala Lumpur? The World's Longest Complex', *Architectural Record,* **2**, February, 30.

Khor, Martin (1996), 'Global Economy and the Third World', in *The Case Against the Global Economy and For a Turn Toward the Local,* edited by J. Mander and E. Goldsmith, San Francisco: Sierra Club Books.

Lachica, Eduardo (1996), 'US Loses Enthusiasm for Dam Projects: Asian Countries Encouraged to Find Alternatives', *The Wall Street Journal,* A1, March 12, 15.

Mander, J. (1996a), 'Technologies of Globalization', in *The Case Against the Global Economy and For a Turn Toward the Local,* edited by J. Mander and E. Goldsmith, San Francisco: Sierra Club Books.

Mander, J. (1996b), 'The Rules of Corporate Behavior', in *The Case Against the Global Economy and For a Turn Toward the Local,* edited by J. Mander and E. Goldsmith, San Francisco: Sierra Club Books.

Mander, J. and E. Goldsmith (eds)(1996), *The Case Against the Global Economy and a Turn Toward the Local,* San Francisco: Sierra Club Books.

Norberg-Hodge, Helena (1996), 'The Pressure to Modernize and Globalize', in *The Case Against the Global Economy and For a Turn Toward the Local,* edited by J. Mander and E. Goldsmith, San Francisco: Sierra Club Books.

Pacelle, M. (1996), 'US Architects in Asia: Only Way to Go Is Up', *The Wall Street Journal,* B3, March 20, 1–2.

Perera, V. (1992), 'Damming Ecology', *The Nation,* **254**, 15, April 20, 508–509.

Petroski, H. (1996), 'The Petronas Twin Towers', *American Scientist*, **84**, 4, July, 322–326.

Pura, R. (1996), 'Will This Great Mall Top China's Wall?', *The Wall Street Journal*, A1, July 11, 12.

Qing, D. (1993) 'The Three Gorges Dam Project and Free Speech in China', *Chicago Review*, **39**, 3–4, 275–278.

Reina, P. (1995), 'No End to Asia's High-Rise Binge', *Engineering News Record*, **234**, May 29, 10.

Reina, P. (1996), 'Bangkok Hotel Setting More Than One Record', *Engineering News Record*, **236**, June 3, 14–15.

Robison, R. (1996) 'The Middle Class and the Bourgeoisie in Indonesia', in *The New Rich in Asia: Mobile Phones, McDonald's and Middle-Class Revolution*, edited by R. Robison and D.S.G. Goodman, London: Routledge.

Rodan, G. (1996), 'Class Transformations and Political Tensions in Singapore's Development', in *The New Rich in Asia: Mobile Phones, McDonald's and Middle-Class Revolution*, edited by R. Robison and D.S.G. Goodman, London: Routledge.

Schulz, D. (1997), 'An Unholy Alliance in East Malaysia: Linking Dams and Logging', *World Press Review*, **44**, 8, August, 8–9.

Schulze, D. (1989), 'Canadian Utility Threatens Cree', *The Progressive*, **53**, 10, October 1, 18.

Sherer, P.M. (1996), 'Thai Villages Fish for Answers to Woes from Dam', *The Wall Street Journal*, A2, March 12, 15.

Sullivan, L.R. (1995), 'The Three Gorges Project: Dammed If They Do?', *Current History*, **94**, 593, September, 266–269.

The Economist (1995), 'Malaysia's Edifice Complex', **336**, 7930, September 2, 34.

The Economist (1996), 'The Erection Index', **339**, 7965, May 11, 69.

Veblen, Thorstein (1987[1899]), *The Theory of the Leisure Class*, New York: Penguin Books.

World Press Review (1997), 'Dammed if You Do', **44**, 8, August, 6–7.

Conclusion

Doug Brown

In *The Theory of the Leisure Class* Veblen stated at one point that capitalism is the 'regime of status.' One thing that should be clear after reading the chapters in this volume is that 100 years later capitalism is still a 'regime of status.' In terms of its relevance for the next century we have yet to work out all of the implications of this characterization. Marx predicted that capitalism would dig its own grave and that the laws of motion of capitalist society would operate in such a way as to bring about both the end of capitalism and a better society to replace it. Veblen was skeptical of this. Although Marx may yet be proven correct, Veblen's evolutionary approach seems more applicable.

Marx was no doubt more ambitious than Veblen in his efforts to project the future and develop a broad theory to explain social change. Marx tried to do more, but possibly as a result, at least some of his ideas have become irrelevant. Now we have the emergence in academic circles of 'post-Marxism,' and this comes on the heels of 'neo-Marxism' as well. With Veblen, although his name is less well known, we have yet to hear about neo- or post-Veblenian views. This suggests to me that starting with *Leisure Class* Veblen has set out to do less than Marx and as a result has had less of his thought judged irrelevant.

One observation about Marx and Veblen that originates with *Leisure Class* is that Veblen seemed to be more concerned with *why* capitalists want to make as much profit as possible. Marx tended to take this for granted for the most part. Marx spent little time trying to analyse the reasons why the business class wanted more and more money. In one respect it can be assumed that with more money and wealth life becomes easier to live, with more comforts, greater ability to experience immediate gratification and instant satisfaction of desires and urges. If this is true of human nature as I think Marx figured it was, then there is little to consider in the question of *why* get rich.

But one unique feature of *The Theory of the Leisure Class* is that Veblen obviously does not take the question of *why* for granted. In fact there is nothing in *Leisure Class* that suggests that Veblen assumed an insatiable human nature. Marx seems to believe that people do have insatiable natures. In fact, it is Marx that embraced the value principle and social imperative of 'the full and free development of the individual.' What Marx condemned about capitalism is that the system of unequal relations allowed those with money and wealth to actualize and realize their self-development at the expense of the exploited working class. Marx was clearly a productivist who would surely today subscribe to the imperative of 'be all you can be.' For him the problem of capitalism was that it did not allow for an equal access to the means for each and every person to realize his or her full potential. Marx had a notion of human insatiability that Veblen, if he had to recognize it at all, would say is culturally-induced and evolutionary in character. So it makes sense that Marx might overlook the reason for why capitalists want to get ever richer.

But Veblen observed that what drives capitalists and those that want to emulate them is important to diagnose and examine. *Leisure Class* suggests that everyone is in a manic race to get rich in order to be one up on their fellows. We want to accumulate as much as possible because that is how we achieve status, social esteem and respect from those around us. Wealth is merely a means to the achievement of a feeling of self-esteem. And our self-esteem, according to Veblen, is largely a function of what others think of us. Marx took the desire for wealth for granted and went on from there to extrapolate the social consequences of a system driven by such a motive. Veblen did not take this desire for granted. *The Theory of the Leisure Class* is a result.

Veblen's analysis leads to a topic for further study. If people want to get rich because this is how they get self-esteem, is it then still the case that our self-esteem is determined by how we measure up in the eyes of others? This continues to be an area of research and debate in psychology. There is evidence today that one's self-respect is not self-validated nor self-induced. We are social beings, as all current psychology points up. At least some part of our psyche is a function of what others think of us, unless we are all latent sociopaths. But this becomes an important question because if we are indeed a function of what others think of us, and if the need for self-esteem is essential for our social and psychic well-being, then it forces us to look at how the economy may feed into this. An economy driven by the insatiable need for status is likely to be proven unsustainable for the next century.

So there is actually another topic for further study that the relevance of *Leisure Class* suggests. If people need self-respect and if much of our self-respect is a function of others, then we need to find a way to obtain this without it being caught up in the 'regime of status.' The way it works now is that we have a global capitalism that is driven by the need to be 'better than others.' Our global economy is one based upon the desire to be 'one up' on one's peers. We have a system of production that is not driven by the need for basic provisions. It is driven by the need to demonstrate our worth and success through the conspicuous display of goods and wealth, by the invidious distinction we can achieve with our financial success and pecuniary prowess. People are driven to seek wealth and possessions using the capitalist wealth-producing machine in order to show that they are okay folks. To show that they are okay folks they feel they have to continually improve themselves so that they can prove they are actually 'better' than others. This irrational logic has not been so much of a concern when for the past 200 years there was an assumption that our global biosphere could sustain unlimited growth with an unlimited carrying capacity.

The logic of this is scary. What we are saying is that we have a system that is based upon the endless search for more wealth. We want more wealth because wealth has become *the* means to win the game of 'I am better than you.' We want to win this game because by winning it, we can achieve status. We need status because it is the means to achieving the respect of others. We need the respect of others because this is how we obtain our self-esteem. We need self-esteem because this is how our natures are built. And what good is an economy that does not facilitate one of life's essentials: self-esteem? This is all present in *The Theory of the Leisure Class*.

The logic of this is not only scary but an economy driven by it is not going to be sustainable in the next century. In my own mind the ultimate relevance of Veblen's analysis in *Leisure Class* is that we need to disconnect several links in the above logic. First we can admit, unless psychological research discovers otherwise, that people need self-respect to live well. It would seem that if sustainability is a value, it requires a humankind with self-respect. Second, we may be forced to admit also that much of our self-respect is going to come from what others think of us. This notion is also reconcilable with a sustainable economy.

But we need to disconnect some of the institutions of the capitalist economy from the endless quest for wealth. An economy whose primary function is to provide the goods and services that we can all agree are the necessities of life is an economy geared to sustainability. Veblen was aware of this too. It comes from his Norwegian agrarian upbringing: self-sufficiency and simplicity. Produce what you need and stop there. You can then be self-sustaining as a world and live a simpler life. We should take Veblen's Norwegian farm mentality and apply it to the global economy! More importantly we need to disconnect the endless search for wealth from the need for status based upon social 'one-upmanship.' But the most important disconnect is the one that links the game of 'I am better than you' to the achievement of self-esteem. We must find a more sustainable and less stressful way to obtain our self-worth than by allowing an economy to be used as a primary mechanism for demonstrating our status. A sustainable economy for the twenty-first century is one that is a means for meeting our agreed-upon material needs, not an economy that is used as a means in an insatiable and competitive struggle for status over others. If self-esteem has become culturally and exclusively a function of winning the status game, and the economy is the means for winning the game, then there is no end in sight. We are then doomed to insatiably produce in order to get ahead of others in order to feel okay about ourselves. This will not work.

So ultimately the question raised by *Leisure Class* that is most relevant for the next century is whether or not we as humans who are culturally evolving species are able to get off the production treadmill we have been using for obtaining our self-esteem. This is no doubt what Veblen was really getting at with his concept of waste. An economy used for a competitive game of self-esteem via status is a tragic waste of resources. Using our time, energy, and precious economic resources for the endless pursuit of status is irrational in a world we now understand to be full of limits.

As long as people are not aware of the fact that our economy is being driven by psychological motives that can be addressed in less wasteful ways, then *The Theory of the Leisure Class* will continue to be relevant and a good read. So little of what Veblen discusses in it seems dated. Given all of the product differentiation that the new high-tech capitalism is able to supply and to do so in a massified way, people the world over are drawn into the consumerist culture where they use the buying of products and services as a means to create their own individual identities. It is obviously very difficult to get much perspective once one is caught up in the process of identity formation using the consumerist paradigm. So it may well be that the only thing that will force the issue is the awareness that consumerism might well destroy our earthly habitat. This suggests that one constraint Veblen would not have been aware of 100 years ago when writing the *Leisure Class* is the environmental limits that would be forced on humankind as a result of overconsumption. Hopefully environmental limits will cause us to reconsider how we go about achieving self-esteem, and if so, then we will read *The Theory of the Leisure Class* in the future as an historical curiosity rather then as a 'penetrating satire' on today's 'regime of status.'

Index

habits of thought, paraphernalia of
learning 161
Hamilton, David 5, 28, 34, 44
Harrods 85
Hartman, H. 142-3, 149-51
Harvey, David 56-7, 60
Harza Engineering Company 200
head count index of poverty 185
hedonistic assumption, pleasure and 15
Heller, Patrick 179-80
hereditary monarchs, economic royalists
and 88-9
Hewison, K. 193-4
high-tech media 54, 83
higher learning
democratization of 167
Veblen and 160-163
Holland 182
home ownership 17
homicide 111
Hong Kong 195
household decisions 124-5
household workers 184
housewives, care of infants and 137-8
Howells, William Dean 28, 34
human activity 30, 65, 76
human nature 11, 15, 41, 57, 143-9,
152, 209
human resources 185-6
hydroelectric projects 195, 197-200
drawbacks of 200-202
hysteresis effects 176-7

identity
crisis 57
culturally-defined feminine 123
emulatory waste 17
enviable 37
formation using consumerism 211
fragmented 46
groups 29-30
images 11, 16-19
imaginative hedonism 22
imperialism, wealth and 186
incentive awards 52, 63, 67, 89
income 20, 31, 44, 98, 101, 110
work and 136-8
India 88, 197-8, 201-2
individuals
consumer culture and 5, 41, 49

'drop out' 51
game of signification and 15
importance of 58
innovation and 173
institutions and 3-4, 144
low status and low assignments 154
pecuniary achievement and 49
productive employment and 140
role of purchased goods and 22
self-expression and 60-61
social group and 10
Indonesia 193
industrial arts 172
industrial efficiency, modern
community and 140
industrialization 35, 81, 119, 176, 196
inequality 62
capital accumulation and 171
education and 181-3
gender 142, 154-5
industrialization and 13, 35
racial, gender and class 182
social capital and 186
socially structured 151, 153
inner cities 42
inner-circle storytelling, exploit and
prowess 100
innovation, upper class and 75, 79-80,
141, 173
insecurity 13, 50, 56-7, 60-61, 64
instincts 144-5, 152-4
of idle curiosity 140, 144-5, 160,
181, 205
of workmanship 60, 138, 140, 144-5,
152, 160, 181, 190, 205
institutional economics 3, 5, 12, 22-4,
141
institutions 22, 144
instrumental behavior 3, 129-30,
138-9, 141, 189-90
instrumental efficacy 23
Intel stock 89
Inter-American Bank 195
'internalist' perspective, consumption's
role and 5
International Monetary Fund (IMF) 80,
118, 191, 195
Internet Gambling 105-6
investment, definition 173
invidious comparisons 7, 55, 58, 147,